JULIET BELL is the collabo...
Janet Gover and Alison Ma...
Juliet was born at a writer...
about heroes who are far from heroic. ...
pizza and wine during many long working lunches, and
finished her first novel over cloud storage and skype in 2017.

Juliet shares Janet and Alison's preoccupation with misunderstood
classic fiction, and stories that explore the darker side of relationships.

Alison also writes commercial women's fiction and romantic
comedies and can be found at www.alison-may.co.uk

Janet writes contemporary romantic adventures mostly set in
outback Australia and can be found at www.janetgover.com

Also by Juliet Bell

The Heights

The Other Wife

JULIET BELL

ONE PLACE. MANY STORIES

HQ
An imprint of HarperCollins*Publishers* Ltd
1 London Bridge Street
London SE1 9GF

This paperback edition 2019

First published in Great Britain by
HQ, an imprint of HarperCollins*Publishers* Ltd 2018

ISBN: 978-0-00-832301-1

MIX
Paper from
responsible sources
FSC™ C007454

This book is produced from independently certified FSC™ paper
to ensure responsible forest management.

For more information visit: www.harpercollins.co.uk/green

Typeset by Palimpsest Book Production Ltd, Falkirk, Stirlingshire
Printed and bound in Great Britain by
CPI Group (UK) Ltd, Croydon, CR0 4YY

To Charlotte

Prologue

According to legend…

The land was empty until the great snake came. He roamed over all the land and, when he slept, deep pools of water formed and flowed into the channels left by his passing. These became the river. As the snake moved from waterhole to waterhole, rainbows formed in the sky.

The lightning man, who the first people would call Namarrgon, came after the serpent. When he was angry, he hurled his spears of light into the ground and woke the fire.

Thousands of years ago, when the first people came to the land, they used the fire. In small groups they moved across the plains, hunting their food and gathering around fires at night to sing and dance, and tell stories of the Dreaming. Sometimes the fire escaped. The trees and the grass burned, and the animals burned. But always the land survived and the first people trusted that the Rainbow Serpent would bring the water back. The plants would grow again. The animals would return and the first men would follow them.

Everything changed when the white men came.

They had tamed the fire. They brought it in guns and trapped it inside the houses that they built, houses that got bigger and stronger as the years passed. They brought new animals too and claimed the land for them. The native animals were driven away by these strange big beasts, just as the first men were driven away by the white men.

In the middle of this plain, a white man built a great stone house. Around that house, there were small buildings and yards for the animals, and, down by the river, the first men had their camp. Sometimes the first men talked of taking back the land that had been theirs. Until then, they worked that land for the white man and for his sons and their sons.

Now the land is dotted with fire. At night, the light gleams from the windows of the white man's big house and figures can be seen moving. There are lights in the other buildings where the white men work and eat and sleep. And small fires still burn where the first men sit by the river and tell their tales.

But, tonight the fire has escaped and it has taken the big stone house in the middle of the plain. The first men and the white men will try to capture it again. But when the fire is set free, it burns until there is nothing left at all.

PART ONE

PART ONE

Chapter 1

Sydney, Australia. 1966

Jane

I was scared. This was my first time in Sydney. My first time in any big city. It was also my first time away from the place where my mother and I had lived since I was a baby. Even looking out of the window of the car was overwhelming – the size of the buildings, the number of cars, the rush and hurry all around me. I sank back into my seat until the car finally stopped and I couldn't hide any longer.

'Come on now, child.' The woman sitting next to me poked me none too gently in the ribs. 'Get out of the car.'

My new home was a huge mountain of red brick. I strained my neck, trying to see how very high it really went. It seemed to reach up almost to the clouds. I desperately wanted to go home. To my friends. To my mother. To the way things were before the police came.

I stared up at the building again. It was truly huge. I would get lost inside it, just as I was lost in this city. The buildings that towered over me seemed to lean in on each other, and there was

3

nothing green. No trees, not even a blade of grass. I hoped I wouldn't have to stay here long. Mum must be coming back soon to take me home to the place with the space and the grass and all the people I knew.

The woman took my two small bags from the back of the car. I didn't own many things. At home everything was shared, so I didn't need my own things. The woman in the car had told me there were other children in this house. My cousins. Maybe I would share with them now.

When we got to the big front door, I pushed it. It didn't open. I tried to pull it, but that didn't work either. The door stayed shut. Puzzled, I looked up at the woman. She rolled her eyes as she reached out to press a button in the wall.

'Yes?' The voice was loud and harsh.

'Child Welfare.'

For a long time there was no answer. 'All right.'

I jumped as a loud buzz and a thunk sounded from the door in front of me.

'Well, don't just stand there. Open the door.'

'But...'

'Open it.'

I pushed the door hard, and this time it moved.

It was dark inside after the bright sunlight in the street. There was a big staircase made of wood that seemed to go forever.

The woman carrying my bags went and stood in front of another door. There were more strange sounds, and that door slid open, revealing a very small room.

'Come on, Jane.' She was starting to sound impatient.

I followed her into the box. I didn't mind small places. That was why I almost always won when we played hide and seek. I was little and could fit into the tiniest places. The door slid shut all on its own. I almost screamed when I felt the little room start to move.

'Oh, for goodness' sake,' the woman said. 'It's only a lift. Your

4

aunt is on the top storey. Far too many floors to use the stairs, especially in this heat.'

Mum had told me to be brave, so I tried to pretend I wasn't frightened as the lift went up and up and up.

When the lift stopped moving, the doors opened again and I jumped out quickly, in case it fell back down to the ground. There was only one other door that I could see. The woman nodded and I tried to open it.

She sighed, before rapping forcefully on the door with her knuckles.

It was opened by a big woman. She had short brown hair and dark eyes. Her dress was grey, with no colours or pattern. Everything about her was so very different to my mum, with her long blonde hair and her pretty clothes and big light skirts that swayed as she walked and ran. The woman peered down at me for a second without smiling. Then she stepped back. 'You'd better come in.'

The room was so pretty that, for a minute, I almost forgot to be scared. There were bright swirling patterns on the walls and a deep carpet that made me want to take my shoes off and let my toes curl into the softness. Everything in the room was new and shiny and clean. There were lace curtains around a big window, and I could see the sky. I felt a bit better then. I had been afraid that in this big brick house, I wouldn't be able to see the sky. There were coloured shiny things on a shelf. I stood on my tiptoes to reach them.

'Jane. Don't touch that. Come back here!' The big woman's voice was loud and screechy. Had I done something wrong?

She looked me up and down. 'I am your Aunt ... I'm Mrs Reed. You're going to be staying here with us, Jane.'

I nodded, but I didn't say anything.

Mrs Reed stared at me, apparently expecting something more. She turned to the woman who had brought me here. 'Is there something wrong with her?'

'I'm sure she's just nervous,' the woman said. 'I'm sure she's a very bright child, really.'

'We'll see about that. Jane, take your bags to your room. It's down that corridor. The last door on the right. You do know right from left, don't you?'

I nodded.

The last door led to a little room, with a bed and some drawers. I put my bags on the bed. It was a pretty room. The bedclothes were pale pink, and felt soft under my fingers.

'That's my old stuff.'

I turned around to see two big children standing in the doorway. The girl was a bit older than me and had dark hair and a little button nose. The boy was even older. These must be the cousins I'd been told about.

'Thank you for sharing your things with me.'

'I'm not sharing anything with you,' the girl said. 'Mum said you could have my old stuff, but don't ever touch anything of mine. Ever.'

'Or mine,' her brother said quietly. 'We didn't ask you here. We don't want you here. We hate you.'

I wanted to cry. But I didn't. I wanted Mum to be proud of me for being brave.

'I didn't want to come here either,' I said.

'Don't you talk to me like that!' His face went pink with anger.

I took a deep breath. 'Mum says everybody should share everything. It's mean if you don't.'

He parroted my words back at me in silly sing-song voice. 'Everybody should share everything.'

His sister laughed.

The boy continued. 'You're not on that hippy farm anymore. Things are different here. This is a proper family, not your druggie commune. You'll have to behave yourself now.'

I didn't know what he meant, but I was suddenly very, very frightened. 'But I'm going back there? Soon?'

'Don't be silly.' Mrs Reed appeared in the doorway. 'The police have shut the whole place down. Thank goodness. The things that were going on there. Drugs. Free love. God knows where my sister is by now. And with who. She's not fit to look after a child.' Her lips pursed. 'She probably doesn't even know who your father is.'

'She wouldn't go anywhere without me!' Mum had always been there. Other people had come and gone but Mum had never left me. Never.

The woman who had come with me in the car was standing behind Mrs Reed, her bag over her shoulder. 'Jane, we explained this. Your mother isn't allowed to look after you anymore. The police have closed the commune down. Some people have gone to jail.'

I shook my head. Nobody had explained anything. 'But...'

The woman had already turned away. Mrs Reed followed her along the corridor and a second later I heard the door open and slam shut.

Mrs Reed marched back into the room.

I jumped up. I was desperate. Nobody had said anything about Mum going away. 'Mum wouldn't leave me. You have to find out what happened to her.'

'Enough.' Mrs Reed folded her arms. 'You're my niece, so I won't have people saying I turned you away, however glad I might be to be rid of you, but in my house you live by my rules. And the first rule is this – you do not ever mention my slut of a sister again.'

'But she's going to come and get me...'

'No. Understand this, Jane Eyre. Your mother will never set foot in this house, and you will never see her again.'

Chapter 2

York, England. 1966

Betty

Betty ran out of Mrs Oakley's house at a quarter past five like always, but it wasn't Mummy standing waiting for her. Instead her father bent down to talk to her as she came towards him. 'Hello, little firefly. I'm picking you up today because Mummy's had to go away for a little while.'

Betty frowned. Mummy always picked her up. She said it was easier that way because Daddy had to work and sometimes people got funny when he came out with them. The front door to Mrs Oakley's neat little house was still open, while the childminder watched her charges go on their way. 'Mr Earl?'

He turned towards the voice. 'Mrs O. What can I do for you?' 'Is Pam not well?'

'No. No. She had to go away for a bit.' He lowered his voice. 'For her nerves.'

'Right.' Mrs Oakley looked away somewhere over Betty's father's shoulder, not at his face. 'Well, I'll be happy to have the bairn back once her mum's all better and can drop her round.'

8

Betty felt her daddy's hand rest on the top of her head. His voice was quieter than usual. 'It's all right. I'm working on the production line at the moment. Regular shifts, so I can bring her before work.'

Mrs Oakley glanced from side to side at the neat little houses that butted up against hers, and the other parents who were picking up their children. They chatted to each other, but none of them spoke to Betty's father. They didn't even look at him.

'I don't think so. It's not really...' She stepped back into the hallway. 'Not really right for you in this area.'

Betty's father's voice raised now. 'But she's my daughter.'

'Well, yes, but...' Mrs Oakley peered around the door at Betty. 'You'd not really know, would you? She takes from her mother.'

The door swung closed with a definite thud. Betty's father stood very still for a moment. The net curtain at the window of the house next to Mrs Oakley's twitched slightly. Daddy took her hand. 'Come on, Betty girl. We'll get a fish supper and listen to records. Shall we?'

Betty nodded. She didn't like fish, but, when Mummy wasn't there, Daddy let her pull the crispy batter off with her fingers and just eat that dipped in the bright green mushy peas. She leant against Daddy's hip while they waited in the chip queue. 'Will Mummy be coming back soon?'

'I hope so, little firefly. I hope so.' He clapped his hands together. 'And until then we'll need to find someone to keep an eye on you while I'm at work.'

'Good. I don't like it at Mrs Oakley's. Sometimes they look at me strangely.'

She felt her father tense for a second, then he stroked her crisp red-brown curls. 'That's only because they don't understand that you are special, my bright little firefly.'

Betty leant more closely into his body.

'It'll be all right. We'll work something out,' he said.

The next morning, Betty clung to her father's hand outside a big red-brick house that she thought she sort of recognised.

'Do you remember coming here, little firefly?'

Betty shook her head.

'This is your grandpa and grandma's house.'

She followed her father up the driveway and stood half behind his legs while he rang the bell.

The door was opened by a tall man with thick black-framed glasses and a big moustache.

'Mr Thompson...' Daddy started.

'What are you doing here?'

'I ... Can we come in?'

The man shook his head. 'I'll not have you upsetting Pam's mother.'

'Right. Well, it's Pam. She's in the hospital. The Retreat.'

The man folded his arms.

'And Betty...' Betty felt her father step to one side so the man could see her properly. 'I've no-one to watch her while I'm at work and so...'

'And so you thought you'd turn up here like nothing had happened.'

'No. I ...'

'We were quite clear when Pamela made her decision. We're happy to take her back and we'll look after the girl. You can leave her here right now and go off and get on with your life.'

Betty's father reached down and took hold of her hand. 'I won't abandon my child. If you could just take care of her for a few hours.'

The man on the doorstep calmly shook his head. 'We'll take her and we'll raise her properly. But we will not have you coming to this house. Make your choice.'

Betty glanced up at her father. His face was creased with emotions that she didn't understand. He knelt down next to her. 'Would you like to stay here, Betty?'

10

''Til you come back?'

Her daddy screwed his eyes shut for a second like Betty did sometimes when she was trying not to cry. When he opened them again, he reached out and cupped her cheek in his hand. 'Don't worry, little firefly. It was a silly idea. Daddy won't leave you anywhere...'

Betty didn't hear the rest of his sentence. Her own wail drowned it out. Even the idea of him leaving her was too much to hold inside her head. Mummy had to go away, but Daddy was still here. She flung herself against his body, throwing her arms around his neck. His hands wrapped straight around her, lifting her up as he stood. 'Well, that's settled, then.'

She buried her face in his neck.

'We'll be going.'

She let him carry her back down the driveway and into the street. Eventually he put her down next to a shiny red telephone box. 'I just need to telephone the office at work, and then we'll go to the park. Feed the ducks.'

Betty beamed. A whole day out with Daddy was so exciting. And maybe tomorrow Mummy would come back and everything would be normal again.

Chapter 3

Jane

It was so quiet when I woke up. At home, it was never quiet. There were always people running around, dogs barking, and children laughing. And seagulls, because we all lived near the beach. But in this new place, it was very, very quiet. I guess that was because there was only me and Mrs Reed and my two cousins. That's not many people for such a big house.

I got out of bed and put my clothes on. My tummy rumbled as I did, so I left my tiny room with its pretty pink bedspread, and went in search of breakfast. I hoped the Reeds had cereal and milk.

I found the milk in the fridge, and put it on the bench. I started opening cupboards and found a bowl, but there was no food. I looked up at the cupboards above my head. I would need a chair to stand on. I found chairs around a big polished wooden table in another room and dragged one into the kitchen.

I took a deep breath then I climbed on the chair. I kept one hand on the back of the chair, and quickly grabbed the cupboard handle until the room stopped swirling around me. I didn't like high places. Mum always kept the cereal in the low cupboards so I didn't have to stand on chairs. I hoped Mrs Reed would do the same if I asked her. But until then, I told myself, I really could do this. And besides, I was hungry.

When I felt better and opened the cupboard nearest to me, there were biscuits. Lots and lots of biscuits. Biscuits were much better than cereal and milk. I dropped two packets of chocolate biscuits onto the bench and then climbed down off the chair. I was eating my second biscuit when I heard a familiar noise from outside.

There were seagulls here in the city too. That was exciting. I hadn't expected to see any birds or animals at all.

I grabbed a couple more biscuits and ran out of the kitchen into the big living room. The seagulls must be out there, through the big glass doors where I could see the sky. It took me a couple of tries to get the door open, but finally the latch clicked and I jumped through the door.

The sky was right in front of me. There were no people, or trees, or cars, or even buildings to break up the big blue open sky. I glanced down and my tummy twisted. I was looking down onto the tops of the buildings across the street and then below that the road was a tiny slither of grey a million miles below me.

I was going to fall. I was going to fall until I was as small as the people in the miniature cars beneath me. The ground was so far away, and the sky was spinning around and around me. I grabbed at the nearest thing I could reach. A little basketwork chair. But that didn't help, the chair fell too and I dropped onto the hard tile floor with the chair on top of me.

All I wanted to do was crawl back through the big glass doors to a place where I was safe from falling. The chair was light. I should have been able to lift it off myself quite easily, but it wouldn't budge. Something, someone, was holding it down. I wriggled as much as I could and caught a glimpse of a pair of feet; feet that were still safely on the soft carpet.

'Help me up.'

The feet didn't move. There was the sound of laughter.

13

'Please...' I pushed against the chair.

'What is going on here?' At last someone lifted the chair out of the way. A rough hand grabbed me by the arm and hauled me to my feet. I darted back into the room where it was safe, backing away from the open door, trying very hard not to cry.

My cousin John was standing just inside the door. He was smiling, not a friendly smile, but a nasty, tight smile. It was the sort of smile I had never seen before. Nobody at home smiled like that.

'What on earth were you doing out there at this hour of the morning? Come on, girl. Stop your snivelling.' Mrs Reed towered over me, and, try as I might, I could not stop sobbing. My whole body was shaking with fear.

'What's that in your hand?' Mrs Reed grabbed my closed hand and slowly prised the fingers opened to reveal the broken biscuit still tightly clutched inside.

'Have you been stealing food?'

'Stealing? No! I don't steal.' My sobs stopped.

'This...' Mrs Reed slapped my hand and broken bits of biscuit fell onto the soft clean carpet. 'You took this from the cupboard, didn't you?'

I nodded. Of course I took it from the cupboard. That's what we always did at home. It wasn't stealing. You took what you needed and everybody shared. 'I was hungry...'

'Hungry? Selfish child. You can't just take food when you want too. Stealing is a sin. And today is Sunday. We go to church on Sundays and we don't eat anything before we go to church. You will be praying for God's forgiveness. You wicked, ungrateful girl.'

'I'm not wicked!'

The slap was as sudden as it was painful. I staggered backwards, clutching my stinging cheek. My eyes filled with tears all over again. No-one had ever hit me before, not even my mother.

'We will not mention this incident again. Go to your room and get ready for church.'

I went to my room.

In the mirror in my room I could see that my right cheek was red where Mrs Reed had slapped me. I had to get ready for church. I'd never been to church before. I wasn't really sure what church was, but I decided to put on the best dress I'd brought with me. Maybe then Mrs Reed would see that I was trying to be good. I turned to get it and saw that John Reed was standing in my open doorway, with that same smile on his face again. He was eating a chocolate biscuit.

Chapter 4

Betty

Betty sat quietly next to Daddy in the cold office. The chair had scratchy material on it and she wriggled in her seat to try to pull her dress down to cover her legs. The grown-ups were talking in low, quiet voices.

'So it will only be for a few weeks. Less than that probably. Her mother…' Daddy turned his head and smiled at Betty. 'She can't look after her just at the moment, but when she's back everything will be all right again.'

The man opposite Daddy on the other side of the big desk nodded curtly. Betty swung her legs while the two men filled in forms and signed papers. Then Daddy lifted her up out of the seat. 'So you're going to have a lovely holiday here with lots of other children. And me and Mummy will come back and get you really soon.'

Betty's bottom lip started to quiver. 'Do I have to go? I want to stay with you.'

'Really, really soon. I promise, little firefly. All right?'

Daddy's eyes looked like he was about to cry. Betty rested her head on his shoulder. 'It's OK, Daddy.'

He took a deep breath and smiled as he set her down on the ground. 'That's right. You need to be very brave for me and remember that everything's OK. I love you, but while Mummy is away, I can't keep you with me. As soon as Mummy comes home, I'll come back. I promise.'

The stranger ushered Daddy out of the office and Betty was alone.

A few minutes later, a lady came into the room and picked up Betty's little case. 'Come on.'

She followed the lady along long white corridors and into a big bedroom with lots of beds in it. The lady popped her case on one of them. 'You'll be here. You can put your things in here.' She pointed at a cupboard next to the bed. 'Quickly now. Chop-chop!'

She flicked the case open and started lifting Betty's things into the cupboard. Betty watched. It seemed silly. She'd just have to put them all back in her case very soon when Daddy came back.

Betty couldn't count how many days and nights she was in the home. She slept in a big room with other children. Little ones, like Betty, at one end, and bigger girls further down. She didn't like having so many people sleeping in the same room. Some of the girls cried at night, and that made Betty want to cry too. During the day they did chores, and the bigger girls did reading. Whatever she was doing, Betty waited. She waited for Mummy and Daddy to come back and take her home. So when one of the ladies who usually looked after the little babies, came and told her to bring her coat and hat, and her little suitcase with her pyjamas and hairbrush, she thought it was time.

She climbed into the back of the car waiting outside and was surprised to find two boys, both a couple of years older than her, already sitting there. The lady sat in the front with the driver, who was the man from the office from the very first day. He looked over into the back seat and frowned when he saw Betty.

'What's she doing here? We're only supposed to send white children.'

'She's white enough.'

'She's half-breed. You saw her father.'

'I did. But they won't. And if you didn't know, you'd think she was white, wouldn't you?'

The driver turned around and stared directly at Betty. 'She's got that hair.'

'Well, stick it under her hat when we get there and tell her not to say anything.'

Betty patted her hair. It had tight little curls like Daddy's but in the sunshine it looked ginger like Mummy's. Daddy said it was special. Daddy said her hair shone like a beautiful flame.

Betty felt her stomach flip. 'Where are we going?'

'On an adventure.'

'Will my mummy and daddy be there?'

The woman twisted in her seat to look at Betty. 'Your mummy and daddy are gone. We're sending you somewhere that you're wanted. You'll have a far better home than with … him. Now be quiet.' Betty did as she was told. She stared out of the window trying to remember the places they were driving past so she could find her way back, but they drove for too long and eventually it got dark. Betty's eyes fell closed.

When she opened them again, the car had stopped. Rain was lashing down, which meant nobody thought it was odd that the woman rammed Betty's hat onto her head and tucked her hair away inside. 'Come on now.'

Betty was dragged along by the woman's tight grip on her hand. The two boys ran along behind. They were by the sea, but not the seaside like when Mummy and Daddy had taken her for a day out on the beach at Scarborough. There was no beach here, just buildings and the ships were much bigger than the fishing boats Daddy had taken her to see. The woman stopped in front of a man with a clipboard, who ticked some items off his list and then pointed them towards a metal bridge leading to the biggest ship Betty had ever seen. She couldn't get on a ship. Ships went over the sea. If she went over the sea, Mummy and Daddy would never find her. 'But my daddy's coming back for me.'

The woman folded her arms. 'You're going somewhere much nicer. Now, on you get. Chop-chop. Off on an adventure.'

There was a sharp shove in her back and Betty had no choice but to follow the wave of tiny bodies making their way onto the boat.

Chapter 5

Jane

Church soon became the best part of my life. On Sundays we would walk up to church. It was a beautiful old building with stone arches and a statue of Jesus at the front door. There was a routine to church, and order of things. At church, nobody would shout or point out what I was doing wrong. At church I could listen to the words of the priest and look at the pictures in the windows and above the altar. Christ on the cross. Mary with her baby. According to the priest she was kind and the most loving of mothers. In the big window she was gathering little children of all nations to her. Sometimes I wished I could step into that picture and be gathered up, safe and loved, far, far away from Mrs Reed.

Each night I knelt beside my bed, and Mrs Reed stood in the doorway and listened to my prayers. I had to thank God that I had a home with her. I had to pray for my cousins, John and Emma. I had to pray for forgiveness for all my wickedness. After Mrs Reed was gone, I always got back on my knees and prayed for my mother. The night before my seventh birthday I prayed extra hard that she would come and find me.

The next morning I got up, wondering if there would be presents on the breakfast table or if I'd have to wait until evening. Mrs Reed hadn't asked me what I wanted to do, but I imagined a trip to the beach, like I'd done on my other birthdays, when the whole community had joined me and Mum for a picnic.

There were no presents on the breakfast table.

There was no day at the beach.

There were no presents after school, either.

At bedtime, before I knelt down to say my prayers, I took a deep breath in and asked Mrs Reed, 'Did you know it was my birthday?'

The woman frowned, but didn't answer my question. 'I don't have time for silliness like that, Jane. Go on, say your prayers.'

That night, in my head, I asked God to take me away from the Reeds.

Two weeks later, Mrs Reed came into my room before breakfast and told me to put my best clothes on because we were going to the cinema. 'It's Emma's birthday day out,' she said.

Emma had grown out of a very pretty yellow dress that was now my smartest outfit. I pulled off my pyjamas and was taking the pretty yellow dress out of my wardrobe when I heard a noise. John was standing in my doorway. He was looking at me in the strangest way. I pulled the dress off the hanger and held it in front of my body. 'What are you doing in here?'

'You can't hide from me, you know.' He was still smiling as he stepped into the room.

'Go away!' I spoke softly. I always spoke softly. Mrs Reed didn't like shouting.

'You can't make me.' He took another step into my room.

'Go away.' I backed away from him, but there was nowhere I could go.

'This is my house and I'll do whatever I want.' He was eleven years old, and much bigger than me. I made to duck past him to run to the bathroom, but he stepped sideways and blocked my way, grabbing my bare shoulders.

'Leave me alone.' I slapped his hands away. Something was very wrong, but I didn't really know what.

'What's going on in here?' Mrs Reed was in the hallway outside the room. She saw my body. 'Jane!'

'She called me to come in here,' John said, the same half-smile still on his face. 'And when I did, she took her clothes off.'

Mrs Reed paled. 'John, leave the room. I'll deal with this.'

'That's not what happened,' I explained as he walked away. 'I didn't...'

'Not one more word from you.' Mrs Reed paced up and down the floor two, and then three times, before she turned to face me. 'You're not pretty, Jane.'

'What?'

'You're like me. Not like your mother. She always had every boy in the town after her. And she let them, you know.' She scowled. 'I thought without her pretty face you might be different. I thought I might be able to teach you how to behave before it was too late, but the apple never falls far from the tree after all.'

'I didn't. John's lying...'

My words were cut off by the crack of her hand across my cheek. 'Never ever blame my son for your dirtiness. Now get dressed.'

I lifted the pretty yellow frock to pull it over my head, but Mrs Reed snatched it away from me.

'Not this. You can't have Emma's pretty things until you show you deserve them.' She took an old brown dress from my cupboard. 'Put this on.'

When I was dressed, she grabbed me by the arm and dragged me through the house. 'You've spoiled this day for all of us,' she said. 'Apologise to poor John and to Emma. We can't go for her birthday treat now. I will not leave you alone in this house and you certainly can't come with us.'

Emma immediately started to wail and stamp her feet.

'Why don't we leave her on the balcony?' John said slowly. 'There's nothing she can steal or break out there.'

I froze. The balcony was a place of horror. There was nothing but that thin railing between me and the ground far below. I'd often sat just inside, desperate for a view of the sky, but I hadn't set foot on the balcony since that first morning. 'No. Please. I didn't do what he said...'

'I told you not to lie.' Mrs Reed dragged me towards the glass doors. 'Well, you will stay out there and think about your sin. John's right. Why should you be allowed to spoil Emma's day?'

She thrust me through the door and I fell onto the tiles. On the other side of the glass doors, the family walked out of the apartment and slammed the front door closed behind them.

I crawled back towards the wall and squeezed myself into the corner, where I couldn't see the edge of the balcony, or the rail or the long fall below it. I sat there for a very long time. At first I tried not to cry. I knew Mum would want me to be brave, but Mum wasn't here. It was just me. Completely abandoned, completely alone. I stopped fighting and let the tears come.

'Are you all right?'

The voice seemed to come from out of the sky. It was soft and kind and full of gentleness.

'Are you Our Lady?'

'No.' The voice laughed. 'I heard you crying. Are you all right?'

The voice floated towards me on the breeze. 'Then are you an angel?'

The voice laughed again. 'No. I'm Jennifer. I'm standing on my balcony, downstairs from you. Are you Jane? I've heard about you, but we've never met.'

I hadn't heard about her, but then Mrs Reed didn't like the people in the building and didn't talk to them very often.

'Are you all right, Jane? Have you locked yourself out on the balcony?'

'No. Mrs Reed puts me here. When I do bad things.'

'Is she there with you?'

'No. They went out.'

There was a long pause. I pressed my back harder against the wall, screwing my eyes closed and not thinking about the drop below. 'Are you still there?'

'I'm here. Would you like me to stay here until Mrs Reed comes home? You can talk to me and tell me all about yourself.'

'Yes, please.' I wasn't quite so scared any more.

Chapter 6

Betty

The days merged into one another. The sea was big and the journey went on forever. Every morning Betty woke up, shivering and sweaty, squashed into the cramped bunk, stomach lurching with the rolls of the ship. Every night before she went to sleep, she clasped her hands together like she used to do at home and prayed that in the morning she'd wake up in her own bed, and go into the kitchen and have bread and jam with Daddy.

'Time to get up.'

Betty didn't have pyjamas anymore. She'd had them in her little case when she'd got on the boat but they'd disappeared, so now she spent her nights and days in one grubby, stinky set of clothes. She hadn't had a bath or combed out her hair for weeks. The ladies with them didn't know how to deal with Betty's curls. One of them had tried but quickly gave up when Betty screamed against the pulling and the pain.

They followed the woman to the dining hall where the children were huddled together into one corner with bread and butter. The other passengers came and went as they pleased, talking about 'ten pounds for all this' or grumbling about their seasickness or the choices for breakfast.

After they'd eaten they were led outside, and told to be quiet and not to bother anyone. At first, Betty sat on her own. Most of the children were bigger than her. A lot of them liked to sit in the sun, but Betty didn't. When the others sat in the sun, their fair skin went bright pink. When she sat in the sun, her skin went brown. She'd started to look different. Like Daddy had looked different. That's when the women had told her to stay inside. They'd said she would look dirty and no-one would ever give her a home. Betty hadn't listened to them. Sooner or later Daddy would come and find her and take her home. But she did stay out of the sun.

After a little while she made a friend.

Her name was Kay, and despite being older, she was the only one who ever talked to Betty. They whispered together in the bunk late at night.

'Where did you come from? Before they sent you here.'

Betty screwed up her face. 'I was in a big house with other children.'

Kay nodded. 'Me too. So your mam's dead, then?'

Betty shook her head vigorously. 'She's not very well but she's going to get better and she's going to come home and...' She tailed off. And what? Betty wasn't sure.

'Nah. She must have died. I heard Mrs Collins say we were all orphans.'

Betty turned the word around in her head. 'What's a norfan?'

'Orphan. It's when your mam and dad are dead.'

'I'm not one of them. My daddy said he would come back and get me.' Betty's face crumpled as fat tears started to run down her cheeks.

'Aw. Come on. Don't do that.' Kay looked anxious. 'Come on. I'll show you what I do when I'm feeling sad.'

They held hands as they walked up on deck and out onto the open area right at the back of the ship. It was cold and windy and dark, but, when Betty looked up, the blackness of the sky was sprinkled with glowing stars.

'They are so pretty.'

Kay nodded. 'But sometimes, it's even prettier. Just wait.'

Betty waited. She didn't know what she was waiting for. Then she saw a golden spark fly across the sky. And then another.

'Look.' Kay pointed to the top of the big funnel that loomed over the ship.

As Betty watched, more sparks, all golden and red, flew from the top of the funnel. Sometimes it was only a few, but sometimes there seemed to be hundreds of sparks, flying up into the air, high above the waves. Away from the ship and all the people on it. Back towards where they'd come from. Back towards home and Daddy. Betty wanted to be one of them.

'They're so pretty. And they're free.'

The girls stood there, holding hands, watching the sparks. But soon the sparks got fewer and fewer. Until finally, they stopped coming at all. The stars no longer seemed pretty to Betty. Tthey were white and cold, and so distant.

'I wish they would never stop.'

'I bet we can make our own,' Kay said. 'Wait here. I won't be long.' She ran back along the deck.

Betty watched the top of the funnels, hoping the sparks would appear again, but they didn't. She felt lost and alone without them.

Kay came running back. 'Look.'

She held some sheets of paper and a box of matches.

'Where did you get them?'

'In the posh dining room.'

Kay scrunched the paper into a ball before setting it down on the deck in a sheltered corner where the wind wasn't too strong. She pulled out a pink-headed match from her box and struck it against the side of the box to no effect. The second time, the match sparked into life. Betty watched the orange flame dance as Kay leant towards the balled-up paper. She set the match to the paper and then bent close in, blowing gently on the tiny hint of fire.

Betty felt her heart pounding in her chest. They weren't supposed to be here. Kay definitely wasn't supposed to have matches.

Betty gazed at the fire. The pounding in her chest slowed. The screaming inside her head quieted. The thoughts of the women and the spanking they were going to get disappeared. She let her mind be filled by the bright, dancing flames, feeling the warmth prickle the skin on her legs, feeling the smoke spike at her eyes, but never looking away. She could feel the warmth of the fire in the hearth. She could hear the sound of Daddy breathing as she rested her head on his chest. This boat, and this journey, and all the confusion she'd been living with, faded away. Then she slowly lifted her head as a bit of paper, glowing with flame, flew up into the night air. Free of the ship, floating back towards home.

'Betty!' Kay grabbed her arm and pulled, but Betty didn't move. She couldn't. The fire had captured her and was holding her in its embrace.

'Betty! Someone's coming.'

Betty ignored her friend again.

'Fine.' She heard Kay's footsteps as she ran away from the fire, but Betty stayed still.

A big brown boot shoved in front of her and stamped away the flames. 'What do you think you're doing, setting a fire on a ship?'

Another voice behind Betty interrupted. 'She's one of them orphan brats, ain't she?'

'I'm not an orphan.'

Large rough hands spun her round. Betty looked at the two men, who towered over her. One of them grinned. 'Is that right?

Well, then, we'd best take you back to Mummy and Daddy. In one of the posh cabins up front, are they?'

Betty shook her head.

'I didn't think so.' The man thwacked Betty hard across the back of her legs. Once. Twice. Three times. And then four. Betty's lip twitched but she bit back the tears. She didn't need to be here. So long as she could see the fire in her head, she could be far away, curled up and safe with Daddy at home. 'Dirty little firebug.' The man grunted the words out as he slapped her again. Eventually he released his grip, and shoved her towards his mate. 'Take her back, then.'

'You're sure she's learnt her lesson?'

The other man had already turned away. 'Don't care anymore. She's not going to be our problem much longer, is she?'

His mate followed. 'I didn't think they took coloureds anyroad.'

Chapter 7

Jane

When school ended in the afternoon, we were supposed to wait for Mrs Reed to come to walk us home. John and Emma would go off and talk to their friends after lessons finished, or play sport. I had to wait by the gate all alone. I wasn't allowed to play in any sports team, or have music lessons or any of the things Emma and John did.

Not long after Emma's birthday, John appeared at the gate before his sister.

'Come with me,' he said.

'We're supposed to wait here.'

'Mum won't be here for ages. Emma has her stupid ballet lesson today. Come with me or else I'll tell Mum on you.'

I wasn't sure what he would tell her, but I knew it would be bad, so I followed him across the playground and around to the sports oval. Almost everyone had gone home for the day, but John opened the door to the sports-equipment shed.

'Go in there.'

I could hear some whispering inside. I started to back away. 'No. I don't want to.'

John grabbed me by the shoulder and pushed me through the doorway. I tripped and fell forward. My arm buckled underneath me and my face crashed into the hard wooden floor.

'Is this her? She's just a kid.'

'She hasn't even got any tits.'

I didn't know how many people there were around me. All the voices sounded like boys. Lying there on the floor, I couldn't see their faces, only their shiny black school shoes.

John's voice rose above the others. 'Well, I did it, didn't I? You said I couldn't get a girl. She's a girl.'

Another of the voices jeered. 'Well, let's have a proper look at her, then.'

John prodded me with the toe of his shoe, trying to get me to roll over. I pulled my arms around my head, keeping my face against the floor, blocking them all out.

'Come on, then.' This time, it was more of a kick than a prod. 'I've already seen 'em. Time to get 'em out for my mates.'

I felt John's hand wrap around my arm. I wriggled instinctively, pulling away from his grip. His shoe caught me as I moved, pushing under my body and forcing me onto my back. There was a volley of laughter as my skirt rode up. I dragged myself to kneeling, pulling my dress down to cover myself. This time another hand grabbed my arm, and John went for my hair. The pain shot through my head. 'Get up!'

I had no choice. It felt as if my hair would be ripped from my scalp if I refused.

Standing in the middle of the jeering circle, I dug my thumbs into the sides of my school uniform, holding it down close to my body.

'Let me go.'

John laughed and reached for the hem of my uniform.

'No.' I slapped his hand away. Another boy grabbed me from behind and held me.

'We won't hurt you,' John said. 'I'm going to show them what

31

you showed me at home the other day.'

He reached for me again, and his cold fingertips touched the bare skin of my neck.

I didn't understand what was happening, but I knew I would be blamed. Mrs Reed would say it was a sign that I was dirty and sinful. I was not dirty. I was not sinful. I would not let this happen.

I screamed as long and as loud as I could. I kicked out at the boys around me. The more they laughed the more I kicked, until I finally heard one of them gasp. I had hurt him. Good.

'What's going on here?'

The boys jumped away, distancing themselves as much as they could, as if they had just happened to be in the shed and not noticed what was going on at all. The sports teacher came into the room. I ran to the door, almost knocking him over as I did.

'Wait.'

He grabbed me by the shoulders. Acting purely on instinct I screamed again and tried to slap his hand away. The noise was attracting other people, including some of the kids and several teachers. I was led away by the lady who taught music. She took me to an empty staffroom and gave me a glass of water. She had a calm, sympathetic voice, but, when she asked me what had happened in the shed, I couldn't tell her. The words sat in my throat, hot and painful, but they refused to be spoken aloud. She looked at me for a long time.

'Are you quite sure you're all right, Jane?'

I nodded, which seemed to stop her asking again. At last there was a knock on the door. The teacher opened it, and I saw Mrs Reed standing there. Her face was hard and cold, and I could see how angry she was.

'Come with me, Jane.'

I did as she said. John and Emma were waiting by the school entrance and we all walked home together, like we did every other day. I didn't look at my elder cousin. Not once. Mrs Reed was silent until we were inside the apartment and the door was closed. 'Jane, this is the worst thing you've ever done.'

'I didn't do anything.'

'They said they found you with a whole group of boys. John said you lured them all there.'

The smirk reappeared on John's face as he watched me, waiting for me to speak.

'That's not what happened.' I clenched my fists. 'He dragged me into that shed with the other boys and told me to...'

'Not another word, Jane! Not one word. This is just like your mother, and I will not stand for it. Not in my house.'

Mrs Reed took my arm and I knew what was coming.

'No. No.' I tried to pull away, but she was too strong. She dragged me to the glass door and pushed me out onto the balcony.

'You'll stay out there until you learn how to behave,' she said. 'And until you apologise to John for lying about him.'

Mrs Reed barely spoke to me in the days after that horrible afternoon. It was impossible to hide from John, but I stayed as far away from him as I could at school, and I didn't go to wait by the gate until Emma was there. I put a chair under the door-handle in my room at night. I don't think I even understood what I was afraid of. I only knew that I was very afraid.

And then I saw Jennifer for the very first time.

On this day, the lift in our building was broken and we had to walk up the stairs. I was glad of this because I hated the lift, especially when I was closed in there with John. Mrs Reed hated the stairs and by the time we were halfway up, she was panting. I lagged behind, even though I wasn't panting at all. As we climbed past the floor below ours, the floor where I knew Jennifer lived, I lagged even more. I still suspected Jennifer was an angel, and I desperately wanted to see her.

Just as Mrs Reed reached the landing, a door opened and a

woman stepped out. I knew at once that it was her. She had long golden hair and a beautiful face, like a real, genuine angel.

'Hello, Mrs Reed,' she said.

'Good afternoon.' Mrs Reed barely glanced her way as she brushed past, finding new energy to climb quickly to the next floor.

'Hello, Jane.'

'Hello, Jennifer.' I spoke very quietly. Mrs Reed didn't like it when we talked to other people.

'Are you all right?' She cast a quick glance up the stairs, but the Reeds were out of sight.

I nodded.

'If you ever need me, you can come down and knock on my door. You know that, don't you?'

Just as I nodded, I heard Mrs Reed calling me from above. 'I have to go.' I hurried up the stairs.

When I first came to live with the Reeds, I used to close my eyes at night and try to remember my mother's face. But this night, as I lay in bed, safely behind my barricaded door, I closed my eyes and pictured Jennifer's face. She was the only person who had been kind to me since I left the home I could no longer remember clearly. And that Sunday, in church, when I closed my eyes to pray to Our Lady, it was Jennifer's face I saw. She was my personal angel. Gentle and kind like Mary, beautiful like my mother. I was drawn to her like nobody I'd ever met before.

Three days later, I was in my room after school doing my homework, when I heard Mrs Reed calling me. I brushed my hair and straightened my clothes, so that I'd be presentable. When I walked into the living room, Mrs Reed was sitting in her chair, looking angry. Another woman was standing by the open glass doors, looking out onto the balcony. She turned when I entered and smiled at me.

'Hello, Jane. Do you remember me?'

I nodded. I could never forget her. It was the lady who had first brought me here, who took me away from my home. I nodded, my heart suddenly pounding. 'Are you here to take me back to Mum?'

She didn't answer. Instead she motioned me to join her in the doorway. Slowly I walked over. I didn't step onto the balcony. The lady crouched down and studied my face. Then she looked at my hands. They were shaking.

'You don't like going onto the balcony, Jane, do you?'

I shook my head. 'I don't want to fall.'

'Of course you don't.' She stood up and closed the doors. 'So, Jane, tell me. Do you like school?'

I looked past the lady to where Mrs Reed was sitting. She had her eyes fixed on me and I knew if I said something bad, she would put me out on the balcony again.

'School is nice.' I said.

'I thought there was some trouble there a little while ago. Trouble with boys.'

I shook my head.

'That's all right. It's good that you like school. Do you like living here too? With your aunt and your cousins.'

I knew what I was supposed to say. 'Yes.'

The woman looked at me for a very long time. She had brown eyes, and there were creases at the sides of her mouth. At last she stood up.

'Thank you, Jane. You can go back to your room now, while I talk to your aunt.'

I sat on my bed, wondering what they were talking about. Then I heard the front door slam and I knew the woman was gone. Mrs Reed opened my bedroom door without knocking. She never knocked. The yelling started before she was even properly through the door.

'How dare you be so ungrateful? You've been telling stories about us, haven't you? Telling lies! And you brought that woman here, asking questions about me. And about my son. You will leave. As soon as I can make the arrangements, you will be out of my house for good.'

Hope leapt into my heart. 'I can go home?'

'Don't be stupid. You have no home other than this one, this home that you choose to treat so badly.'

'But Mum…'

'I told you never to speak of her in this house.' She took a deep breath in, and lowered her voice. 'You, Jane Eyre, will go to boarding school, and just be grateful I am willing to spend so much money to get you away from here.'

Chapter 8

Betty

Betty was hungry as she stepped off the ship. She'd been hungry for weeks now, but this was different. Today they'd been told there was no time for breakfast because today was A Very Important Day. Today, the women said, they would start their new lives. Some of the children had cried. Some of them had asked if their parents would be there. The women had shaken their heads, and said that their parents were gone now. Betty hadn't cried. Whenever Betty felt like tears were pricking at her eyes, she thought as hard as she could about the orange flames dancing in front of her and the sparks lighting the night sky, and flying away back to her real home. That always made her feel calm.

The sun beating down on the dockside made it easy for Betty to think of the fire. It felt hot on her face and she longed to peel off her cardigan and feel the warmth on her arms. But she had been told to keep her cardigan on, because her arms were already too brown. And she had a hat, too, that almost hid her hair. She followed the rest of the children along the concrete path and stopped in front of two big buses. A tall man in a neat grey suit stood in front of them. The women shushed them into near silence, before he started to speak.

'It's my honour to welcome all of you to Australia today. You're here to help us build a brave, forward-thinking nation, filled with the right sort of people. You will learn to work the land. You will learn trades. You will grow up to have fine Australian children of your own. You have come on a great adventure to this great land. Work hard. Grow into decent young men and women, and Australia will become your home.'

Betty didn't really listen to what he was saying. She didn't understand a lot of it. She understood the heat beating down on her face. She understood the hunger in her belly. She understood that it was weeks and weeks since she'd got onto the ship and that, wherever she was now, it was not her home.

The women from the boat clapped politely as the man finished talking, and then they started quickly shoving the children into different queues. Betty felt a hand reach out and take hers. She looked up and saw Kay frowning down at her.

A moment later, the hand was pulled away. 'Older girls on this bus. Little ones wait here.'

Betty concentrated hard on the warmth and the flickering flame inside her head. She heard Kay complain. 'But I want to go with Betty.'

'That's not how it works.'

'But...'

'On the bus.'

For a second it looked like Kay would refuse. She sucked in a deep breath and folded her arms. The woman turned away from her and Betty watched her friend deflate like an old balloon.

'It's OK. When Daddy comes to get me, I'll tell him we need to find you.'

Kay didn't reply. She stepped forward and up the stairs onto the bus. She didn't look back.

Betty waited until all the big children had been sorted onto buses, and then there were only four of them left. Three boys a year or so older than Betty, and Betty herself.

Betty heard whispers and muttering among the adults. She edged closer.

'Just boys, you see...'

Betty moved even closer to get a better look. There were two men who looked like they had their white collars on backwards, like the priests back home did. Maybe they were priests too. The man in the grey suit who'd given the little speech was still there, with a woman in a smart pink dress clutching his hand. The woman stepped towards Betty.

'This little thing?' she asked incredulously. 'This little one's causing all the trouble?'

One of the priests nodded. 'We only take boys. There weren't any younger girls on the docket. She should have gone on the bus to the nuns.'

The other man shook his head. 'That's over eights.'

The woman squatted down and looked at Betty more closely. 'How old are you, doll?'

'Five.'

The woman nodded and turned her head away, suddenly blinking hard. She looked up at the smartly dressed man. 'Charles?'

The man shook his head.

The woman stood. Betty listened carefully to their whispers. 'Charles, you know I've always wanted a little girl.'

'Don't be ridiculous.'

'She's pretty.'

'She's a...' He stared at Betty. 'I mean, look at that hair.'

One of the women from the boat interrupted. 'The children don't normally go to private homes.'

The other woman glanced at the watch on her wrist. 'But Mr and Mrs Mason are very respectable people. I mean, he's a councillor. That's why they send him down for the welcome.'

The first woman stared at Betty and then back to the couple. 'But one like her? I mean, she's a...'

'She's a child who needs to go somewhere.' The priest's voice was cold. 'And the Masons are very generous benefactors to our mission. It would be as if the girl was in our care...'

'Like it says on the docket?'

'Like it says on your docket, but living somewhere more appropriate for her...' The priest glanced at Betty. 'For someone like her.'

The smartly dressed man, Mr Mason, folded his arms. 'I don't know.'

His wife wasn't listening anymore. She was leaning towards Betty, reaching out her hand as if to pet a charming puppy dog.

One of the women shrugged. 'They're excellent workers, though. With a bit of discipline.'

The man nodded. 'And there are payments for her support?'

The grown-ups huddled around in deeper discussion. Betty turned her attention to Mrs Mason, who was looking at her with absolute delight. Betty smiled slightly. 'What's your name, darling?'

'Betty.'

Mrs Mason frowned. 'What's that short for?'

Betty shrugged. Daddy had called her his little firefly because she burned brighter than anything else in the world. Mummy had said she was just Betty, and Elizabeth on Sundays. 'Elizabeth on Sundays?' she guessed.

'Elizabeth. That's better.' She stared at Betty a bit longer. 'But it's a bit much for such a little thing. Eliza. Would you like to be Eliza?'

Betty shook her head, but the woman turned away and shouted over her shoulder. 'Charles! We shall call her Eliza.'

Mr Mason broke away from the rest of the group. 'She'll have to earn her keep. Cooking and cleaning.'

Mrs Mason pursed her lips at her husband. 'We'll see about that.' She turned back to Betty. 'Come along, then, Eliza. I'm Mrs Mason. I'm going to be your new mummy.'

Chapter 9

Jane

I only saw Jennifer once more.

Two weeks after the visit from the child-welfare woman, Mrs Reed told me to pack all my things into an old suitcase because I was leaving to go to my new school. I was so happy to be escaping the Reeds, but I could not go without saying goodbye to Jennifer.

I sneaked out of the front door and darted down the stairs. I'd never normally dare, but I had to see her and what could Mrs Reed do now? She'd already decided to get rid of me.

I banged on Jennifer's door, my heart pounding in my chest just as loudly as my knuckles on the wood. She was home.

'Jane, is everything all right?'

'I wanted to say goodbye.'

'Where are you going?'

'To boarding school.'

She smiled. 'Well, I wish you all the best. Do come and see me when you are home for the holidays.'

I half-opened my mouth. There was so much more I wanted to say. Jennifer was my angel. I was desperate to leave the Reeds, but the idea of leaving her behind was so incredibly sad.

'Jane. Jane Eyre. Come back here at once,' Mrs Reed shouted from the landing above.

'Goodbye.' I threw myself at Jennifer, wrapping my arms around her. She patted me gently on the back and then stepped away.

'Take care of yourself, Jane.' And then the door swung closed.

'Don't keep me waiting, girl.' Mrs Reed pouted. 'Get your bag. It's time you left. And I don't want you to talk to that interfering woman again. Ever. Do you understand?'

'Yes, Mrs Reed.' For the first time in my life I realised that I'd told a lie. If I got a chance to see Jennifer, I knew that I would.

A taxi took Mrs Reed and I into the centre of the city, and pulled up in front of a large building. There were several big buses parked there, and people everywhere. A lot of them were carrying suitcases too. Mrs Reed told the taxi driver to wait for her.

She was leaving me here. I looked around at the crowds and the bustle and the strange faces. I didn't want to be with Mrs Reed, but I was suddenly a little bit afraid of being alone in such a busy place.

'Now, where is that teacher who's supposed to meet you?'

When we found her, the teacher looked very old to me, with short grey hair and a narrow, pinched face. She looked at me through her glasses when we were introduced.

'*Bien*. Come, child. Say your goodbyes to your mother and we will find our places on the bus. It is a very long way to Dubbo.'

'She's not...'

'Behave yourself at school,' Mrs Reed interrupted me. She looked at the floor for a second, and opened her mouth as if she wanted to say something more, but then she turned and walked away without once looking back.

The bus was not crowded, so the teacher left me sitting alone while she found her own seat. The journey took hours. We stopped a few times for people to get on and off, and to buy food and use the toilet at a petrol station. After a couple of hours, we were out of the city and driving through open spaces. I liked the open spaces. They reminded me of the home that I was starting to forget. I slept sometimes as the bus went on and on and on into the night.

The teacher shook me awake at last.

'We are here, Jane Eyre. Come along.'

It was very dark and my head was still fuzzy with sleep as we walked up to the gates. I looked up and read the name of the school.

Our Lady of the Rosary Girls' Boarding School.

A light over the gate gave off a soft golden glow as I walked beneath it. Perhaps here things would be better for me.

Chapter 10

Betty

'Come and sit by me, Eliza.' Betty squeezed onto the seat next to Mrs Mason. 'That's right. Sit by your mummy.'

Betty did as she was told. She didn't remind Mrs Mason that she was not really her mummy. Or that her name was really Betty. She had learnt that Mrs Mason didn't like it when she did that. Mrs Mason liked to have her close by, and liked to be called Mummy. She liked hugs and kisses. And if Betty did all those things, she was given treats and pretty clothes. And she could avoid Mr Mason and his son. That was something else she had learnt in the past weeks, or was it months? It was best to stay away from them.

Mrs Mason opened a magazine on her lap, circling one arm around Betty to keep the magazine open in front of them both. The magazines Mrs Mason bought had pictures of women who looked like Mrs Mason, living in houses that looked like the Masons' house. She liked to show Betty the pictures and tell her about what was in style and what was out. Today the magazine was open at a recipe page. 'We need to pick the dessert for Mr Mason's dinner on Friday. There are important people coming. What do you think?'

44

Betty peered at the pictures before thrusting a stubby finger at the one that looked the most chocolatey.

Mrs Mason scanned the text. 'Golliwog Biscuit Cake?'

Betty nodded.

'And will you help make it?'

'Yes.'

Mrs Mason tickled Betty's tummy. 'Good girl. I'll let you lick the bowl.'

Mr Mason strode into the room. 'Is our son home yet? Where's Richard?' He stopped. 'Why do you always have that little thing sitting right on top of you? She should be making herself useful.'

Mrs Mason pursed her lips. 'She is. She's helping me plan supper for Friday evening. We're going to make Golliwog Biscuit Cake.'

'Don't be stupid, woman. You can't serve that to my guests. Make a proper dessert.'

Betty shrank back a little, trying to hide behind Mrs Mason like she always did when Mr Mason was home.

'Is Richard home?'

Mrs Mason glanced at the clock. 'He should be here any minute.'

The front door clicked open right on schedule, and she heard the Masons' teenage son stomp into the hallway and then into the front lounge. His habitual slouch straightened instantly when he saw his father.

'I thought Richard should join us on Friday night.'

The boy grew another few inches.

'He needs to start learning the business and meeting the right people.'

Mrs Mason frowned. 'Isn't he a bit young?'

'Let me decide what's best for our son. He's ready. You'd keep him in nappies if you had your way.' He strode towards the door. 'And you've got your pet now if you want something to baby.'

Mr Mason marched out of the room and a few moments later

the front door swung open and closed again. Richard's demeanour shifted as soon as his father was out of the house. He slumped onto the couch, swinging his legs up onto the cushion.

'Richard, don't put your feet on the cushions.' Mrs Mason's voice quivered as she murmured the instruction.

Richard laughed at his mother's feeble attempt to tell him off. 'You don't tell my dad what to do.'

'He's the man of the house.'

'And one day I will be.' Richard laughed as he stood up again and headed towards the door. 'Let me know when dinner's ready.'

The lounge room fell into silence after the door slammed behind him. Mrs Mason patted Betty gently on the head.

On Friday evening, Betty was sent to her room early. Mrs Mason gave her banana sandwiches and a couple of golliwog biscuits that she'd bought ready for them to bake into a cake. They'd do that tomorrow, and the cake would be just for them, not for Mr Mason's guests. She sat up in bed, leaning on the wall, pulling her knees up to her chest with the covers over her legs. She munched on her biscuit, dropping crumbs on the sheets. She wasn't at all sleepy.

Her room was right above the front door. She wriggled to the end of the bed and reached to crack the window open a little bit. She could hear people arriving. The men all had big, brash voices like Mr Mason. The women were quieter. She tried to remember. She didn't think Daddy was loud and brash. Had Mummy been quiet?

She couldn't remember. She thought that Mummy did used to shout sometimes. She thought that sometimes Mummy used bad words that made Daddy frown. Betty could remember Daddy's big, strong hands, and his deep, warm voice, but she couldn't remember Mummy properly anymore at all. Betty screwed her eyes closed and tried to bring Mummy's face into her head. It was almost there, but, when she tried to look closely, the image blurred and wafted away.

The voices outside the front door had subsided to just two now. Mr Mason and Richard. Betty opened her eyes and listened.

'Now, these blokes own some of the biggest properties in the state. These are important people and they need to know that we're men they can do business with. You understand.'

'Yes, Father.'

'Right. So tell me again. Who are you sitting next to?'

'The old guy. Rochester.'

'Less of the old. He's only a few years older than me.'

Betty thought she heard Richard snigger, and the noise was followed by the sharp crack of Mr Mason's hand across his son's face.

'You'll take this seriously.'

'Sorry, Father.'

'The Rochesters are important people, and I've heard they're not happy with Halligans. So you're going to charm him. He's got a son not much older than you. He'll inherit the property one day, like you'll inherit all this. That's what we want Rochester to see – that we're a nice, respectable family business that he can trust for years to come.'

'Yes, Father.'

There was another short moment of quiet. 'Now, get your face cleaned up and get inside.'

Chapter 11

Jane

Waking up on my first morning at Our Lady School, I found myself surrounded by girls my own age. They stood beside my bed, looking down at the person who had magically appeared in the middle of the night.

'You're the new girl.'

'Yes. I'm Jane.' I sat up in bed, pushing back the thin sheet and scratchy blanket, conscious of their eyes on me. Back when I lived with my mother, there were always lots of people around, and lots of kids to play with. It would be good to live like that again.

'Why didn't you come on the first day of school like we did?' The girl asking the questions was very pretty. She had long, shiny brown hair tied in two plaits, with pink ribbons. She was wearing pink pyjamas too.

'I don't know. I was at school in Sydney. Then Mrs Reed said I was coming here.'

'Who is Mrs Reed? Is she your mother?'

'My aunt. I just lived with her.'

'Why don't you live with your mum and dad?'

They were all staring at me, waiting for the answer.

'I don't know.'

'Maybe she's an orphan,' a red-haired girl suggested. 'Are your mum and dad dead?'

'No!' My answer was automatic, but the question lodged somewhere deep inside me. Why hadn't Mum come to take me home from the Reed house? As for a dad... I wasn't sure. I'd never called any of Mum's friends 'dad'.

'I bet they are. I bet they're dead,' a blonde girl said. 'Or maybe they just don't love you and they gave you away.'

Something snapped when she said that. My mum had loved me. I was sure she had. Before Mrs Reed, before this school, I'd been happy.

'Don't say that.' I jumped out of bed. 'You take that back.'

'I bet you're right,' another voice chimed in.

'Nah.' That was the first girl again. 'I think she's an orphan. I think they're dead. Dead. Dead. Dead.'

The first girl started the chant, but the others picked it up quickly.

'Stop it!' I screamed. The shouting was ringing in my ears. Another school. Another set of kids who seemed to hate me. For a second I was back in the sports shed with the jeering and the fear. 'Stop it...' I pushed the dark-haired girl. She staggered backwards and fell over right at the feet of the nun who had at that moment entered the dormitory.

'What's going on here?' The nun was tall and thin, and dressed all in black.

'She pushed me, Sister.' The dark-haired girl immediately began sobbing.

'We don't allow pushing here.' The nun looked me up and down. 'And nor do we allow girls to sleep in their clothes.'

I tugged at my nightie. It wasn't really a nightie, it was just a big t-shirt that was a hand-me down from Emma, but it was all I had.

'Now apologise to Miranda.'

The girl still sitting on the floor turned towards me with a really nasty smile.

'No. I won't. She said a horrible thing about me.'

'I didn't, Sister, honestly.' Miranda turned her doll-like face to the nun.

The nun took me by the shoulder. 'You will apologise. Now. And then you will write out one hundred times, "I must not tell lies". Do you understand?' When I didn't answer, she shook my shoulder hard. 'Do you understand, Jane Eyre?'

All around me the other girls were smiling and giggling. The nun shook me again, gripping my shoulder so hard it hurt.

It wasn't fair! I had thought being at a school with no boys to bully me would be better. I was wrong.

Chapter 12

Betty

Betty was pulled along by Mrs Mason's tight grip on her hand, through the mass of bodies rushing and pushing their way through the shops. Betty had never seen anything like this.

Bankstown Square, Mrs Mason said, was the biggest shopping centre in the whole country, with all sorts of new and interesting shops that everyone wanted to see. That's why Mrs Mason had to come here to buy Betty's new summer clothes. Betty had thought it was summer already, but apparently that wasn't right. Summer and winter were backwards here and even winter wasn't really cold.

Betty's legs were tired and Mrs Mason was laden with carrier bags from all the shops they'd been in. Mrs Mason hadn't let her try on one of the new miniskirts that were so popular. She was apparently too little for that sort of thing, whatever that sort of thing was. Her dresses were all pretty and frilly. Betty didn't really like them, but she didn't tell Mrs Mason that. She thought that that would make Mrs Mason sad.

They swept out of the big sliding doors into the sunshine. Mrs Mason pulled her hand away for a second to reach into her pocket.

That was it. Betty was too tired. She shuffled backwards away from Mrs Mason and sat down on a low wall outside the shops. The sun was hot on her face and she closed her eyes for a moment, away from the bustle and the noise. It was almost warm enough to imagine that she was back in her real home in front of the blazing fire.

It couldn't have been more than a few seconds before she opened her eyes again, but when she did she couldn't see Mrs Mason anywhere. Betty clambered up onto the wall, but even up on tippy-toes she couldn't see Mrs Mason. There were too many people pushing their way into the shopping centre, or fighting their way to the car park.

'Eliza!'

She heard the voice and jumped off the wall. She tried to run towards the voice, but there were too many people in the way.

'Eliza!' The voice was further away now. It seemed to come from outside the car park, near the street.

Betty stopped and tried to listen. Where was Mrs Mason? She had to find her. Mrs Mason was the only person she knew, the only person who cared about her.

'Eliza!'

The voice was closer this time. Betty set out more confidently, striding in what she hoped was the right direction.

The next sound made her stop. It wasn't a voice. It wasn't Mrs Mason calling for her. It was a growl of an engine, then a screech of brakes, and then a cry. The crowd around her stopped milling in all their different directions and turned, like Betty, towards the cry.

Then the voices all started up at once. 'Someone go into one of the shops and call the ambos.'

'What happened?'

'Is she all right?'

'Oh my God.'

Betty pushed and shoved as hard as she could to get to the

front of the crowd. Mrs Mason must be in the crowd, so if she could get to the front Mrs Mason would see her, wouldn't she? And then everything would be all right.

But she couldn't get through. The throng of people was too great. Eventually she called out. 'Help me!'

A woman's face appeared, ducking down to her level. 'Are you all right?'

'Mrs Mason....' Betty gulped out the words but couldn't finish.

'Mrs Mason? Is that your mother?'

Betty shook her head. 'I live with her.'

'OK. I'm sure we can find her.'

Betty let the stranger lift her up and carry her through the crowd, shouting at people to let them through.

'Can you see your lady now?' The woman turned around so Betty could look at the people gathered.

Betty shook her head. The woman turned again. Then Betty saw Mrs Mason. She was lying in the street. There was a motor-bike on its side right next to her, and a man dressed in black leather sitting on the pavement. A truck was stopped on the other side of the road, its cab twisted away from them at a funny angle. Betty cried out.

'What's wrong?'

She couldn't make the words. She stuck out a hand, finger pointing towards the figure stretched out on the road.

'Oh dear God,' the woman muttered. She turned her body so Betty couldn't see Mrs Mason lying on the road, but it was too late. The image was fixed inside her head. Eventually a siren sounded and a couple of cars with flashing lights pulled to a stop in the empty street alongside the abandoned truck. The woman who was still holding Betty stepped forward to the men who jumped out of the cars.

'I think this is her little daughter,' she whispered.

53

Chapter 13

Jane

In those first weeks at school, I tried to keep to myself, but it was hard. There were two hundred girls at Our Lady, and very few places to be alone. All the girls ate together in a large dining room and slept six to a dormitory. We kept our clothes in small cubicles, but even then three girls shared a single space.

I never minded sharing my space when I lived with Mum, but here it was different. Here, instead of letting one another be, it felt like everyone was competing to be the best and the most popular. And I hated getting changed in front of the other girls. Showing your body was wrong. Mrs Reed had said that when John had looked at me, and I'd known that she'd been right.

This meant I was sometimes late for chapel or late for class. I hated it when the nuns got angry, and sometimes I was punished for lateness, but I still was not going to get undressed in front of the other girls.

On weekends, we were allowed to wear ordinary clothes instead of uniforms. I only had three dresses. They were hand-me-downs from Emma and when I first got them, I thought they were pretty. At school I learnt differently.

'Oh look, Jane is wearing the same dress she wore last weekend.'

'Look! It's been ripped and mended. She's got no-one to buy her a new one.' Miranda was the most popular girl in our class. Where she led, the others would follow. 'Because she's an orphan.'

'I am not an orphan!'

'Then why don't your parents come to visit you like mine do?'

'Because they live a long way away.'

'No. It's because they're dead and you're an orphan.'

They all started chanting. 'Jane is an orphan. Jane is an orphan. Dead. Dead. Dead.' I tried to ignore them and walk away, but they stood in front of me, just chanting.

'I am not!' I struck out at the nearest girl. Not Miranda. She'd learnt by now not to stand too close to me.

The girl screamed very loudly. I hit her again. Then one of her friends pulled my hair, so I hit her too. Then they were all screaming, and pushing and shoving me.

'Girls. Stop it this instant!' Sister Mary Gabriel was the deputy headmistress of the school.

'They started it.' My words rushed out. 'They said I was an orphan, and I'm not. I hate them!'

'She hit me,' one of the other girls wailed.

'Enough!' We all fell silent. 'Jane Eyre, did you hit her?'

'Yes, but…'

'But nothing. We do not hit people. This is wrong. Our Lord teaches us that. You will go to the chapel and pray to the Holy Mother to forgive you. Miranda, you and your friends will go to the library. I want a one-page essay from each of you about the virtues of being kind to those who are…' She glanced back in my direction. 'Less fortunate than ourselves. Now go, all of you.'

When I got to the chapel that day, a girl called Helen from my class was there. I had never spoken to her before, but I'd always wanted to. She wasn't into make-up and gossiping like the other girls. She didn't have fancy clothes either, but she did have lovely reddish hair. She didn't smile very often, but when she did, her face seemed to glow. She kept herself a bit separate from the others. She never joined in with their chants. And she was so clever. She always knew the answers to the teachers' questions, and she wasn't afraid to put her hand up to answer, even though the other girls called her 'smartie' and teacher's pet.

I didn't say anything. I slipped into the next pew and knelt down. I didn't pray for forgiveness for hitting the other girls. I prayed for forgiveness for whatever I'd done that meant I'd deserved to be sent to Mrs Reed's house and then here.

'You shouldn't fight with them.'

I sat back and turned to look at Helen.

'How did you know I was fighting?'

'Your dress is torn. Why do you always fight them, Jane?' She frowned as she looked at me. 'You can't win.'

'I hate them all. They said I was an orphan…and I'm not.' Perhaps I thought if I said it often enough, it would be true.

'Why would that be a bad thing? I am an orphan.'

'Oh. I'm sorry. I didn't know.' I couldn't help but ask, hoping for an answer that would prove that my situation was different to hers. 'What happened to your mum and dad?'

'I don't know. I was very small. I have been an orphan as long as I can remember.'

'Don't you hate not having a home or a family? I hate it.'

'But I do have a home. It's here. I've been at boarding school since I was tiny.' She twisted in the pew to face me properly. 'We could be family, though, if you wanted, Jane. You and me.'

I couldn't put my reaction into words. Someone wanted to spend time with me. I managed to nod and reached my hand towards her across the pew.

She took it and smiled. 'Good. Now we're together, you won't have to fight all the time.'

Chapter 14

Betty

'I don't know why Mother thought she was pretty.'

Richard didn't even look at Betty as he spoke about her. He'd learnt that from his father.

'Neither do I.' Mr Mason fell quiet for a moment. 'But she was like that. She always saw the good in people.'

Richard snorted.

Mr Mason rose from his chair and walked over to where Betty was sitting on a couch, reading a book.

'You can't just sit around here all day.' He straightened up. 'Maddie!'

The housekeeper walked into the room. She was the third or fourth since Mrs Mason's death. They came. They stayed for a little while and they went away. Only Betty was stuck here.

'I need you to sort this one out.'

The girl glanced at Betty uncertainly. 'What do you mean? I get her off to school every day. What else am I supposed to do?'

'She's old enough to start pulling her weight around here now.'

'Yes, Mr Mason.'

'And after school she can work with you in the kitchen. She

needs to learn what you do. Cooking, cleaning…' His voice trailed away as if he was unable to imagine what else might need doing around the house. 'She'll be someone's wife if we're lucky one day. Or she can work for someone if she has to. Like you.'

Maddie's face set in a stony look. 'Yes, Mr Mason.'

'Right. Off you go, then.' He turned to Betty. 'Both of you now.'

Betty scurried after the cleaning girl.

'And do something about her hair.' The final words were shouted after them as Maddie pushed Betty towards the kitchen, where she took a long, hard look at Betty's hair.

'How'd you get hair like that anyway?'

Betty tugged at her dark, tight curls and shrugged.

'I don't understand. I can't see someone like him taking in a half-caste.' She stared again at Betty's hair. 'This needs sorting out, though.'

She opened and shut cupboards for a minute. 'Now, you don't tell anyone I showed you how to do this. OK?'

Betty nodded. Maddie mixed milk and honey together in a pan and smoothed them onto Betty's hair, before combing her kinks and curls away. Eventually she lifted Betty up so she could look at herself in the mirror that hung high up next to the door. 'See. No more frizz.'

'It looks like your hair.'

Maddie narrowed her eyes. 'Don't say that.'

Betty did her hair like that every day when she went to school. It didn't make any difference. Nobody at her school talked or looked like her. Maddie was unsympathetic. 'You've just got to fit in.'

But Betty didn't fit in. Betty didn't talk the same as her classmates. Betty had cracks in the skin at the end of her fingers from the dish soap and the oven cleaner she used when she cleaned the kitchen after school. Betty had bags under her eyes from getting up so early to smooth down her kinky hair. Betty had cheeks that erupted into freckles at the slightest hint of sun, and arms that turned a rich brown when she stayed outside at break-time. Betty wasn't like this Eliza Mason whose name was written on the class list.

Eliza Mason, she imagined, would be a good girl who fit in and knew how to behave with all these strange children who treated her like the foreigner. Eliza Mason would belong in the living room at the big house with Richard and Mr Mason, not out in the kitchen with the cleaning lady.

One day, Maddie held out her finger to Betty. There was a thin gold band with a tiny sparkling clear stone at the centre. 'He's called Mick. He works for his dad in construction. But he can sing. He's auditioning to go on the cruise ships and then we'll both be off.'

Betty never found out whether Maddie's Mick got his job on the cruise ships and whether Maddie went with him, but she went somewhere. And then there was another woman, and another, and another. And they never knew that Eliza used to be Betty, or that she used to sit in the nice living room with Mrs Mason. They just saw a girl who didn't belong. As the years passed, her world got smaller. School. The kitchen. The tiny bedroom well away from Mr Mason and Richard. And the yard outside the kitchen door. The yard was her escape. She would go there and listen to the music and the voices on her cheap plastic radio. Sometimes she heard a voice that sounded like her dad, or like the way she thought she remembered her dad talking. She listened to the Beatles and the Stones, and then to Bowie and Queen, and The Who. Something about them made her think of another home and another world from a long, long time ago.

In the yard the sun would beat down on her skin and she could imagine the warmth of the fire. In the yard she didn't have to behave a certain way. She could touch the ground with her fingers and feel the air on her face, and stare up at the sky. And she could imagine what it would be like to launch herself into the clouds and fly free like the sparks that were now almost all she remembered from the big ship that had brought her to this life. She wished she was a shining spark against the night sky, flying far away from this place and these people that held her down. Flying back to that half-forgotten place she still thought of as home.

Chapter 15

Jane

Another Christmas was approaching and once more I stared out the window at the coaches parked in the school's circular driveway. They were very different from the old bus that had brought me to Our Lady years ago when I was just a little kid. These coaches had air-conditioning, and toilets. And music played during the journey. At least, that's what the girls who rode them home for the holidays said. I wouldn't know. In all the years I'd been here, I'd never been 'home' for the holidays. I hadn't even heard from the Reeds in years. They had probably forgotten I ever existed, and that thought didn't bother me at all. Our Lady was home now. The only person in the world I cared about was here.

'They'll all be leaving soon.'

I could hear the happiness in Helen's voice.

Below our dormitory, the front doors of the senior-school boarding house opened and girls poured out, bubbling with excitement at the thought of going home. We watched them as they fought for the best seats on the coaches. Helen and I were anxious for them to leave too. For the next six weeks we would be the only students at the school. It was our own private heaven.

'Come on, I want to show you something.' Helen moved away from the window.

'What?'

'It's a surprise.'

Together we started down the big wooden staircase that led to the main entrance of the boarding house. As always, Helen didn't hurry. She never hurried. When I was smaller, that had bothered me and I'd wanted to grab her hand and drag her along at my speed. But now I was used to it. I was content to walk beside her.

'Oh look, it's the orphans.'

'There'll be no Christmas for you.' Miranda and her friends were standing near the front door. 'It'll just be you and the nuns. And all those prayers.' She rolled her eyes. 'No Christmas dinner and no presents for you.'

'She might get some more of last year's hand me down clothes.'

'Maybe this year she'll get a training bra.' I fought down the urge to tug at my slightly too small dress. I was still wearing hand-me-downs from the Reeds, although occasionally, at the nuns' urgings, Mrs Reed sent some money to buy me things I needed. A bra was not one of those things. At fourteen, I was still flat chested. The girls sniggered, flexing their shoulders to show off their developing busts.

The anger I'd got so used to carrying with me since I'd arrived at school flared up. I didn't care about Christmas dinner or growing breasts, but I wanted to shake them and shout at them until they saw that not having those things didn't matter one bit. Helen and I were perfectly happy without them.

Helen's fingers closed around my hand and I pushed the anger aside.

'Girls – don't dawdle. The bus won't wait for you.' We all turned to see one of the nuns coming down the stairs, followed by a woman we had never seen before. 'And Miranda, perhaps during Christmas you could think about our Lord and his teachings about being kind to others.'

'Yes, Sister.' The girls left quickly.

The sister smiled at Helen and I. 'So girls, you will both be with us for the summer again?'

'Yes, Sister.'

'Well then, I would like to introduce you to our newest member of staff who has just joined us. This is Miss Temple.'

Miss Temple smiled. Her hair was dark red and her eyes were golden brown. She had painted fingernails. They were a soft, shiny pink and when she moved her hands, as she did when she talked, the pink caught the light. She wore a blue dress with a white collar, not unlike our school uniform, but on her it looked elegant. 'You're not a nun.' The words were out before I could stop them.

'No.' Miss Temple's smile spread wider.

'Miss Temple is the first of our lay staff,' the Sister explained. 'We will be taking on a few lay teachers and house mistresses in the future. Miss Temple will be joining us as an English teacher when school resumes in February.'

'And I will be house mistress here in the junior school,' added Miss Temple.

Helen nodded. 'Can we go now, please, Sister?'

'Of course.'

We left. We slipped around the back of the boarding house towards the gymnasium.

'Don't you think Miss Temple is pretty?' I was still a little dazzled by her.

'I suppose so.' Helen frowned a little bit. 'Come on..'

'Where are we going?'

I followed her along the edge of the sports field to the furthest corner of the grounds. This area wasn't used for anything and it was overgrown with bushes. Helen pushed her way past the bushes and I followed her into a small open area.

'Oh.'

There were flowers growing all around me. Yellow and red flowers that were in full bloom because summer was just starting.

I could smell them too. There was something familiar about that smell.

'It must have been a garden once,' Helen said. 'When I found this place, there were weeds everywhere. I pulled them out and the flowers grew.'

'When did you find it?'

'A couple of months ago. I wanted to surprise you. Miranda is wrong, Jane. This is your present.'

'My present?'

'Your Christmas present, silly. We can spend all our holiday here and no-one will disturb us. We can grow even more flowers together.'

'It's beautiful.' I flung my arms around Helen and hugged her. As I did, I remembered where I had smelled the flowers before. My mother. I could barely remember her face, but I did remember the flowers she'd grown. The garden smelled like home and freedom, and memories, and Helen had made it for me.

I hugged my best friend even tighter as I said words I hadn't said since the day I was taken away from my home.

'I love you, Helen.'

Chapter 16

Betty

Betty leant on the veranda railing. It was a hot January day. Most people would be inside in the shade, but, even after all this time, Betty still loved the way the heat of the sun warmed her as it touched her skin. And she even secretly loved the way it turned her skin darker – it reminded her that she wasn't Eliza Mason at all, no matter what everyone else might think.

The girls from school would go to the beach on the weekends and come in on Monday all red and sore, and complaining that they could never get a tan. Betty wasn't like them. That meant they hated her. Betty had decided not to care. She'd decided that she hated them too.

A car pulled up to the garage. Richard's new car, a present from his father for his birthday. She'd heard Richard boasting to his mates about the big red muscle car. It was a 1971 Falcon GTHO with racing stripes. He thought it made him powerful. It didn't. It was the car that was powerful. Richard was nothing.

She slipped back inside before Richard got out of the car. She tried to avoid Richard as much as she could. He had ignored her for years, but just lately he'd noticed her again and she didn't like the way he looked at her now.

She tied her hair out of her face and went down to the kitchen. The cleaning woman only came twice a week now. Mr Mason had decreed Betty old enough to manage most of the cooking and tidying. He only got someone in to help if he was having his disgusting work people over to the house. Then Betty was confined to the kitchen. She didn't mind that too much. It was better than sitting at that table with the Masons.

It was time to start making dinner, so she put a pot of water on the stove to boil and started peeling potatoes.

'What are you doing?'

The tone of Richard's voice made her freeze.

'Go away. I'm starting dinner. Your father will be angry at me if it's late.'

Richard shrugged. 'He's not home yet. Went out with clients and won't be back for ages. Plenty of time for a bit of fun.' His smirk made Betty's insides clench. She was sixteen. She knew exactly what he was talking about.

'Piss off.'

'I don't think so. We've fed and clothed you all these years. It's time you started paying us back. And I know just how you can do that.'

Betty shook her head. 'No.'

Richard lunged towards her. She staggered backwards, cracking her hip on the corner of the big table. She stumbled. That was enough for him to get to her. He pushed her back onto the table and trapped her there between his arms and his body. She wriggled backwards. He laughed.

One hand grabbed her wrist. The other dug into her thigh. 'You can pretend you don't want to, but we both know you do, don't we?'

His arm pushed down across her chest, and his free hand

pulled at her knee, forcing her thighs wide. 'Come on. I know you give it to the boys at school.'

His hand starting pulling at her skirt. Betty stared up at the ceiling, her panicking mind searching for something... anything.

She twisted her shoulders as hard as she could. It unbalanced him and she sat up, leaning forward, trying desperately to push him away. It wasn't enough. She just ended up closer against his body. He laughed again. 'I knew you'd be up for it.'

He held her tight against his body now, while he struggled with his own clothes. 'I bet you like to suck cock, don't you?'

A wave of nausea hit her. She leant forward as far as she could. One last effort. The pot for the potatoes was still on the stove. If she could reach that, then she'd have something she could hit him with. She reached and her fingertips brushed something – the handle? She tried to grab. The burning pain seared through her hand. She screamed without thinking. Richard looked behind himself. He pulled her hand into his grip, staring at the red welt that was appearing across her palm. 'Does that hurt?'

Betty had no fight left. She nodded silently.

He smirked again. 'Good.'

He tipped her back onto the table. Looking into his eyes, she saw a kind of madness there. Nothing would stop him now. Not her pleas, or her injury. Not even fear of his father finding out. She'd had boys before, but this was something else. They'd wanted her. Richard just wanted to have her, to show her that he could. Betty closed her eyes and pictured the fire. She concentrated on the burning sensation in her hand, and in her mind that grew into flames dancing in front of her, warming her. Carrying her away.

'What in God's name...?'

Richard was off her in an instant. 'Father?'

Betty pushed with her uninjured arm, and pulled her knees up onto the table, dragging her skirt down to cover herself.

'What in God's name is going on here?'

Betty stared down at her blistering hand. She didn't speak.

'I was... she...' Richard stumbled and stuttered over the words as he stuffed himself back into his trousers.

'She what?' His father's voice was cool.

'She started it.'

Betty shook her head.

'She came on to me. Been coming on to me for months now.'

Mr Mason nodded. 'And you couldn't resist the urge?'

Richard bent his head towards the ground. 'Sorry, Father.'

Betty waited for the consequences. She'd heard Mr Mason shout at his son through the walls sometimes. But instead of anger, Mr Mason just nodded. 'Young men have needs.'

He stepped forward and slapped his son briskly across the shoulder. Then he looked at Betty. 'And you fancied this one.'

Richard shrugged. 'She was up for it.'

Betty burned with rage. 'I was not. I...'

Mr Mason held up a hand. 'Quiet. You've done enough.'

The older man was staring at her, though not with want, like she'd had from Richard such a short time before. This was something else.

'My mates all want a go with her. That's half the reason they all want to come round here.'

Mr Mason nodded. 'That's interesting. Very interesting.' He turned back to his son. 'I forgot the contracts for the Northam land leases. Could you fetch them? Should be on my desk.'

Richard hurried out of the room.

Betty still sat huddled on the table.

Mr Mason folded his arms. 'I'm thinking I might get a new cleaning girl in.'

Betty nodded, confused.

'Maybe it's time you played more of a part in the business, if you know what I mean? Does that sound good?'

Betty didn't know what he meant, but it seemed to mean less cleaning, so she nodded.

'Good. We'll have to get you some new clothes.' He looked her up and down. 'Nicer things so you're nice for my associates to look at. I'll give you money to go shopping. Would you like that?'

Now Betty understood. She was to look pretty and make people happy. 'Yes, Mr Mason.'

Chapter 17

Jane

'Sue says she did it with her boyfriend on New Year's Eve. At a party.'

'I bet she's lying.'

'No, she told me it didn't last long, but they definitely did It.' The two girls giggled wildly as they carried their bags up the stairs to the dormitories.

I watched them go. I hated the start of the new year. During the summer holidays, Helen and I got to be alone at Our Lady. For ten years now, summer had been my favourite part of the year. We would read and talk, and now we had the added joy of watching our garden flourish. The Christmas services with only the two of us and the nuns, rather than with a chapel full of giggling girls, were beautiful and I was able to feel the presence of the Lord in the calm and the music.

Then school would start, and all that peace was shattered.

This year we were moving into grade twelve. I was almost seventeen, almost a woman, according to the calendar, but nowhere near what the other girls would consider being a woman. I'd barely talked to a man outside of the priests at confession, and that certainly didn't count. Those giggling girls gossiping about who had and hadn't done it already lived in a different world.

I let myself out the back door of the boarding house. As a senior boarder, the nuns didn't seem to mind if I went where I liked around the school grounds after lessons were over. The garden was wilting a bit in the late summer heat, but it was still beautiful. The roses were continuing to bloom, and we had trained a white bougainvillea from the neighbouring garden to climb to our side of the fence. Helen had said that that was a sort of magic – it was like stealing, but nobody lost anything. The more people loved and cared for the plant, the more there was to go around. There were tall sunflowers, their faces raised to the clear blue sky and delicate blue Agapanthus. Helen and I had made a shady bower, with green grass to sit on, and she was there now, resting against the garden wall and reading. Throughout the summer, this little oasis had given me so much joy, but now I found myself looking at the scene with a sense of disquiet. 'What's wrong?' she asked as I dropped onto the grass next to her.

'This is our last year at school. What do we do at the end of the year?'

She put her book down and looked at me. 'Will you go back to live with the Reeds?'

'Never.'

She took my hand. 'You're still thinking about John, aren't you?'

I nodded. It had been a long time before I'd even told Helen about that day in the sports shed and about my cousin coming into my room. Even now I couldn't make sense of what he'd been doing. 'He probably goes after prettier girls now.'

'Oh, Jane. You are pretty. Don't you know that?'

She always said that, and I always wanted to believe her. But when I looked at the other girls, I knew it wasn't true. I was bony where they had curves. My plain brown hair was flat and fine, not glossy like some of the others. I barely dared to try putting on make-up. I didn't know how to stop it looking like a painted mask. At best, I hoped to be forgettable.

'I don't know anything, Helen. I've lived here since I was just a child. We both have.' I was realising rapidly that in a few short months we'd have to leave this place. We'd have to leave this garden. We'd have to leave the nuns and lay teachers who'd been our guides through life so far. And we'd have to go... where? I tried to explain what I meant.

'The only time we leave is to go on school trips. We really don't know what's out there.' The idea was overwhelming – there was a whole world waiting to chew us up. 'Maybe we should stay here and become nuns?'

Helen laughed. She had a lovely laugh, soft and sweet, like her.

'You would not make a good nun, Jane.'

'Why not?' I had faith. It was my touchstone – one of the only things I could always trust, and I didn't care about missing out on all that stuff with boys. That would be a relief, if anything.

Helen shook her head. 'You have too much energy and curiosity to be happy settling for life here as a nun.'

She was missing my point. 'But I don't know anything about life. I've never even kissed anyone.'

'You've kissed me.'

I fell silent. I had kissed Helen. On the cheek. And once she'd planted a kiss on my lips after we came out of a really hard exam where she was convinced she'd passed. That wasn't what I meant. 'Not like that.'

'So how do you want to kiss me?'

I didn't reply. I didn't know the words. But I wanted to kiss her. I wanted to know what it felt like to touch her. I wanted to stay in this garden forever with Helen. And I didn't have the words to explain that, so I needed another way to show her.

I placed my lips gently on hers. They tasted like honey, just as sweet and soft as she was. Her fingertips brushed my cheek. It was a perfect moment. There was me, and there was Helen. And no one to hurt us.

Then she pulled away.

I almost didn't dare open my eyes, but when I did she was smiling. I kissed her again, longer and harder, and, for the first time, our tongues touched. My heart began to beat a little faster. No part of me wanted to stop. I'd had one kiss, and now another. I wanted to keep going, keep exploring. I wanted more of her. I wanted to give her more of me.

Something stopped me. This time, I pulled away.

'Jane?'

'I can't.'

'Why not?' Helen sat up and looked at me.

'It's... It's wrong.' I hated saying it out loud. It sounded like a rejection and it wasn't. It wasn't at all. She was all I wanted, but I loved God. I loved the feeling of safety and community that I'd experienced from the very first time I'd been part of a church. We laughed at the nuns sometimes, but, I knew in my heart that what they taught us about Jesus, about the gospel, was true. And they taught us that what I'd done with Helen was wrong.

'It's not.' She took a deep breath in. 'I love you. When we're together, nothing else matters. I thought you felt the same?'

It was the hint of uncertainty in her voice that was my undoing. Helen had always had a certainty about her decisions that I couldn't match, but now she was looking to me for reassurance. I looked around the garden that the two of us had built. We'd made something beautiful.

'I do feel the same.'

Her smile was so wide I thought it might crack her face. 'It's not wrong, Jane. Nothing that is based on love can be wrong.'

I nodded. In my head I pushed all thoughts of God and the church to one side, and gave myself totally to my feelings for

Helen. The two things were separate. Helen and I together was something wonderful. It was just something that needed to be kept private, separate from everything else. I bent my head towards her, and kissed her again.

Chapter 18

Betty

'Hey. What you doing?'

Betty turned towards the voice. The boy had been in her year at school. They'd made out after school once, ages ago now – just pashing, kids' stuff. Betty hadn't seen him at all last term. 'Nothing much. Where you been?'

'The parents moved me to a private school.' He fell into step beside her as they walked across the park. 'Boor-ring. No girls there. No-one like you.' He glanced at her, looking up and down until his eyes came to rest on her boobs.

This was the thing that made her powerful; the thing that set her apart from everyone else. She might have to follow a lot of other people's rules most of the time, but, when it came to this, she could set the rules. The other girls might look through her as if she wasn't there, but the boys didn't. All she had to do was smile. Or bend over to flash them a look at her boobs. Or her backside in a miniskirt. Then they were in her power.

She wasn't like those neat little girls with their perfect bouncy ponytails and their posters of David Cassidy and the Bee Gees.

They talked earnestly about how far they'd gone with some boy. And how he wanted more, but they weren't the type of girl who did that. And sometimes they'd shoot a look at Betty when they said that. And inside, Betty would just laugh.

Those girls didn't understand. It didn't have to mean anything. It was fun. And you got to decide who and when. Sex was power. Betty ran her hand over her hair, smoothed by the milk and honey mixture, like she'd done three mornings a week every week since she was six years old. They could make her look like them but that didn't mean her body belonged to them. It was hers. And she could do whatever – whoever – she liked with it.

'Do you wanna have some fun?'

He nodded. She grabbed his hand as a rush of excitement took her. She led him away from the path into a bit of the park that was overgrown with bushes. She knew this place well. She spun around and leant back against the tree. That look was on his face. The look that told her he wanted her. He grinned as he moved towards her and pressed his lips to hers.

Betty responded hungrily. This was her favourite thing to do. She clung to him as he pushed his hands under her loose, thin skirt and hooked his fingers around her knickers. Her own hands went to his waistband, pulling at the buttons on his jeans.

'Eliza...' He grunted the name into her neck.

'Call me Betty.'

'What? But?'

'Just shut up.' She pressed her lips against his, thrusting her tongue into his mouth to stop him talking. If he wouldn't call her Betty, she didn't want him to call her anything.

He took the hint, moving his hands to his hips and easing his jeans and grundies down.

She reached into the pocket of her skirt and pulled out a small packet.

'Put this on.'

'What?' He glanced down at the condom. 'No way. Not gonna wear one of those things.'

She placed her hands on his shoulders and pushed him away. 'Then you don't get to do this.'

He didn't even hesitate. He just did as she ordered and her blood surged with the feeling of power. She had him. She pulled him back to her body. She ground her crotch against him, pulling him deeper into her, searching for that release. She heard his breath growing ragged and felt his fingers digging deeper into her butt. He wasn't any good. He was done within seconds of getting going. He gasped for breath and his knees sagged. That made Betty feel even stronger. When she felt the energy drain out of him, it was as if she had taken it from him.

She put a hand firmly on his chest and pushed him back. He stood there, staring at her, daks round his knees. She could see something like awe in his eyes, and she knew she was his first. He would never forget her.

'When can we… you… again?'

He liked her. He wanted to do it again. She felt a deep satisfaction that had nothing to do with physical release.

'Maybe.'

She stepped out of her knickers, picked them up and stuffed them in her pocket, and made to walk away.

She stopped.

Richard was walking across the park towards her. She ducked back into the bushes and signalled to the boy to be quiet. She listened as Richard's footsteps slowly went past.

She had avoided him as much as possible since that day. She wasn't afraid that he'd try and have her again. Mr Mason had plans for her, so Richard wouldn't be allowed to touch her again. But she didn't want him to tell his father what she was doing with the other boys. She understood that her being pure and clean was important to Mr Mason's plans.

Mason wanted her now he had a use for her.

The boys wanted her.

She wasn't someone to be passed around and abandoned anymore.

Chapter 19

Jane

The clear note of the bell cut through the muted conversation in the dining hall. Everyone fell silent as Sister Mary Gabriel stood up.

'Girls, immediately after the meal, everyone in the senior school is to make their way to the assembly hall. Teachers, if you could please ensure the younger girls are escorted to their dormitories early. Lights may be kept on for an extra half hour to allow the girls to read or study.'

There were a few questioning glances around the room as the sister sat down again. Sunday evening assemblies were reserved for important announcements, like the retirement of one of the sisters, or the arrival of a new teacher.

I looked across to the next table, where Helen was sitting. School rules determined that we must all rotate around different tables, to get to know our fellow students and to develop the art of conversation. At least, that was what the teachers said. I always thought it was just designed to stop friends sitting together and being too rowdy. Not that I cared. Helen and I were often separated by the daily goings on at school, but when classes were over, we had our garden and we had each other.

I was happy, so happy that some days it was a struggle not to shout out how I felt to the whole school, but I knew I couldn't. Publicly, we were best friends, so of course we were together as we sat in the assembly hall. Every now and then, we would let our hands brush, or our fingers touch, but I was confident that our secret was safe.

The nuns had seats on the stage in front of us. Surprisingly, Father Brook wasn't there. He'd given a very loud sermon in chapel about sins of the flesh, before hearing confession and then dining with the sisters at the head table. I went to confession each week, but I never said anything about Helen. The two things were separate. I loved God and I loved Helen. The only way that made sense was if I never let the two mix, even in my own thoughts.

'Silence, please.'

Sister Mary Gabriel, who was now our headmistress, got to her feet. She looked around the room, her gaze not resting on anyone in particular.

'I want to talk about something very important, and I want you to pay attention. This is a very serious matter.'

The hall fell silent. All eyes were on Sister Gabriel.

'You are no longer really girls. You are young women and I know Matron has assisted some of you as you reach this milestone in your lives.'

While the nuns on the stage looked perfectly composed, a few of the girls giggled or stared at their hands. Some of us might talk about periods to one another, but the idea of Sister Mary Gabriel giving a lecture on the subject was mortifying.

'This is also the time you begin to experience… feelings. Such feelings are given by God to a man and a woman for when they enter holy matrimony. Feelings that lead to the joy of children.'

A few more of the girls sniggered now.

'But…' The forceful word brought an end to the giggles. 'Sometimes, when you are young, these feelings can become confused.'

I was sure my heart had stopped beating. I didn't dare look at Helen sitting next to me.

'It is possible that these feelings might be directed at another girl among you.'

Heads began turning as the girls looked from one to another, wondering who was 'confused'.

Sister Mary Gabriel looked sternly over us all. 'Our Holy Father, Pope Paul, says that any act between two people of the same gender is depraved and counter to God's word. It is sinful and those who act this way are condemned to damnation. But if you feel this way, and do not act upon it, then we are here to help you. Our Blessed Pontiff and the Church know that such deviant feelings can be cured, with proper teaching and adherence to church law. With confession and the love of our Lord Jesus Christ.'

A wave of nausea swept through my body. I swallowed hard, trying to look straight ahead. I didn't want to listen to any more. Somehow they knew. My two nice separate worlds – my love and my faith – were colliding. Sister Mary Gabriel thought we were sinners. We had acted on our feelings so we were beyond saving now. Depraved. Deviant. Those were her words for us.

I sat, trapped in my seat, until the lecture was over, and then stood up and joined the line of girls leaving the hall. Miss Temple escorted us back to the boarding house. Normally she chatted to the older girls quite happily, but tonight she was silent, her mouth fixed in a thin line, presumably shocked by what we'd all heard.

I had to know if we had been found out, but I had to sound casual, as if I wasn't asking for any reason at all. 'Miss Temple? Do the sisters know of anyone who… ' I wasn't sure how to end the sentence.

Miss Temple folded her arms, and dropped her gaze to the floor. 'Jane, I think you and the other girls should go to your rooms and prepare for bed. I don't want to discuss what the headmistress said. It's a matter for each of you to reflect on individually.'

The boarding house took a long time to settle that night. Girls whispered together long after lights out. I lay in my bed waiting until all was quiet and everyone was asleep. Helen and I slipped silently out of our beds and tiptoed through to our cubicle. With the door shut behind us, we sat down side by side.

'That was us she was talking about,' I whispered. 'The sisters know.'

'No, they don't.' As always, Helen was more confident, more definite than I. 'If they knew, we'd have been called into the office. They'd have just talked to us about their holy cure.'

I knew that what I was going to say next would hurt her, but I couldn't lie to Helen, even by omission. 'What if they're right?'

'They're not.'

'But what if this is a sin? What if we could be cured and made normal? The pope said...'

'If the pope said that, he was wrong.'

Those words shocked me. 'I thought you believed?'

'I did.' She put her hand against my cheek and turned me to face her. 'I do. I believe that God made us, but I think he made us capable of love. I don't believe love is a sin. Not ever.'

She kissed me, and I let her, but my eyes were filling with tears. I wanted to believe her. I truly did.

Chapter 20

Betty

Betty ran along the street, rain soaking through her thin blouse. Rain. Rain was delicious. If only the air would turn cold to go with it, she'd be able to imagine she was somewhere else entirely. The thought stopped her dead in her tracks. She turned her face to the sky, mouth open wide, and let the rain fall onto her face, between her lips, dancing on her skin. There was a hint of a memory there – snow falling, white and cold, and Betty turning her tiny face upwards, trying to catch a flake on her tongue. Her father laughing in the background. In her imagination she tried to turn and look at his face, but the image blurred and faded away.

'Eliza! Eliza! Come inside.'

Mr Mason was standing on the porch, glancing quickly one way and then the other along the street. Betty stomped towards the house.

'What are you doing out in this weather?'

'It's just rain.'

He shook his head. 'And dressed like that.' He pointed towards her skirt and blouse, both stuck tight to her body and going see-through in the rain.

'It's not cold.'

'Go and get changed. And then come and find me.'

Betty did as she was told. The new order in the house hadn't really settled yet. Since Mr Mason had caught Richard trying it on with her in the kitchen, Richard had been nice as pie. And Betty had been eating with the family. She was being included, though not in everything. Mr Mason's lectures about the stock numbers and auctions and land leases were reserved for Richard. Sometimes he muttered that if Mrs Mason had been there, she could have shown Betty how to do things.

But Mrs Mason wasn't there.

When she'd changed her clothes, she found Mr Mason sitting on his own in his office, a large room at the back of the house. He called it his study, which sounded very serious and important for a big plain room, with square shelves filled with box files and dull grey filing cabinets that didn't quite close properly. This was where Mr Mason did his actual work, rather than at the big dining table where he talked about work.

He didn't look up when she came in. Betty waited, uncertain what to do next. He didn't acknowledge her. She cleared her throat. She thought she saw a hint of a frown cross his face, but nothing else.

'You wanted to…'

He held up a hand. 'Wait.'

Betty stomped angrily across the room and threw herself into the chair opposite Mr Mason.

'I told you to wait.'

'I'm waiting here.'

'This is what we have to deal with.' He folded the map he had open on the desk and stared at her. 'This wilfulness has to go. You're not stringing along some yahoo you met at the beach. The

84

men I entertain are powerful people. Rich people. They have some standards.'

Betty didn't answer. In her experience, men didn't have standards. Men had lust and that's what led them. Mason was probably no different. She licked her lips and leant forward, letting him get a good look down her top.

He turned away. 'Stop it. Silly girl.'

Betty sat up straight.

'You're not going to be doing any of that sort of thing.'

'Most blokes like that sort of thing.'

'I'm sure they do. But you're of no use to me if you've got a reputation. And if the men I work with have seen what you're offering. You're a Mason. Now act like it.'

Betty frowned.

'The Mason family is going somewhere, you know. My father didn't have two coins to rub together in England. He came here with nothing. Years before you and the rest of these ten-pound Poms. And he worked. And I took what he worked for and turned it into all this.'

Betty followed the sweep of his hand around the room. He didn't mean this scruffy office. He meant the house. And the name. And the wife who'd gone to meetings with other wives and talked about what charities to support and other good works. He meant Betty. She was one of the good works after all.

'And I'll pass it on to Richard and he'll make even more of it. And you'll play your part too.'

There was a look in his eye that Betty hadn't seen before. An intensity, a determination. 'It all comes down to land in the end. We're only agents.' He laughed. 'We take their money but it's just money. We don't have part of the place. Do you understand?'

Betty nodded. A place that was completely yours – that mattered. She understood that. If you had somewhere you belonged, nobody could take that away from you.

'But if you were there, one of them, having their babies, then we'd be one of them, wouldn't we?'

'One of who?'

He shook his head, and unfolded the map again across his desk. 'You've got no idea. Look.'

She did as she was told, bending her head over the map. Different sections were outlined by thick, coloured lines. Mr Mason traced a purple line. 'That's the Harold estate.' He moved to a green line. 'Crossthwaite.' And then a red line. 'Thornfield – the Rochesters' property.' He jabbed at the red line at one extreme and then the other. 'More than a day to drive from one side to the other. Can you even imagine?'

Betty gulped. 'And one man owns all that?'

Mr Mason nodded. And then he smiled. 'One man. And his sons.' He smiled more widely. 'Would you like to meet his sons, Eliza?'

Chapter 21

Jane

'Lezzos. Look at the lezzos.'

I halted in my tracks, my heart pounding. We had been found out. Please, God, no. Not now. Not when I was struggling...

'Lezzo...'

The chants were coming from behind me. I curled my hands into fists as I slowly turned around. The hallway was empty. I heard the words again, and this time someone was crying. I was spared. I could walk away, but someone else was suffering.

I pushed open the door to the communal bathroom. There were four shower cubicles along one wall, and three or four middle-school girls crowded around an open door. The crying was coming from inside.

'Stop that.' The anger burst from me. 'Leave them alone.'

The crowd turned to face me. I was older, but I was not a prefect. They weren't scared of me. But they should have been. I leant over to see who was in the cubicle. There were two girls, both younger than their attackers. They were cowering, fully dressed but wet through, as though they'd been shoved in there and had the water turned on above them.

The rage that I thought had peaked grew stronger. They could be me, but not just me – Helen. The thought of her shivering and humiliated fired my anger again. I turned back to the group of bullies who were tormenting the two girls. 'Get out of here!'

I grabbed the nearest girl by the shoulder and pushed her towards the door. She fell against it with a heavy crash.

One of the other girls reached for me. I took half a step back and slapped her across the face. Hard. The smack of my hand against her skin made her stagger back. There was a moment of quiet. I didn't dare speak. Eventually the girl I had hit shrugged. 'Come on.'

She led her little group away. The two girls shuffled out of the cubicle. In an instant, the anger left me. 'You'd better go and get changed.'

They edged past me. One of them turned back. 'We're not... you know...'

I must have frowned.

'We're not lezzoss.'

Her friend nodded emphatically. 'Course we're not. That's gross.'

I spent that afternoon waiting for the detention that never came. The girl I slapped must have realised she'd get into just as much trouble as me if she said anything. I was cross, though. I deserved to be punished. I'd lost my temper. I'd lashed out, but it was worse than that. Really I was just as bad as the girl I'd hit. I'd done the same as thing as her. Since Sister Mary Gabriel's lecture I'd turned away from Helen. I hadn't been brave enough to say anything to her, but I found excuses not to go to the garden during our free time. I pretended I was busy when she suggested studying together. At night, I went quickly to bed and pretended I was asleep if she tried to talk to me at lights out. I was hurting the person I loved most in the world because of who she was. How was I any better than those girls shouting insults in the bathroom?

At the end of lessons I took myself to the chapel. I could pray. I could seek forgiveness. I could rely on my faith, but something wasn't right. I didn't know why, but the chapel didn't bring me the comfort I craved. The church viewed Helen as depraved. That was the thing that hurt so much. Seeing myself as depraved was easier, but I couldn't see Helen like that. She was not sinful. She was kind and pure and good. Absolutely good.

And I had denied her. I'd let my doubt override my faith in our love.

I'd been stupid. I'd let fear hold me back from love. The only fear I had left was the fear that Helen might not forgive me. I had to find her. I had to tell her that I was sorry, that I was ready to fully accept her love. I would beg if I had to. The school year was almost over. This place, these rules, didn't have to mean anything to us anymore. We could go anywhere.

I left the chapel and set out for the small garden behind the gym. I didn't dare run and risk being caught, but I wished myself there quicker than my legs could carry me. The garden was in full bloom. I hesitated as I pushed through to our hidden spot. The flowers were beautiful. And there, in the filtered sunlight, Helen was beautiful too. It felt like fate. She was exactly where I'd pictured her. I could only hope she was waiting for me to come back to her.

Helen didn't stir as I walked across to the bower and sat down beside her. I reached out to touch her face. The skin was damp with sweat. Her breathing was heavy and uneven.

'Helen? Helen!'

I shook her shoulder and slowly her eyes opened. Something was wrong.

'Helen. What's happened?'

She tried to say something, but then whimpered in pain as her whole body suddenly twitched violently. I took her hand and then I saw it. The bite marks on her arm were swollen and red. Congealed blood spotted her lower arm.

My throat tightened with a fear so strong I thought for a moment my heart would stop beating. But Helen needed me.

'Was it a snake?'

She shook her head. Her lips moved soundlessly, but I knew what she was saying. A spider. We all knew about redbacks and funnel webs.

'Lie very still. I'll go get help.' I started to get up, but her fingers reached for me.

'Please. Don't leave me.'

The words tore me into little pieces. I had to go – it was her only hope – but I was desperate to stay.

'I'll only be a minute, Helen. I have to get help. I have to.'

I gently took her hand away and leapt to my feet. I was shouting for help as I ran past the gym onto the big open lawn at the centre of the school. There was no-one there. Still shouting, I ran towards the main boarding house. Miss Temple was the first to appear.

'Jane. Jane. What's wrong?'

'Helen, you've got to get help for Helen.' I was sobbing as Miss Temple grabbed me by my shoulders.

'What's happened?'

'I think she's been bitten by a spider.'

'Where is she?'

'In our garden.'

'Jane, go and tell Matron to call an ambulance.'

I shook my head. 'I have to get back to Helen. She needs me.'

I had done what I had to. Help would come and now, more than anything else, I needed to be with Helen. I ran back to her. Behind me, I heard Miss Temple calling out for someone to phone for an ambulance.

Helen was moving as I dashed back into our little garden. He body was twisting painfully in violent spasms. I dropped to the grass and pulled her head onto my lap. She was moaning in pain, and her breathing was becoming more and more ragged.

'Helen. Please, Helen. Hold on. Help is coming.'

She opened her eyes, but didn't seem to see me.

'Helen, I love you. Please don't leave me.'

'Jane…' I barely heard the whisper.

Tears were streaming down my face as Miss Temple ran into the little garden. She gasped when she saw Helen and knelt swiftly beside her.

'The ambulance is on the way,' she told me. 'Helen? Helen, can you hear me?'

Helen didn't reply.

More teachers arrived, trampling over our carefully tended garden. They tried to pull me away, but Miss Temple stopped them. Their voices sounded loud and harsh, and I wanted to tell them to be quiet – I didn't want them to disturb my sleeping love.

The ambulance arrived and she was finally taken from me. The men knelt next to her, shouting and moving with such urgency. But soon, too soon, the quiet returned to our garden. The men slowed. Their voices dropped to whispers and then they stood, quietly shaking their heads.

Chapter 22

Betty

She let Mr Mason steer her by the elbow through the crowd of people pouring through the gates of the showgrounds. 'Now, I don't have time to babysit you, so you need to get your bearings.'

He stopped in a large open area, and pulled her around to face the way he wanted. 'The main cattle pavilions and ring are over there. That's where I'll be for most of the morning.'

'Looking at cows?'

Mr Mason gave her a look that mixed pity with disgust. 'Doing business with the people who own the livestock. Anyway, sideshow alley is down that way. Stay away from there. That's for the city people and the kids. The Country Women's Association does afternoon teas in a pavilion on the other side of the main ring. That's the sort of place you need to be seen. Make people think you'll make a proper grazier's wife. The cattlemen's bar is also there, but you stay well clear of that too. I don't want you getting mixed up with the types that hang out there. The people we care about are in the members' rooms.'

Betty scowled.

'Father! Father!' Richard hurried over to them. 'Mr Rochester's waiting for you in the beef cattle pavilion. He's as mad as a cut snake about something.'

Mr Mason glanced at Betty.

Richard hadn't finished. 'And his son's with him. The older one anyway. They're barely talking to each other.'

Mr Mason nodded curtly. 'Probably not the right time for you to meet them, Eliza. Go and see about the Country Women's Association. Make yourself useful. Remember the names we went over. Keep your eyes and ears open. There'll be people there you ought to get to know.'

Betty nodded mutely and watched the two men stride away. Mr Mason turned back. 'The Grand Parade is at midday. Be at the members' enclosure entrance before that. I'll come and get you in.'

Wow – a parade of cows. She could barely contain her excitement. She could hear music and wild screams, and see the flashing lights of sideshow alley. That would be much more fun than cows. Besides, if she wasn't supposed to be there, it was probably the place she really wanted to be. Betty set off in that direction.

'Come on, girl. Fancy a ride?' The leering sideshow hawker wasn't referring to the Ferris wheel and she knew it. She ignored him and walked on. Most of the people around her were kids, eating fairy floss and dagwood dogs. They'd be throwing that up again later when they hopped on those rides. Betty watched the Octopus for a few minutes as it swung people high into the air. That wasn't what she wanted. The people on the rides were squashed together and held down by iron bars. Betty felt her chest tighten at the idea. She preferred to be free. She wanted wide open spaces. The sun on her face and the rain on her skin. She couldn't be trapped. She wouldn't be held down.

She turned away from the rides and walked along the aisles between the freakish wide-mouthed clowns and the kewpie dolls on sticks, with their bare butts showing under their glittery dresses. She watched a young couple holding hands and giggling as they bought tickets to the Tunnel of Love. For a heartbeat, Betty wondered what it would be like to be that girl. Happy and in love. She'd never had that. And she didn't want it. She pushed that bit of weakness aside. That wasn't for her. She turned away from the couple. She'd had enough of this. What she really wanted was to find some good-looking bloke and flirt with him. She wouldn't do anything, of course. She understood Mr Mason's plan for her and she wasn't going to risk her chance to get away. But right now, nobody was paying her any attention. She was starting to feel invisible, and she didn't like that feeling.

Betty headed back towards the livestock areas. They weren't hard to find. She just followed her nose.

As she approached the ring, a horse pranced into view. It was a big, beautiful creature, dark brown with a small white star on its forehead. The rider on its back was struggling to control it. The animal tossed its head, its mouth white with foam. The horse half-reared and Betty flinched as the rider brought down her whip with a smart crack on the horse's rump. The horse leapt forward in protest. Betty turned away. She couldn't bear to watch a moment longer, because she knew just how that poor animal felt.

Then she saw him. He was standing on his own, leaning on the fence at the side of the arena. Betty paused before she went over. He was older than her. Maybe twenty-five. He had thick dark hair that skimmed the collar of his tan checked shirt. He'd taken off his Akubra and it was hanging from his fingertips. She moved closer, edging forward to get a look at his face. He was staring at the ground in front of him, but she could see the sharp angular lines of his cheekbones and jaw. He could make her day more interesting. He could make her feel better.

'Hi.'

He stood to his full height and turned towards her. He was tall and broad. Betty felt a moment's uncertainty. Mostly she went with boys. It was easier. You knew who was in charge.

'G'day.'

His voice was deep, and he looked at her with piercing grey eyes. This was not the same way the boys looked at her. It was … more. Betty felt a hint of something moving deep inside her. She dropped her eyes to the ground. This time it wasn't because of anything Mason had told her to do. It was because of this sharp-eyed man and the way he looked at her.

'Are you looking for someone?'

She shook her head, still not quite meeting his eyes. 'You're here for the show jumping?'

He laughed without any humour. 'No. I'm here because my old man is mad at my brother, and because he says he'll cut off my allowance if I don't do what he wants me to.'

Here because he had to be. She understood that. 'Same for me.'

'Your dad's threatening to disinherit you too?'

Dad. For a moment he was there again. Those strong arms. That deep, melodious voice. That wonderful safe place. And then it was gone. She looked directly at the stranger beside her. 'No. I'm here because I didn't have a choice.'

He met her gaze. His deep grey eyes seemed to pin her to the spot. He started to smile. 'At least I'm only here today.'

'Edward!' The name was shouted from across the showground. The man sighed under his breath, and pushed his hat firmly over his hair. 'Back to it, then.'

The man called Edward strode off towards the older man who was calling him. Betty watched him leave, feeling an almost physical pull to follow. She reached her hand out and gripped the fence to ground herself. He might be a bit older, but he was no different to the others. Except he wasn't. He was like her. He understood.

Richard and Mr Mason were hurrying towards her. 'What did you say to him?'

Betty shrugged. 'Nothing.'

'What did he say?'

She shrugged again. 'Just that he was here because of his father – who is mad at his brother for some reason. I don't think he's enjoying it much.'

Mr Mason turned towards his son. 'So Freddie Rochester's definitely out of favour. Good to know. Did he say why?'

Richard giggled before Betty could respond.

Mr Mason narrowed his eyes. 'What's so funny?'

'One of Rochester's stockmen told Terry Harolds that Freddie's shagging one of their Abos.'

Mr Mason looked blank. 'So?'

'And he says Freddie wants to move her into the big house. Like she was his wife or something.'

Mr Mason took a tiny step backwards as if to distance himself from the very idea. Then he looked back at Betty. 'That explains it. All the more important that his sons meet a nice, suitable Australian girl, then.'

'I'm English.'

'You're a Mason. So long as you're not one of them...' He jerked his head towards a group of young Aboriginal men leading live-stock out towards the ring. 'I don't care.' He looked her up and down. 'Make sure you smooth your hair down properly tomorrow. And for goodness' sake get yourself a hat and stay out of the sun. We don't want them asking questions about you. We'll make sure Edward sees you again tomorrow.'

'He's not going to be here tomorrow. He said he was only staying today.'

'And Freddie Rochester's no use at the moment.' Mr Mason folded his arms. 'Then let's make sure next time you meet one of them they're absolutely desperate to get to know the feted Eliza Mason.'

Chapter 23

Jane

'I don't think this is good for you, Jane.'

Miss Temple stepped through the gap in the hedge into the garden. My garden. Mine and Helen's, except now Helen was gone.

I brushed the tears away from my eyes and picked up the gardening fork I had dropped some time ago.

'I can't let it all die, Miss Temple.'

'She wouldn't have wanted you to sit here all alone crying either.' Miss Temple came to sit beside me. She'd been kind to me since Helen died, kinder than I deserved.

'I had to repair the damage done by all those people tramping through here that day. But it's hard with just me.'

'I know.'

We sat for a long time in silence.

'It wasn't your fault, you know, Jane. There was nothing we could have done to save her.'

'If I hadn't been distracted. If I hadn't gone to chapel that day…' It was the thought I kept torturing myself with. If I'd never rejected Helen; if I'd been there with her; if I'd realised how stupid I was being, a week, or a day, or even just an hour earlier; if I'd run; if I'd simply run, through the school, rather than walked because of my fear of getting into trouble. If I'd done any of those things she'd still be with me now.

'Then you might have been the one bitten,' said Miss Temple. 'You heard what the doctors said. The antivenin they use isn't very good. And if it's left too late, it doesn't help.'

'If I'd been here...'

'We can all think like that. Helen often helped in the chapel – if I'd asked her to help that day, she wouldn't have been here in the garden. You can't blame yourself. It won't bring her back.'

I couldn't answer. She was trying to help, but I knew I couldn't bring Helen back. Every waking hour of every day, I knew that.

'And you need to start thinking about what you're going to do when school finishes. It's only a couple of weeks now.'

I shook my head. Without Helen I couldn't imagine what I would do. She had been the only fixed point in my future.

'Have you thought about staying here?'

'As a nun?' I almost smiled as I remembered Helen's reaction to that idea. 'I'd be a terrible nun.'

'I was thinking as a teacher or a house mistress.'

My fingers stopped their relentless pulling at the blades of grass in front of me. I let the idea settle in my mind and found that it sat there very easily. For the first time since she had joined me, I looked at Miss Temple properly. She looked happy. Content. I wanted to feel like that.

'I might like to be a teacher.' Like you, I thought. Since Helen's death, Miss Temple had been the one person who hadn't seemed to want to steer me away from my grief. And school was where Helen had been. At least I wouldn't be leaving her all over again.

I thought some more about the idea. 'To be a teacher, I'd have to go to university. I don't have any money.'

'Would your family help?'

'No.' I'd had one letter from Mrs Reed this year, simply stating that now my final tuition fees had been paid, her duty to me was complete. Effectively I had no family.

'Well, maybe you could stay here as an assistant, and study on the distance-learning programme. That's how I trained. I could help you.'

'Would the sisters let me?'

'I can't promise, but I think maybe if I told them I'd be your mentor. The lower-school assistant is leaving at the end of the year, and you already know the school. There wouldn't be much money, but you'd have somewhere to live included.'

It was so much more than I deserved. I felt tears in my eyes again. Grief for Helen and gratitude towards Miss Temple merged together.

'But, Jane, I want you to promise me something.'

'Ok?'

'Promise me that you won't sit here on your own all the time. I understand. I do. But this isn't good for you. If I help you, you must promise me you'll stop coming here like this.'

I closed my eyes and pictured Helen's beautiful face and then took a deep breath. I wasn't ready to say goodbye, but at least this way I had a friend to help.

'I'll try.'

That transition from pupil to teacher was easier than I expected. The nuns were very happy to take me on as a trainee and I quickly enrolled in distance education. I now had my own small flat at the school, and had learnt to drive the school's station wagon, so I could pick up new girls from the train station. This task and the occasional school outing were the only times I ever left the grounds of Our Lady. On my days off, I mostly studied. I was determined to become a teacher. The lessons I received in the mail weren't difficult, and I had passed my exams easily. Less easy was the thought that at some point, I would have to go to Armidale for on-campus lessons and exams.

And every day I would go and sit in the staff room. At first, I was almost too nervous to go there. I still felt like a student, invading the teachers' private space. But when I walked in that first time, Miss Temple was there, with a pile of students' exercise books on the table in front of her.

'There's a fresh pot of tea made, if you want some, Jane.'

'Lovely. Thank you, Miss Temple.'

Her hand stopped moving and she placed her pen beside the stack of books. 'Jane, don't you think it's time you stopped calling me Miss Temple? At least in private. You're not my student anymore. You're my friend.'

She was right. We were friends. I felt closer to her than I had to anyone since Helen. She was so different to Helen, but there was a tiny streak of the rebel in both of them. Miss Temple hid it well, but there were moments when I caught her rolling her eyes at some pronouncement from one of the nuns.

'I would use your first name,' I said as I sat down next to her. 'Except for one thing.'

'What's that?'

'I don't know what it is.'

She started to laugh. 'Really?'

'In all these years, I've only ever heard you referred to as Miss Temple.'

'Well, my name is Gail.'

'I am very pleased to meet you, Gail.'

Chapter 24

Betty

Betty checked her appearance in her compact mirror. What a difference twelve months made. And a bit of money. Her hair had been done properly at the hairdressers' and there wasn't a hint of frizz to be seen. Her skin was creamy and smooth, freckles painted away with powder and concealer. She didn't like her new dress, though. It was plainer and homelier than the clothes she liked. But it was what Mason had ordered. Now she was ready.

She followed Mr Mason through a gate into the showgrounds, ignoring the crowds and the noise and the smells. She knew what she had to do. She was to be polite, well-behaved and amusing with the property owners and clients she'd met during the year. She was to talk to their wives and daughters. She was not to flirt. She was not to have opinions. She was not to, in Mr Mason's words, make a show of herself. They all had to think well of her. They were her references, and, if the week went badly, her fall-back plan.

Richard was already in the members' enclosure, walking around briskly, giving out business cards and shaking hands. Betty scanned the crowd. There were a smattering of faces she recognised. She smiled like she was supposed to. She waited for Mr Mason to call her over. She was not to be bold, not to be forward. She came when beckoned and not before.

'Eliza, this is Mr Rochester who owns Thornfield.' He turned to the older man alongside him. 'My wife, God rest her soul, and I adopted Eliza when she was just five years old.'

Betty didn't flinch at the word 'adopted'. Let him make like she'd always been part of the family. If it got her a ticket away to somewhere with wide open spaces and nobody looking over her shoulder then she wasn't about to complain.

The older man nodded. 'Adopted?'

'Eliza was orphaned.'

That word stabbed harder, but she didn't let the smile shift from her lips.

'Sorry to hear that.' He looked her up and down. 'You know much about cattle, Eliza?'

She shook her head. She knew she wasn't expected to know anything.

'My wife never knew a thing about cattle. Grew up on a cattle property and then married me, and she couldn't tell a Hereford from Brahman. She looked after us, though, didn't she?' He directed the question to the young man who was approaching from the other side of the arena.

'Didn't she what?'

'Your ma – she looked after us.'

The younger man nodded slowly. He turned to Betty. His brow furrowed. 'I don't think we've met.'

He didn't remember. Betty felt a twist of disappointment. Why would he remember? It had been a moment, less than a moment, a whole year before. She held out her hand very properly. 'Eliza Mason.'

'Edward Rochester.' He took her hand and shook it. His skin was smoother than she'd expected. He was dressed like his father and the other property owners, but she was quite sure those hands had never done a proper day's work.

'My son, Edward.'

'Eliza!' As slowly as she dared, she pulled her hand away. Mr Mason put his hand on her arms. 'Eliza, Mrs Weston is here. She's very keen to show you the craft stalls.'

Betty nodded and allowed herself to be shepherded away by a buxom woman in a brightly patterned polyester dress. She listened to Mr Mason making her excuses. 'Eliza's first full year at the show. This is all new to her.' She strained to hear as he lowered his voice. 'So innocent. Mrs Mason put a lot of store on girls being raised properly. If you know what I mean.'

Betty suppressed a giggle. Just like that her purity was reborn. She shot a quick glance back over her shoulder, enough to make sure that Edward Rochester knew that she'd seen him watching her leave.

The next few days were similar to the first. Freddie Rochester wasn't even at the show this time. The gossip was that he was now even further out of favour than the year before. So, she was dangled like a carrot in front of Edward and his father, and then sent away to engage in some chaste and appropriate activity. It was so boring she wanted to scream. She drank tea, and ate scones, and looked at patchwork quilts until she thought her stomach would burst and her eyeballs would bleed.

On the fifth day she was back at the side of the arena, Mr Mason on one side of her, the Rochesters on the other. Mr Mason cleared his throat. 'This must be very boring for you, Eliza.'

She sensed an exchange of glances above her head. Mr Rochester spoke next. 'Edward, why don't you take Miss Mason for a look around? Stretch your legs a bit.'

Edward looked at her. Again she found herself pinned down by his gaze. She'd heard of men undressing women with their eyes, and she thought she knew what that meant. She'd thought it was the look of lust she was used to, but this was something else. She didn't feel coveted. She felt undone. Eventually he nodded. 'Why not?'

She followed him around the arena. Edward didn't speak. He strode across the ground, confident that nobody would be in his path. Betty followed. She didn't know anyone who moved like that. Mr Mason was stiff, always upright, always watchful. Richard tried to act like he owned the place but it was a façade that anyone could see through. Edward Rochester behaved like a man who was entitled to go wherever he chose.

Eventually he stopped. 'I want a beer. Come on.' And off he went again, doubling back on his route to get to the bar. Betty followed him inside. He was greeted with shouts and laughter. He disappeared for a moment into the crush of bodies. A second later he reappeared, grabbing her wrist and pulling her towards a huddle of men next to the bar. 'Max, Gordo, everyone, this is Eliza.'

There was a volley of cheers and a single wolf whistle. 'She's all right, mate.'

Betty smiled. This she understood. These were little boys dressed up like men. She dipped her head and looked up at them through her lashes. Even dressed up as nice, demure Eliza Mason she knew how to deal with boys.

Rochester thrust a glass of wine into her hand. She'd have preferred a long cold beer, but Mr Mason had told her that a proper lady would drink wine, and he'd made her practice until she could take an elegant sip without pursing her lips against the sharpness in her throat.

For a time, Rochester ignored her while his mates all had a go at chatting her up with their cheesiest lines. Rochester had just watched and she'd thought maybe she'd blown it. Then he grabbed her wrist and dragged her out of the tent. She stumbled after him, blinking against the bright sunlight. His lips were on hers before she'd had time to adjust. She was frozen to the spot, unable

104

to respond, mouth clenched closed in shock. He pulled back before she could gather herself to respond to his lips.

He smiled. 'They were telling it like it is, then.'

She frowned. 'Sorry?'

'You really are as pure as your old man said.'

Her confusion when he kissed her had been interpreted as something else. She didn't know if this was a good or a bad thing.

His smile widened, wolf-like and hungry. 'It's all right.' He took her hand. 'We should get back anyway if I'm going to talk to your father.'

The deal was done while Betty drank another of the interminable cups of tea in the CWA tent. The Rochester and Mason men were gathered at the cattle ring, and, just as the beasts were bought and sold, so was Betty.

The women around her whispered and nodded knowingly, but Betty ignored them. Behind the tent, someone had started a barbecue. The smell of cooking meat was thick in the air, but Betty ignored that too. Through an open tent flap, she occasionally caught an explosion of brightness, as the sizzling fat burst into flame. Betty longed to walk over there; for the release of the fire warming her skin and the flames dancing in front of her, and the sparks flying away into the sky. She wanted to fling off these stupid neat clothes Mr Mason had put her in and feel the heat on her body. In her body.

Then they were back, all four men beaming as they called her over. Edward Rochester's smile was faint, and he looked at her as if he was looking inside her, taking her apart one bit at a time. She almost shivered.

She stood as they entered, like a proper lady was supposed to.

'So, Mr Rochester has decided to make Mason's his sole stock and station agent.' Mr Mason's smile was triumphant.

The older Rochester patted her arm. 'You're a pretty thing.'

His hand was shaking slightly. Betty wondered if he was drunk, or maybe sick.

'Shall we retire to the bar and drink to our new partnership?' Mason led the man away, but Edward stayed with her.

'My old man's right.'

Betty's brow furrowed.

'You are pretty.' He reached and lifted her hand in his. 'But you're not happy, are you?'

'I don't know what you mean.'

He stared at her. 'Yes. You do. You're like me. You're restless stuck here. You want to get away.'

She knew what she was supposed to say. She was supposed to say that she was very happy living here, being Eliza Mason. She didn't reply.

'You wouldn't manage, though. Not on your own.' He continued. 'You've probably never seen anything outside of your nice house and your nice life.' There was a spike of bitterness in his voice.

Betty's mind drifted back to her daddy – her real daddy – and to the long boat trip, and to the years of working for her keep in the kitchen, and to the boys in alleyways, on tree stumps, against walls. She stayed silent. Eliza Mason hadn't seen any of those things. Eliza Mason was the perfect, appropriate, respectable bride for a rich man's son.

His fingers moved to her face. 'It's all right, though. I can show you everything.' He smiled. 'You're not like anyone I've been with before. You're so innocent.'

Betty let him continue.

'So when we're married, we'll have a place in Sydney. As long as Freddie is at Thornfield, we're free to do what we want.'

So that was that. She would finally be free of Eliza Mason. It didn't matter that she had not been asked if this was what she wanted. Edward Rochester could give her the freedom she ached for. She was never going to say no to that.

Chapter 25

Jane

'Miss Eyre, I think I left my swimming togs at the pool. Can I go and look, please?'

It felt strange to be giving detention rather than receiving it, but that was what I was doing. Some girls had been discovered swimming in the school pool without teacher supervision, which was strictly forbidden. Two of them had been tasked with setting all the tables in the dining hall as punishment, and I was overseeing them, keeping a sharp eye open for left-handed table settings, which had been a trick when I was still a student.

The girls had finished their detention, and now one of them was asking to go back to the pool.

'You know you are not allowed at the pool without a teacher there.'

'But I won't go in the water.'

'Why don't I go and get them for you?' I had to check the pool anyway. When it was this hot, girls were always sneaking in for a swim.

The pool had been built a few years before. It was a gift from a former student, and was a blessing during the hot summer months. It sat in a far corner of the grounds, with a thick hedge hiding it from view. There was a fence and a gate also protecting it, but as I approached I saw the gate was open. The pool, however, was empty, with not even a wet stain on the concrete surrounds to indicate a recent hasty exit. The door to the changing shed, however, was open. I walked over, my soft-soled shoes making no sound on the pool surround.

As I stepped through the doors, my eyes took a few seconds to adjust to the dim light. Two girls were sitting on the wooden benches at the far end of the room. It looked as though they had not long been out of the pool. Their hair was wet and their bathers had been discarded on the floor. Before I could speak, the girls embraced.

I backed soundlessly out of the shed. It was a private moment. I had no business being there. At the gate, I stopped. I grasped the fence as if it was a lifebuoy that could stop me washing away on a tidal wave of emotion. I'd been telling myself I was over my grief. I thought I had locked it down where it couldn't hurt me anymore. I'd accepted Gail's kindness and help, and convinced myself that I was doing all right now. Seeing those two girls together, so simply and so totally together, was all it took to put me right back at the centre of my pain. My arms almost tingled with the emptiness of not being able to hold the person I loved.

'Jane. Are you all right? You look quite pale.' Sister Bernadette, a nun who'd been at the school since long before I arrived, appeared on the path.

With great effort, I focussed on the nun's concerned face. 'I am fine, Sister, thank you. Perhaps I've had a little too much sun, that's all.'

'Well, child, go back to the boarding house and rest. I was just coming to check that the pool and the changing shed were properly locked.'

My thoughts raced to the two girls inside the shed. I could remember sitting in that assembly with Helen, the words depraved, sinful and deviant echoing in my head. I could still feel the horror and humiliation, and I still regretted how I had let that change my relationship with the only person I had ever truly loved.

'I've already checked, Sister.' I blurted the words out too quickly. The nun frowned.

I forced myself to calm down, to slow down. 'Everything is as it should be.' I put my hand to my forehead. 'I do actually feel a bit unwell. Could you walk with me back to the house, please?'

'Of course.' The sister took my arm and I allowed her to lead me away from the gate, the fence and the girls in the changing room.

Chapter 26

Betty

Something was wrong. Betty knew it the instant she walked into the church. Edward was standing at the end of the aisle, his father by his side. Where was Freddie? His brother was supposed to be his best man. Old Mr Rochester's face was thunder. And Edward was staring at the wall. He didn't even turn as Betty approached in her long white dress and veil.

Look at me! Edward didn't hear her silent scream. She wanted to shout out loud but she was supposed to be the perfect bride, in the perfect dress, in a perfect ceremony.

Edward looked at her as he said, 'I do,' but his eyes were glazed. Betty felt a pull she wasn't familiar with. His face was tight and anxious. Her arms ached to be around him. Her lips yearned to whisper to him that whatever the trouble he was carrying might be, everything would be all right.

When the ceremony was over, they walked back down the aisle, her hand on Edward's arm. The reception was a blur. She didn't know anyone there, except the Masons, and all she wanted to do was get away from them. A lot of people came over to talk to Edward, but he remained stony faced. There was no sign of the charming, handsome man she had met at the show.

After the wedding, they flew to the Great Barrier Reef for their honeymoon. On the plane, Edward stared out the window and silently drank. She tried to reach him with the happy chatter that Mr Mason had taught her was proper, but her new husband might as well have been a million miles away. Finally they reached their resort. Finally they got past the volley of welcome hosts and porters and smiling staff. Finally they were alone.

Eliza's cheerful manner wasn't getting her anywhere. Betty stuck out her bottom lip. 'Tell me what's wrong.'

'He's gone.'

'Who's gone?'

'Freddie. He's run off with that Abo woman. She's up the duff and he says he's going to marry her.'

She didn't need to ask what that meant. Edward's father wasn't going to let an Aboriginal baby inherit his property.

Edward looked at her properly for the first time. 'So Freddie is gone. He's free. I'll inherit Thornfield now. I'll have to go back and run that bloody place.'

The silence hung between them for a second before Betty rallied. 'But that's years away.' She moved closer to her husband. 'We have time to have fun now.'

She leant towards him, so that he could feel her warmth, as her breast brushed against his arm. She saw it then, the look in his eyes.

'Let's change and go for a walk on the beach,' she said. 'I love the beach.'

She chose a bikini, even though it was too late to swim. And a silk sarong that wrapped around her body like water. She looked good and she knew it. She walked very close to him. 'I love being outside.'

He wrapped his arm around her, so she was walking pressed into his side. 'I love the ocean. We'll get an apartment in one of those new blocks overlooking the sea.'

An apartment sounded small, enclosed. Betty tensed.

'With a balcony that goes all the way along so it feels like you could dive straight off.'

She nodded. That would be all right.

'Yeah. We'll get somewhere near the water, away from my father.'

'And away from the Masons!' Betty pulled away from him and spread her arms wide to the heavens, declaring her freedom to the world.

Rochester laughed. 'Away from all of them.'

She spun around, losing her balance and careering back into his body. They fell onto the sand, breathless and laughing. She turned onto her side, raising her head up on her hand. Her husband had flopped onto his back. She reached a hand onto his chest and traced a line with her fingertips, down over his ribs, and onto his belly. She watched him watching her. Her gaze met his. Neither of them spoke.

She pushed herself up onto her knees and swung one leg over his torso, straddling him. He was still watching her, his calm expression giving way to something else – desire, of course – but something else as well. There was a questioning look in his eyes.

Betty looked one way and then the other along the deserted beach. She could hear voices from the hotel bar, but they were out of sight. She untied the halter at the back of her neck and removed her top, letting it drop to the sand beside them. Then she reached for him.

'Stop.'

She froze. He wanted her. She could see it in his face and hear it in his ragged breathing.

'I don't think Mason told the whole truth to my old man about you.'

'What?'

'The innocent young virgin?'

Betty froze. That was still what she was supposed to be, wasn't it?

'I don't know what you mean.'

'Yes, you do.' He pulled himself up onto his elbows, and then rolled, turning her under him and pressing her into the sand with the weight of his body. His fingers tore at her bikini bottom. Betty clawed at his back, pulling him to her. He grabbed her wrists. One hand and then the other, were pulled above her head and pushed hard down into the sand. And then he took her. She lifted her groin to meet him, thrusting against him. She welcomed his anger and his hurt and his passion.

When he was done, he straightened his clothes and stood up. Looking down at her spreadeagled in the sand, he smiled.

'I'm not complaining. Being all proper during the day, and then a wildcat in bed. Are you sure you're real Eliza Rochester?'

Betty slowly recovered her clothes and stood up beside him. He wasn't disappointed in her, though. He wasn't angry. Maybe she could try. 'I've never really liked being called Eliza.'

'Why not?' He nodded before she could answer. 'You're Elizabeth, aren't you? They said it at the wedding.'

They had. And it was right, she supposed. 'People used to call me Betty.'

'Short for Elizabeth again. Elizabeth.' He rolled the word around in his mouth. 'I like it. It's regal. Elizabeth Rochester.'

Another life. Another name. Maybe this was just what happened.

She let him take her hand and lead her back to the hotel.

'Mr Rochester!' The voice called out to them as soon as they came close to the lights of the resort. 'Mr Rochester!'

The messenger was a short Aboriginal boy. 'Mr Rochester. There was a telephone call for you to the front desk. We've been looking for you everywhere.'

'Did they leave a message?'

'Yes.' The boy handed over a folded piece of paper. His eyes dropped to the ground and he hurried away.

'What is it?'

Edward read the words, then let the paper slip from his fingers, to be carried away by the sea breeze.

'My father. He's dead.'

Chapter 27

Jane

From the window of what used to be my dormitory, I could see the gym and I could feel the small garden behind it calling to me. True to my word to Miss Temple – to Gail – I had not been back there, but the urge to go was getting stronger. It was as if after months of being too overwhelmed to think about Helen at all, the thought of her was at the centre of everything once again. I missed her. I missed being close to someone, being kissed, being touched.

'Jane? Is everything all right?' Gail's voice was warm. 'It's very hard to forget, isn't it?'

That surprised me. 'You think about her too?'

'Of course I do, Jane. Helen was a lovely girl, and her death was an utter tragedy.'

I nodded, my throat too tight to speak.

'I think she would have been pleased to see how well you are doing now, Jane. And she wouldn't have wanted you to brood over what happened.'

I wasn't so sure. Helen would not have wanted me to brood over her death, but I think she would have wanted me to reflect on how I'd let my guilt tear us apart. I hoped that by protecting those girls by the pool I had somehow started to right that wrong. I prayed that Helen was proud of me.

'Come on, Jane, why don't we get some tea? I have cake in my flat.'

I followed Gail, glad of her invitation. I'd never been inside Gail's flat before. When she opened the door, I found myself walking into a modern, comfortable place, larger than my own living quarters but still compact. There was a sitting room, complete with a television, bookshelves and a single large sofa. I could see her bedroom through an open door. Another open door led to a small kitchen and somewhere, no doubt, was a bathroom.

It felt like a home. While Gail made tea, I browsed her books. Titles by Germaine Greer and Gloria Steinem sat next to D H Lawrence and Jacqueline Susann. I raised an eyebrow at a couple of the titles.

'Have you read many of those?' she asked, setting the tea tray down on the coffee table.

'I think the nuns wouldn't be too happy to see some of those books.'

She shrugged. 'What I read in my own time is my own business.'

'But...'

'But what? There is more to this world than the sisters here will tell you about. There are so many ideas to be explored.'

As she spoke, she poured the tea into big white mugs and laid out two slices of cake onto mismatched plates.

I examined a shelf decorated with a series of framed photographs.

'Is this your family?'

'Yes.'

The picture showed a couple and two teenage children. The woman had long dark blonde hair, and a happy smile. I peered

116

closely and saw that the girl was a young Gail. 'You look a lot like your mother,' I said. 'She's pretty.'

'Thank you. When I was a little girl, all I wanted was to grow up like her.'

I studied the photos some more. There was one taken recently of Gail and a man with his arm around her shoulders. I glanced at the boy in the family picture. Perhaps they were the same person; it was impossible to tell.

'Jane, your tea is getting cold.'

I returned to sit next to Gail on the sofa. We drank our tea and ate our cake, talking about books and films. It turned out she loved old Hollywood – Katharine Hepburn, Bette Davis, Cary Grant and Clark Gable. She was horrified by how limited my knowledge of the movies was. 'Well, I've lived here since I was little,' I protested, when she discovered that I hadn't even seen *Gone with the Wind*.

'Then you must come and watch some with me next time there's something on TV,' Gail said. 'When we both have the evening off. We could even sneak some beer in as well.'

I didn't risk further teasing by admitting I'd never had a beer, but, as I left her flat later that evening, it occurred to me that I had just had a couple of hours of something approaching a 'normal' life.

My first real experience of normal.

I liked it.

I wanted more of it.

Chapter 28

Betty

Their long journey began the next afternoon.

Betty tried to be helpful. She repacked the few things they'd got around to unpacking, folding Edward's clothes as neatly as she could. But the husband she'd only had a day to get to know was already a ghost to her. He moved silently around the hotel, only speaking to make arrangements or on the telephone. Finally he'd gone for a walk, leaving Betty alone in the room amid the remains of her honeymoon.

When he didn't return after an hour, Betty set out to look for him. She found him sitting alone at one end of the bar, whisky in front of him. She perched on the stool alongside him. 'Are you OK?'

'Of course not.'

He wouldn't be, would he? Betty didn't know how to comfort another person. Her daddy had comforted her, and then Mrs Mason, but that was a long time ago. Since then, she'd never had anyone to comfort her. Nor had she ever taken the role of comforter herself. But that was what a wife did, wasn't it? It was what Mrs Mason had done. She'd taken care of everyone. That was the role Betty had to play now. She had to take care of her husband.

'I'm sorry.'

The barman placed a lurid pink drink in front of her. 'Complimentary cocktail of the day,' he announced. She took a sip. The sweetness was cloying and out of place.

'Everything's screwed up now,' Edward said as he turned his glass in his hands.

She didn't answer.

'It won't be the way we planned. It won't be an apartment on the beach. It'll be the property. The land. And the workers. And the cattle. All of that to manage.' He downed his remaining drink. 'That's who I am now.' He looked at her. 'And that's who you are now, too.' He laughed bitterly.

'But you've got a manager and agents and workers.'

He shook his head, and glanced at her, and then looked away, over her head, out towards the beach. 'I have responsibilities.' He cleared his throat. 'Not just the property.'

Betty felt her freedom starting to slip away. She would go where she was taken. Again.

An hour later they were in the air, the twelve-seater plane coughing and sputtering on the runway before gliding into the sky. Betty watched the beach and the island get smaller and smaller until they disappeared from view.

'What did you mean?'

Her husband didn't look at her. 'When?'

'When you said 'not just the property'. You said you had responsibilities.'

He shook his head. 'You'll see.' He turned his shoulder away from her, closing the conversation.

Betty turned back to her window. For a while there was only sky and sea and cloud. They were suspended in nothingness. Betty's stomach clenched. A person could drift away entirely here with nothing to hold on to at all.

They had to wait for a connecting flight in Townsville, and it was dusk by the time they took off for Sydney, where they would spend the night before flying to Edward's home the next day.

As they rose above the city, Betty gasped. The land all around was on fire. Bright red and orange flames flickered and leapt in the evening dusk. She could see sparks rising into the sky, flying away just as she had so longed to do.

'Edward. Look.'

Her husband glanced dully out of the window. 'There're burning the cane. That's all.'

That's all? How could he say that? The fire was beautiful. Betty stared at down at the flames, feeling as if she was being drawn into the light and the heat. She forgot where they were going. She forgot what was expected of her. She was miles away and years before, safe on her father's lap watching the flames dance and jump in the hearth.

Chapter 29

Jane

Gail rapidly turned me into something of a film buff. I grew to share her love of the golden era of Hollywood. For me, Lauren Bacall and Audrey Hepburn were my favourites. There weren't a lot of modern films on television, and I didn't like what there was. Things like James Bond were so violent, so cruel. Give me Elizabeth Taylor and Richard Burton in *Cleopatra* any time.

At least once a week, Gail and I would sit in her tiny flat and watch a film while we drank tea and ate cake. Very occasionally we'd tempt fate with a beer or two. If we got caught, we'd both lose our jobs, but Gail said that I got too hung up on rules, and that it was nobody's business if we had one drink.

Gail and I laughed at the same jokes and cried over the same movies – I even contributed some of my meagre wages so we could buy a brand new VCR machine for her flat. Then we watched more and more movies, sharing a box of tissues strategically placed on the sofa between us for the weepies and giggling helplessly at the comedies.

It was fun. It was like having family.

It was like being normal. I could lock away thoughts of Helen and the love we had shared.

One evening, reading the paper in the staffroom, I saw that a film we had been eager to see was on television that night. I put the paper down and hurried to Gail's flat. I knocked, but, as I so often did, walked in without waiting for her answer.

I froze just inside the door.

Gail was half-sitting half-lying on the table, her skirt pulled up around her waist, her blouse and bra gone. Her bare legs were wrapped around the naked hips of a man who was towering over her, his shirt hanging open. As I stood rooted to the spot, he thrust into her. I heard her cry out, not in pain or protest, but in pleasure as she reached for him.

I fled, slamming the door closed on what I'd seen.

Chapter 30

Betty

It was evening by the time their small plane began the descent towards Thornfield. Betty had long since stopped looking out the window, bored by the endless empty red-brown landscape passing below them. But as they sank towards the ribbon of graded earth that served as a landing strip for the homestead, Betty leant towards her window. There was a river that seemed to curve around a cluster of buildings. Nearest to the water the buildings were rough tin things – not much more than huts. Further back she saw sheds, though not like the backyard sheds in the city. These were vast. The word Thornfield was written in large white letters across one of the iron roofs. And then she saw the house. She heard herself gasp. She knew the Rochesters were rich, but she hadn't realised that they lived in a whole other world.

The plane sputtered to a halt. Edward threw the door open and jumped out, leaving Betty to scramble down on her own. A tall, dark-skinned man was leaning on the side of a ute a few metres away. He stepped forward and took their bags from the plane. Edward frowned at him. 'I thought Jack would be here.'

The man shook his head. 'He went into town.'

Edward nodded. 'Right. Up to the house, then, Jimmy.'

The man held the door of the ute open for Betty. He didn't speak, but briefly touched the broad brim of his dusty brown hat.

Betty smiled as she slid onto the passenger seat. She was somebody here. She was at the top of the tree rather than the bottom.

Her husband got behind the wheel and started the engine. The Aboriginal man jumped into the back of the ute with the bags.

Betty peered forward and then twisted around. The land was flat, with low scrubby trees. She knew Edward had cattle, but there weren't any to be seen. She gazed out towards the horizon. 'I can't see any fences.'

Edward frowned. 'What do you mean?'

'A fence, to show where your property ends. How do you know when the next farm starts?'

'There aren't any fences.' Edward's voice was flat and without emotion.

'What? Why not?'

'All this is Thornfield.'

Betty twisted again in her seat. She remembered the map Mr Mason had shown her. On paper was one thing, on the ground it was mind-blowing. 'Everything?'

'As far as the eye can see and then some.' Edward lifted his chin. 'All of this belongs to my... to me.'

Betty was still struggling with that as they arrived at the house.

Edward threw his door open. 'Well, here we are.'

He didn't go in. He just stood beside the car and stared up at the house. Betty stopped beside him and stared too. The house was even more imposing close up than from the air. She'd thought the Masons' house in Sydney was big, but this was like one of those big English houses she'd seen in magazines and on TV. A wide veranda encased the front of both the floors of the sandstone building, edged with intricate wrought-iron railings. The window frames were painted a bright, shiny white, which was impressive given the red dust in the air. Edward swallowed hard next to her. This wasn't where he'd planned to be, either. She took his hand. 'Shall we go in?'

He nodded curtly and she let him lead her up the two shallow steps, across the wooden veranda and into the hallway. Jimmy followed, carrying their bags from the car. He placed them carefully inside the door and left, touching his hat in Betty's direction once again.

Betty spun slowly around, her mouth falling slightly open as she took in the big entrance hallway, with its high ceilings and grand staircase leading to the top floor. The stair rails and doors and furniture were all dark polished wood, gleaming red in the late afternoon light against the pale cream walls. The Masons' house was a shack compared to this.

'Edward!' A middle-aged, grey-haired woman bustled into the hallway. 'I didn't hear the plane. I had the radio on. I don't hear anything. Have you had something to eat?'

Betty was starving.

Edward shook his head. 'I'm tired. It's been a long journey. We might just go straight upstairs.'

The stranger patted his arm. 'I understand.' She turned her attention to Betty, holding out a hand. 'I'm Mrs Fairfax. Grace Fairfax.'

'I'm Bett... Elizabeth.'

'Mrs Rochester.' Edward spoke over her.

'Welcome.' Grace smiled at her. 'I've made up the blue room, Edward's room, for the two of you.'

'The blue room?' Edward hesitated. 'I should have the master bedroom.'

Grace looked at the floor. 'That was your father's room. It's where he...'

Betty's stomach lurched. Was Grace saying...?

'What happened?' Edward's voice cracked slightly. 'He was with us for the wedding in Sydney. How...?'

'He flew straight home after the wedding,' Grace told them. 'When I went to ask him if he needed anything...' Her voice trailed off.

Edward nodded curtly. 'The blue room will do for now. And...' He gave Grace a questioning look.

'Oh. Fast asleep. I didn't tell her you were coming tonight. She would've wanted to wait up.'

'Good.' He nodded, abruptly ending the conversation, before taking Betty's hand and almost dragging her up the stairs.

'Our bags?' Betty pulled back.

'They can wait until tomorrow.'

The grand staircase ended in a hallway that ran at right angles to the stairs. There were several doors leading to rooms at the front of the house and what could be other hallways leading back behind them. Edward paused for a second at the tightly closed door directly opposite the stairs. His fingers tightened around Betty's hand. She winced but didn't pull away. He needed her support now. This must have been his father's room. Edward turned away and led her to a door at the far end of the house. Inside, a large double bed and polished wood wardrobes didn't begin to fill all the space between the pale blue walls.

Rochester slammed the door shut behind them. Betty watched and waited as he pulled his shirt loose from his jeans and wrenched it off over his head. 'This place...'

'What about it?'

'It just... It makes me feel like a child again. It's a trap.'

Betty shook her head. How could you be trapped when you owned everything as far as the eye could see? No fences, no boundaries. In a house as big as a castle, he was king of his own universe. He had no idea what being trapped really meant. She pushed the thoughts away. She was being unkind. He'd just lost his father. And she was his wife. She was supposed to be taking care of him.

She closed the gap between them and pressed her body against his.

126

He grabbed her, hard and tight around the waist, and smashed his mouth against hers, pressing his tongue between her lips urgently, before pulling away to give himself space to drag at her clothes. Within seconds she was on the bed, raising her hips to meet him. This was something she could do. This was a way that she could make them both feel better.

Chapter 31

Jane

'I know you didn't say anything, Jane. But they found out anyway. I guess they were bound to.'

I didn't know what to say. For the past two days, I had been struggling just to look Gail in the eyes. Every time I looked at her, I saw her face as it had been – burning with life and passion and ecstasy. I had apologised for walking in on her, of course, and she had brushed it off as not important. But then word had somehow got back to the nuns, and, after a meeting with Sister Mary Gabriel, Gail was packing. She had to be gone that very day.

'Where will you go?' Those words at least I could speak.

'Matt and I have decided to go to Queensland.'

'Queensland?'

'Yes. There's a job for Matt in Townsville. We'll swim every day and walk on the beach and I'll never have to walk to chapel in a heavy frost again.'

'Are you going to marry him?'

'I don't know. Maybe. Maybe not.'

'But you and he…' I couldn't say it out loud, but surely she knew what I meant. Men and women only did...what they did if they were married or at least going to get married. Didn't they?

Gail stopped packing. 'Seriously, Jane, how old are you now?'

'I'm twenty. I'll be twenty-one this year.'

'And this is 1979, not 1929. You've never lived out in the real world, have you?'

I shook my head.

'Maybe you need to leave Our Lady? There's a lot of world out there. You need to meet people...meet men...you need to fall in love and make mistakes, and live your life. I don't want you to end up a lonely old woman.'

I helped her carry her things to the car. Two suitcases and three cardboard boxes, one small television and, of course, our well-used video player. Once it was all safely stowed, Gail turned and hugged me.

'Goodbye, Jane. Good luck. I hope you get away from here and I hope you have a happy life.'

I held her tightly for a second longer, then let her go.

She got in her car and drove away without a backward glance.

Chapter 32

Betty

The next morning was bright and warm. Sun danced through the curtains long before Betty woke up. When she did wake, the bed beside her was already cold. She found her suitcase standing against the wall. Half her clothes were still at the Masons' house. They were supposed to have been going back to Sydney. She pulled out a cotton sundress – the best thing she had that wasn't a bikini – and got dressed.

She found the bathroom. As she washed her face she looked at the water running over her fingers. Where did the water come from all the way out here? Tentatively she took a sip. It tasted strange. The door at the top of the stairs, the one that had been tightly shut last night, was ajar. Betty pushed it open. Her husband was standing alone at the foot of the bed.

'Edward?'

He started as she said his name. 'It was right here.' He nodded towards the bed. 'She found him just lying there, like he was asleep.' His voice cracked but didn't break.

Betty moved towards him, but she was bustled out of the way as a little girl, blonde curls bouncing, whirled past her and bowled into Edward's legs. His demeanour changed instantly. He scooped the child up into his arms. 'Hello, you.'

'Did you bring me a present?'

His face tensed. 'Sorry, doll. Not this time. We had to come back in a hurry.'

'Cos of grumpy Grampy?'

'Don't call him that.'

'Mummy calls him that.'

A hint of a smile tugged at Edward's lips. 'Well, Mummy is a very naughty lady.'

The little girl giggled, her blue eyes sparkling. What was Betty supposed to think? She knew Edward had a brother but this little girl was too big to be the baby that had been whispered about. Was there another brother? Or a sister? Or was this Grace's daughter? Maybe she was just treated like one of the family. Betty didn't know anything about how Thornfield worked. She was supposed to have time – time to learn, time to get used to being Mrs Rochester – before she had to understand any of this.

Edward set the child down on the floor. 'Adele, there's someone I'd like to introduce to you. This is Elizabeth. She and I are going to be living here all the time now.'

Adele beamed. 'All the time?'

Edward nodded.

The little girl trotted over to Betty and held out a podgy hand. 'Are you my new nanny?'

Betty shook the hand that was offered. 'No. But I'm sure we'll be friends.'

The little girl giggled. 'You're funny.'

'Adele!' Grace's voice from the stairway sent the child scurrying for the door.

'Bye bye, funny Lizzybeth,' she chorused. 'Bye bye, Daddy.'

Betty reeled. 'Daddy?' she stuttered.

Edward nodded.

Something hot was rising in Betty's gut. 'You didn't tell me.'

Another thought clicked into place. 'You didn't invite her to the wedding? Your own child.'

Her husband bristled at that. 'I'm a good father. I would have had her there if...'

'If what?' Suddenly the explanation was obvious. Betty might not understand Thornfield, but after years with the Masons she understood these people. They all had their secrets. 'You didn't tell the Masons about her, did you?'

Edward looked at the floor. 'My father thought it better not to.'

Betty could imagine. Nothing improper. Nothing human that might get in the way of business. Adele was like her – another inconvenient little girl. 'So you lied. Where's her mother?'

'Celine? God knows. She's an actress so probably off on tour somewhere. Adele lives here. My father had one of the Aboriginal women look after her.'

'Were you married?'

Edward gave a sigh of disbelief. 'Of course not. Celine was not what my father wanted for his son.'

Betty understood. 'But you still lied.'

He shrugged. 'They told me you were a virgin.'

'So now we both know.'

He nodded curtly.

'And that's it? Nothing else.'

'Nothing else.'

She felt herself calm. Maybe she could manage this. If the two of them had time together to learn how to navigate this strange new world, maybe that would be all right.

'Lizzybeth! Lizzybeth!'

'What is it?' Betty leanet over the railing on the veranda at the front of the house and let her gaze follow Adele's finger up towards the sky, where the mail plane was turning above the property, getting ready to land.

'Is that Mummy's aeroplane?'

Betty nodded. 'I guess so.'

Adele's mother, Celine, would be the first new face on the property since Mr Rochester's funeral, where Betty had met some of Edward's neighbours, if you could call someone who lived fifty kilometres away a 'neighbour'. They were two hour's drive from the nearest town. A full day's drive from Sydney. Neighbours didn't just drop in. Edward's brother Freddie had snuck into the back of the church at the funeral and sat on his own. The brothers had only exchanged the briefest of nods, before Freddie departed. It didn't seem like he was in any rush to revisit the family home.

The mail plane came twice a week, and there were people around, but nobody who could be Betty's friend. The Aboriginal workers had their own camp down by the river. Mr Jeffries, the property manager, had his own house between the stables and the landing strip. Edward spent all his time either out on the property with Jeffries or shut away in his office. Grace wasn't friendly to Betty. She wasn't unfriendly, but, like all the workers, she was assessing the new boss and his new wife. Betty's confidence in the kitchen, and her willingness to clean up after herself seemed to irritate rather than endear her to Grace. They weren't quite on the same side yet. Which just left Adele. Edward had sacked the Aboriginal nanny the day after the funeral. Betty was here now, and caring for house and child was a wife's job after all.

And Betty did care for the little girl at least. Adele was wonderful. Betty knew the child had her new stepmum wrapped right around her little finger, but Betty didn't care. She was completely in love with the little girl.

'Can we go and meet it?'

The ute was sitting next to the house, where it always was. Betty could drive over to the landing strip herself, but the keys were kept in Mr Jeffries' house and she hadn't worked out how to ask for her own set. She stuck her head back through the door to the house. 'Mr Jeffries. The mail plane's here!' she shouted.

'Mr Jeffries has taken the other car to town.' Jimmy, the stockman who'd met them on the first day, was standing in front of the house. His t-shirt, once white, was stained red by the dust and the earth, and his wide-brimmed hat topped a face half-hidden by a thick dark beard. 'He said I should bring them to the house.'

'I could drive,' Betty offered.

Jimmy shrugged. 'I don't mind doing it.'

'Adele asked if she could come too.'

'No worries.'

Betty climbed into the passenger side of the ute with Adele squeezed in between her and their driver.

'You're looking forward to seeing your mum?'

Adele nodded eagerly. 'She brings me presents.'

'Does she?' Jimmy chatted easily with the little girl.

Betty fixed her gaze out of the window. The vastness of the land hadn't yet sunk in. She'd married a man who owned a whole world.

Jimmy pulled the ute to a stop alongside the landing strip. They climbed out and the little girl skipped away. 'Don't go too far.' Betty could hear the note of worry in her own voice. She needed to keep the things she cared for close, so they couldn't slip away.

'She'll be right.' Jimmy folded his arms and looked to the sky.

'All this takes a lot of getting used to,' Betty said as she watched the plane drop towards the dirt landing strip.

'I guess for city folk it does.'

'They told me the Rochesters owned all this land. But I didn't even imagine how big and remote it is.'

'They do not own this place.' Jimmy's voice was quiet but firm. 'They are not part of this land.'

Betty frowned. What was he talking about? Edward did own this place. His father's will had been very clear. Before she could ask, Jimmy started walking towards the plane, which had landed and was now parking at the end of the airstrip.

'Lizzybeth! They're here.'

Betty let Adele grab her hand and drag her towards the plane. The first person to jump out was a man. Betty frowned. They weren't expecting anyone else, were they? The second figure was a woman.

'Mummy!' Adele broke free of her hand and ran towards the stranger. Betty hung back. The woman was beautiful. She was tall, with long red hair rolling down her back. Her skin was as pale and as smooth as alabaster. Compared to her, Betty was too short. She looked too dark. She was just all wrong.

The third passenger made Betty gasp. Jumping from the plane behind beautiful Celine was another man. This one she knew only too well. Richard Mason. Here. In her brave new world.

Chapter 33

Jane

I missed Gail. But more than that, I missed the feeling our friendship had given me. The feeling of belonging. Of having a family. Of being normal. The more I thought about it, the more I realised how abnormal my life had been. Born into a commune to a mother I now barely remembered. Living with the Reeds, and treated like an unwelcome stray that had wandered in off the street. Living here, behind the high walls of Our Lady.

Then I found the picture of Helen.

I was sorting through some paperwork in the staffroom, and I found a box of annual class photos that had never been collected. I'd never had a class photo. Students had to pay for their pictures and Mrs Reed would never have given me money to waste on such frivolity. The photos in the box had accumulated over the years and I held my breath as I sorted through them, not daring to hope…then I saw Helen's face looking back at me.

It is surprising how quickly we forget even the ones we love the most. I pulled the photograph from the box and stared at her beautiful face. It was as I remembered her, but it wasn't. I had forgotten the confidence in her eyes and the certainty with which she had faced a world that offered so little to her. Tears pricked the back of my eyes and I felt ashamed. I had let her down. I had let guilt and fear stop me from being with her. And now I was doing the same again.

I carefully put all the other photos back into the box, and slipped the photo of my class – the photo of Helen – between the pages of one of my books. That night, asleep in my tiny room, I didn't just dream. I decided.

The next day, I found a copy of the *Sydney Morning Herald*. I turned to the employment section. I wasn't yet a qualified teacher and I didn't want to return to Sydney, so finding a new job would be difficult. But I would find one because I had to. I needed to get away from Our Lady and the memories that haunted me. I needed to experience the outside world that was still very much a mystery to me. I needed to move on and find a normal life.

Chapter 34

Betty

Edward greeted all three of the guests like long-lost friends. The man Betty hadn't recognised was introduced as Max Hardy – an old school friend of Edward's, who she had apparently met before at the Sydney Show. She smiled politely, but didn't remember. Max knew Celine already, and Richard could toady his way in anywhere. They all made themselves totally at home. Being Mrs Rochester was supposed to stop this. It was supposed to mean that Betty was never the outsider again.

The friends sat up late at night, drinking and talking about places and people Betty didn't know. Betty always sat away from the others. She didn't want to be too close to Celine. Next to that alabaster perfection, her own skin looked as dark as that of the Aborigines, who were a major topic of conversation.

'Bloody Gough Whitlam and his commie government,' Edward would say. 'Giving our land away, back to those people. They did nothing with it, until we came. Not a building, not a fence. They didn't graze a single animal. Without us, this land would be nothing. Well, they're not getting Thornfield.'

Betty was never game to ask him if that was what Jimmy had

meant when he said the land wasn't Edward's. She didn't care too much about their conversation. All she cared was that every night, Edward came to their bed and reached for her. As long as he needed her, she was safe.

Of course, there wasn't much to do at Thornfield, and, within a couple of days, Edward was searching for ways to entertain his guests. Adele squealed in delight at Edward's suggestion of driving out to the horse paddock to look at the new foals. Max also nodded his assent. Edward turned to Betty. 'Will you come with us?'

Betty wanted to say yes. She wanted to be part of the group. But she was afraid to spend too long in the sun. Mr Mason had been strict about that. She was a white woman now. Betty shook her head.

'What about you, Richard?'

He shook his head. 'I'll let you go. Give me a chance to catch up with my sister.'

Betty frowned at the word. She was used to the façade, but didn't like the idea of being alone with the man who really wasn't her brother.

'Adele, dear, maybe you should stay behind.' Celine absently patted her daughter on the head.

It had been like that since the plane had brought these new people among them. Both Adele's parents doted on her in small doses, then put her aside to drink, or play cards, or go out for whatever fun they could find elsewhere. Betty pulled the little girl close to her.

'I'm sure she'd like to spend more time with her beautiful mother.'

Celine preened a little. 'Oh, all right, then.'

They set off, Max leading the way with Edward, Celine and Adele looking for all the world like a family.

'You've got to do something about that.' Richard appeared at her shoulder.

'About what?' She stepped away from him.

'I talked to Father last night. He's worried.'

'What about?'

'About her. Them.' He waved in the general direction the group had taken. 'Nobody ever said he had a kid. We only found out after the old man died.'

'I know.'

'So it makes it even more important that you get on with things.'

Betty was confused. 'Get on with what?'

'You know. Getting yourself knocked up. He needs an heir. A son. A legitimate son. Then he won't be able to get rid of you, will he?'

Betty shook her head in disgust. 'Get rid of me? I'm his wife.'

'And that Celine woman's the mother of his child. And she's prettier than you. And cleverer than you.' His face was a picture of contempt. 'If you don't give him a kid, he can chuck you out whenever he likes. At least if you've got a baby, he'll have to give you something. Money. Somewhere to live. And we'll have the son.'

This wasn't right. This wasn't her new life. She wasn't just a body to be bought and sold anymore. She was Mrs Edward Rochester. That was supposed to be enough.

Richard sneered again. 'And we know he can get a woman pregnant. So maybe you're the problem?'

Betty felt something contract inside herself like she was going to throw up. She turned away from the house and started to walk. She needed to get away and be by herself. She walked quickly towards the river, not slowing until she was sure Richard hadn't followed. How dare he talk to her like that? She wasn't a waif who they'd taken pity on anymore. She had a position. She was Elizabeth Rochester. He couldn't talk to her like she was silly little Betty dressed up in Eliza's clothes.

She stopped when she heard the voices.

'We are of this land. We know how to wait. We should go on strike like the Gurindji.'

'How long do we wait? It took 'em ten years at Wave Hill.'

Betty moved closer. There was a group of Aboriginal workers standing together at the edge of their camp.

'But they made a law. The land will come back to us. That Gough Whitlam, he said so. We just need to wait.'

The group gradually noticed her presence, glancing towards her and falling silent. Eventually Jimmy stepped out of the crowd, and, as he always did, touched his hat. 'Mrs Rochester, were you looking for someone?'

Betty shook her head to clear the confusion that had settled on her. She didn't know why she'd come down here.

Jimmy moved closer, staring into her face. 'Are you all right?'

She didn't reply. She didn't know quite whether she was all right or not for a moment. She was angry with Richard. And she didn't really know why she'd walked away from the house. Sometimes she just needed to get away from people with their expectations of how she had to be.

'I'll take her back up. Come on, Mrs Rochester.'

'Betty.' She muttered her name. She let him lead her back towards the homestead. It was easily twenty minutes' walk. She'd come further than she'd thought.

'Mrs Rochester.'

'Yes?'

'I don't wanna be... Well, my wife, Peggy, she says...'

Peggy had looked after Adele before Betty arrived. She still sometimes brought her own fat little baby and sat in the kitchen, bouncing him on her knee while Grace made them both cups of tea.

'What does she say?'

'She says you've gone really brown since you got here, you know, in the sun.'

Betty didn't reply. She thought she'd been careful.

'Peggy had a cousin. He was mixed. Real pale, he was. They had to cover him in mud when he was a kid to stop them police taking him, but, when he grew up, he could pass. You know. As white.'

Betty knew exactly what he meant.

'Maybe you don't wanna come out in the sun too long?'

She gathered herself. They were nearly at the house now. This was where she was in control. This was where she was Mrs Edward Rochester. 'Thank you, but I don't know what you're talking about.'

'Right.'

'I'm from England originally.'

He nodded. 'I didn't mean anything by it, Mrs Rochester.'

'It's Betty.' She said it louder this time.

He smiled. 'Betty, then,' he said.

The smell of baking biscuits hit her as soon as she opened the kitchen door. She smiled. She loved the heat of the oven, and Richard would never find her if she waited there until Edward returned.

Everyone came back for lunch. Grace laid out a meal on the veranda. Betty sat opposite her husband, who was flanked by Celine and Max. Adele babbled enough to keep the conversation going, but her mother was past the point of hiding her boredom with the child.

'I'm desperate to get back to Sydney,' she declared, as she flicked open her second beer. 'Seriously, Edward, I don't know how you put up with this day in, day out.'

Edward shrugged.

'And now Elizabeth is taking care of Adele, you don't really need to be here all the time, do you?'

Max interrupted. 'He's still got a property to run.'

'I thought he was paying you for that.'

142

Betty shook her head. 'Sorry? Edward's paying Max for what?'

Edward took a long swig of his beer. 'As property manager. Jeffries was stuck in the past, y'know. I had to let him go.'

'When?'

'Last week.'

'You didn't say.' She fought to keep the irritation out of her voice.

'Ooooh!' Celine slapped her hand down onto Edward's thigh. 'You're in trouble now.'

Edward glared at Betty. She'd shown him up in front of his friends.

Richard jumped in. 'Hardly your concern how Edward runs his business, is it?'

It was her opportunity to back down, to say she didn't mind. She could say she was just surprised. Eliza Mason would have, but Elizabeth Rochester was someone with more about her than that. Elizabeth Rochester was supposed to be someone who mattered.

Edward shifted on his seat to let Celine lean in closer to his body. He was goading her. She could see it now. Well, she wouldn't be goaded. Eliza would have turned a blind eye. Betty would have screamed and yelled. Elizabeth wouldn't do either. She pushed her seat away from the table. 'Excuse me.'

She didn't have to sit and watch. She made her way into the house. She could hear the voices out on the veranda getting more raucous now. She could hear Grace clattering about in the kitchen as well. She headed upstairs. Instead of going into the big bedroom that she and Edward had now taken over as their own, she turned to the right. The house was arranged in a U-shape. The right-hand leg of the U had Grace's rooms at the corner, but the other rooms were unused. There was even a door that separated that section from the rest of the house. Betty opened the door and went through. The air was still and

143

quiet. She sat down on the floor, leaning against the door, which clicked closed under her weight. She was alone. No-one was watching, judging, or expecting anything of her. Here, for a moment, she could simply be. Betty exhaled.

Chapter 35

Jane

Dear Mrs Fairfax
I write in response to your advertisement in the Sydney Morning
Herald *regarding the position of live-in tutor.*

I am currently working as a house mistress at Our Lady of the
Rosary School in Dubbo as I complete my distance teacher training
with the University of New England in Armidale. I have enclosed
a resume and copies of my university records.

In your advertisement, you mentioned the isolation of the posi-
tion. Let me assure you that such remoteness would not give me a
moment's concern. I have no immediate family and no ties to any
one place.

My telephone details are enclosed, and I would very much appre-
ciate a chance to discuss this further with you at your convenience.
Yours sincerely
Jane Eyre

I read the letter one more time. It was brief, but what more was
there to say? I'd never applied for a job before and I had little
hope of getting this one, but I had to start somewhere. It was the

145

first job that had looked even vaguely possible for someone with my limited qualifications and experience in all the months that I'd been looking. My resolve to get away from Our Lady was fading fast. I needed a job, and I needed one soon.

I picked up the pen and signed my name, then folded the letter and my resume, and slid them into the envelope. I checked the newspaper ad one more time and then carefully wrote out the address.

Mrs G. Fairfax
Thornfield
Via Bourke
NSW 2840

Chapter 36

Betty

Jimmy carried the last of the bags from the ute and put them down on the kitchen table.

'Thanks for this.' Grace was supposed to do the fortnightly run into town for supplies, but had retreated to her bedroom with a migraine this morning. There was no way Betty could wait. It was Adele's birthday and she'd promised her a cake. So a cake there would be, whether Grace was around to make it or not.

She waved Jimmy off from the back step, nodding a greeting to Max who was striding from the stables towards his own house, and then turned her attention to her task. She hadn't baked a cake on her own since she'd been elevated to polite company from the Masons' kitchen, but it was easy enough. She remembered Maddie's voice telling her – *four ounces of flour, four ounces of sugar, four ounces of butter, two eggs.* Four, four, four, two. Butter and sugar first, then the eggs, and then the flour.

She mixed her ingredients quickly. When it was baked she would layer it with buttercream and strawberry jam, and serve it with peaches. They were canned peaches, but they'd have to do. It was the only fruit she could persuade Adele to eat.

She slid her cake pan into the oven and glanced at her watch. Twenty minutes before she needed to check on it. Probably thirty before it needed to come out. Adele was with Peggy, learning how to do laundry, which she seemed to think was fun. Betty had time for a rest.

She headed upstairs, but stopped at the doorway to the bedroom. It was ajar. She pushed it open. Edward was sitting on the end of the bed. 'Where have you been?'

'In the kitchen.'

'With whom?'

Betty frowned. 'On my own. I was making Adele a birthday cake.'

'That's Grace's job.'

'She's not very well.'

Edward snorted. 'Well, isn't that convenient.'

'What do you mean?'

'Max saw you.'

Betty was genuinely confused now. 'Saw what?'

Edward stood up and stalked towards her, leaning past her to slam the door shut. 'With that Abo you're so keen on.'

'Jimmy? He carried the shopping in for me.' Her mind was reeling. 'Because Grace is sick.'

'Don't treat me like I'm stupid.' Edward took another step towards her, closing the non-existent space between them and forcing her back against the wall.

Betty's whole body tensed. 'I don't know what you're talking about.'

'I know you go down to that camp of theirs.'

This was insane. Betty screwed her eyes closed, trying to give her mind a moment to think. It didn't help. Edward was king here. She was his queen only because she pleased him and now she didn't know what he wanted her to say. 'I don't. I did once, maybe. But I was going for a walk. I wasn't going to see anyone.'

When he spoke again his voice was quiet – the loud anger of a moment before replaced with something colder and more definite. 'I cannot have my wife associating with those sorts of people. Did I tell you what Max said about you?'

Betty shook her head.

'He said that when he saw you waiting for the plane that first day – with Adele and Jimmy – he thought...' He stepped back from her, just a fraction, and looked carefully at her face. 'He thought you were one of them.'

Betty froze.

'I should have married Celine. At least I'd have known what I was getting.'

She could make this all right. She still could. 'I'm your wife.'

'More fool me.'

She shook her head. 'You don't mean that. It's been a difficult few months.' She pressed her hand against his chest, determined now. 'I can make you feel better.'

She wrapped a finger around his button. 'I can, can't I?'

The anger in his eyes turned to something else and she pressed on, flicking the button open, and then the next. Whatever fight was going on inside his head, she knew she'd won. His hand went to her thigh, pulling her dress up, and then she was against the wall again, lifting her legs around his waist and welcoming him into her.

Afterwards, they sank to the floor, breathless. Betty was calmed. She still had this. Whatever else he did, she had the marital bed, the marital bedroom. This was still where he returned to at the end of the day.

'What's that smell?'

The smell was burning. The cake. Betty scrambled to her feet, pulling her underwear up, and smoothing her skirt down. She ran down the stairs and to the kitchen. Max had already pulled her blackened cake from the oven and was tossing a wet cloth over the remains.

Edward followed behind her. The two men exchanged a look.

'You know how dangerous a fire is out here? Even a small one can spread in seconds.' Max didn't try to hide his anger.

'I'm sorry. I just lost track of time…' She looked to her husband.

'I'll deal with this.' He dismissed Max and closed the kitchen door. 'He's right. You could have burned the house down. That could have spread for miles.'

'I was a bit distracted.' She'd been with him. He couldn't blame her.

'Yeah. Maybe that's all you're good for.'

The words hit her in the gut. Not because they were unkind. Because they were true. That was all she was good for.

'I'm getting someone in to look after Adele.' He looked her up and down. 'Someone a bit more stable. Celine thought…'

That was it. That was too much. She fled from the room. She didn't go outside. Max was there. And Jimmy. Whatever she did would be wrong. Instead, she ran upstairs, past the bedroom and into the small corridor she'd escaped to before. She slammed the door closed behind her. She sucked the air into her lungs. She needed to be calm. She rifled through her pockets for the box of matches she carried. It wasn't there. She could see them in her head. She'd put them down before she started baking, up high on a shelf, out of reach in case Adele came in. They would still be there in the kitchen.

She sat down, leaning against the wall. It was OK. She could close her eyes and think of the flames dancing as she threw more wood into the stove's firebox. If she thought really hard, that would be enough. She could imagine the flames dancing in front of her and she could breathe in and out. In and out, and feel the warmth entering her lungs. In and out. And she could do that until her mind was quiet. Until Eliza and Elizabeth and Betty

150

had stopped telling her what to do and how she'd failed. She could be quiet and she could be still.

Eventually she was ready to venture back into the house. She still had time to make a second cake for Adele. And she could talk to Edward and make him understand that there was nothing going on. She could be the woman he wanted her to be. She stood up and turned the small round door-handle. It clicked but the door didn't open.

She pulled harder.

Nothing.

She banged on the door with the flat of her hand. Grace's rooms were was just along the corridor. She'd wake her up if she was resting, but she had to get out. 'Grace! Grace!'

She didn't hear footsteps but Grace's voice responded straight away. 'Mrs Rochester.'

'Can you let me out, Grace? The door seems to be stuck.'

There was a moment of silence. 'I don't have the key.'

'OK. Well, can you find Edward and get it, please?'

Another moment of silence. 'Mr Rochester has taken Adele into town for a treat.' She heard Grace clear her throat. 'He said you were to stay in there until he got back. So you could calm down properly.'

Betty was perfectly calm. So calm that the scream that forced its way from her lungs to her lips was a surprise to her. A good surprise. It felt loud. It felt powerful. She tried another one, sending a long loud wail out into her prison. She balled her hands into fists and banged harder and louder on the door. It was exhilarating. Locked in here she could let everything go. If she wanted to be quiet, she could be quiet. If she wanted to scream and shout and rage, then she could do that too. She could be anyone at all behind this door.

Chapter 37

Jane

I had expected the garden to be dead or just covered over with weeds. It wasn't.

I stepped through the hole in the hedge into a wonderland of colour and life. The roses that Helen and I had planted had flourished even without our care. They had climbed the hedge and entwined themselves with its branches, which were now clothed in glorious red and gold flowers. The garden beds we had tended so carefully were overgrown, but the wildness made it more beautiful rather than less. The flowers we'd planted had taken hold and now waved defiantly in the light breeze. The riotous bougainvillea capped it all with a white cloud of blooms. Our garden was at its most beautiful.

I drank it in, trying to lock every image in my memory. When I was gone this place would still be here, a little part of me, and of Helen, blooming here forever.

I sat down on the grass and pulled the letter from my pocket. I opened it and read it one more time, even though I'd read the two brief paragraphs a hundred times already. I was expected at Thornfield as soon as was possible.

'I'm leaving, Helen,' I said softly. 'I am finally going to take my life into my own hands, just like we always said we would do. I am so sorry you won't be with me.' The idea of leaving still felt unreal, like something out of a film. I let myself smile at the idea. 'Maybe the father will fall in love with me and ask me to marry him, like in *The Sound of Music*.'

Some part of me believed that was possible. Away from Our Lady, away from all these memories, I'd be normal, wouldn't I? There was a pang of guilt at the thought.

'I'll never forget you Helen,' I whispered. I had my photograph now, still pressed safely between the pages of a book.

I sat there for a short time, knowing that I didn't have long.

'I have to go, Helen. I have to catch the train to Bourke and then I'm taking the mail plane to Thornfield. It's a long way west of here. Right in the outback.' I'd never been on a plane before and I felt sick at the idea of being up in the sky with nothing around me but a tiny metal case. I thought of Helen, who was never scared, never uncertain. I needed to carry a bit of her spirit with me for this journey.

There was no reason to stay any longer. I got to my feet and pushed the letter back into my pocket.

'Goodbye, Helen.'

I made my way back to the boarding house, where my two small suitcases were waiting for me inside the door. I had already said goodbye to the nuns and the other lay teachers. One of them offered to drive me to the station, but I said no. My suitcases weren't heavy, and it felt important that I walked away from the school under my own steam. These were my first steps out into the world alone.

I walked back down the path and under the arched gateway where I had arrived more than fourteen years ago. I hesitated for a fraction of a second, as a tiny voice at the back of my mind told me that going to an isolated cattle station was just another way of hiding. Pushing that voice away, I took a firmer grasp on the handles of my cases and strode purposefully toward the rail station.

Chapter 38

Betty

'I'm going away for a little while.' It was an innocuous statement over the breakfast table, but it was the longest sentence her husband had spoken to her since Adele's birthday. You couldn't say that they'd drifted apart, not when he came for her every single night, and she welcomed him, nails dug hard enough into his back to draw blood. But he didn't speak to her anymore. They didn't make plans together. He didn't pretend that she was his partner anywhere other than the bedroom.

Betty nodded. 'How long for?'

'As long as necessary.' He put down his coffee cup. 'Grace will look after things here until the new tutor arrives for Adele.'

'Tutor?'

He nodded. 'Tutor. Nanny. She needs someone who can help with her schoolwork.'

'No.' Betty was adamant.

'What do you mean, "no"?'

'I mean, I can look after her. I can help.'

Edward shook his head and pushed his chair away from the

table. 'It's already arranged. I hope you're not going to make things difficult.'

'What do you mean?'

'Just be reasonable.' He walked straight past her into the hallway and set off up the stairs.

Betty followed him into the bedroom. He couldn't take Adele away from her. She wouldn't let him. 'What will I do?'

Edward shrugged. 'Whatever people's wives do. But don't make a display of yourself.'

Was that what she did? She didn't know how. She wore the clothes Mr Mason had bought her. She was polite to Grace and Max. She adored Adele. There was nothing else for her to do. She went for walks so she could feel the heat on her skin. She talked to Jimmy and Peggy because nobody else would tell her how a property like Thornfield worked. Nobody else would talk to her much at all. Her husband pulled his shirt off over his head. For a second she thought he was undressing, but then he threw the wardrobe open and pulled a fresh shirt out instead. He didn't look at her as he spoke. 'People keep seeing you wandering about the place, talking to the wrong sorts of people.'

He was fastening his buttons. Betty darted towards him, sliding her fingers under the fabric. 'I'm trying.'

He hesitated for a second and she thought she had him. She thought, if she tried, she could take him back to the beach on their honeymoon before it all fell apart.

He shook his head. 'That's all you can do, isn't it? I should have sent you back to the Masons when I found out you were soiled goods.'

The words were like a slap. The fingers that were under his shirt tensed, and, before she had time to think, her nails dug into his flesh. He grabbed her wrist and pulled her hand away. With the other hand, she directed a hard slap at his face, but missed, catching just the side of his neck.

155

'Bitch.'

He swung his arm around her middle. Betty kicked and writhed but he was stronger than her, and he started moving, dragging her out of the bedroom towards the door that sealed off the unused rooms. The hairs on the back of Betty's neck sensed the danger. 'You're going to lock me in.'

'You need to learn to calm down.'

She twisted, thrusting her heel back towards his shin, but it was no use. The door was already standing open. She'd wonder about that later. That door was never open, but on this day it was, wide open and ready when he tossed her through and slammed it closed behind her.

She waited for a second in silence, waiting for herself to shout or knock and thump. But she didn't.

His voice carried through the door. 'It's for your own good. You'll be safe in there.' He was silent for a moment. 'It's for the best.' And then his footsteps disappeared away along the hall.

Safe. A safe place. For her own good. The silence was welcoming. It was restful to be completely alone. And it would only be for a few hours. He'd done this before, and when he'd calmed down he'd let her out. She padded along the corridor. There were two rooms and a bathroom along here, so she wouldn't be uncomfortable at all. Maybe Edward was right. Maybe this was for the best, just for a little while.

PART TWO

Chapter 39

'You'll feel better if you do something.' Grace's voice was soft and calm. It was always soft and calm when she brought Betty her tray, but it grated on Betty's nerves like nails down a blackboard. 'I've brought you cross-stitch. You haven't tried that.'

Betty didn't move off her bed in the corner of the room. 'He's locked me in.'

Grace looked at the floor for a second. 'Don't be silly. You've got lovely rooms.' She nodded towards the window. 'And a very lovely view.'

'I'm a prisoner.'

The older woman put the tray down on the table and folded her arms. 'It's for the best. Mr Rochester said…'

Betty rolled over, turning her back on the room, and pulled the pillows over her head. She'd had enough of Grace parroting what Mr Rochester had said. That this was for her own good. That she needed to calm down. That she needed to control her temper. It was all lies anyway. Her husband loved her spirit. He'd told her that himself, well, not told her exactly, but shown her in his own way, she thought.

She didn't know why Grace was keeping her here, but she knew that Edward had gone away. Edward wouldn't have meant her to be here all this time. As soon as he got back she'd be free. She was Elizabeth Rochester. She was Edward's wife. She wasn't supposed to be shut in here like this. She was supposed to be free.

I loved flying. It wasn't terrifying as I'd expected – it was exhilarating.

The plane was tiny and the only place for me to sit was up front, next to the pilot. We hurtled down the runway, and my stomach rolled in a most uncomfortable way as we leapt into the air. I'd been torturing myself every time I thought about getting on the plane, with the memory of that balcony at Mrs Reed's apartment still far too clear in my mind. But as soon as we were in the sky, something changed. Despite the noise of the engine, everything felt unutterably calm.

The sky was the most brilliant blue and the world was spread out beneath me. I almost believed that I could see forever, tracking the changes in the landscape from my vantage point thousands of metres above it all. At first everything was green. There were rivers and roads and houses. Gradually the colours changed and the world became brown. The roads were fewer and the distances between the houses grew ever greater. Even from all this way up in the sky, there were moments when I couldn't make out a single house.

'There is it. Thornfield.' I heard the pilot, brisk and definite above the growl of the engine. The plane swept in a wide circle, slowly descending towards the earth, and, for the first time, I had a clear view of my new home.

A tree-lined river swept in a long gentle curve across a landscape that was almost as red as it was brown. I could make out the line of a dirt track cut through the plain, leading to a cluster of buildings nestled in the curve of the river. It took me a few minutes to realise this track was the main road leading to the property. At the end of the track, there was a large house, set slightly back from everything else, and another cluster of buildings, and stockyards. The name *Thornfield* was painted in large white letters on the roof of a huge shed.

Apart from those stockyards, there were no boundaries. Not a single fence as far as I could see.

The plane dropped lower and I looked for people moving through this strange new world I was about to enter. There were none. The pilot and I could have been the very last people on earth.

Excitement overwhelmed any fear I ought to have had as the plane bounced to a rough landing on the dirt airstrip. As we came to a standstill, I looked out the window and saw a car approaching. It stopped a short distance from the plane, and a tall, slim man got out.

'I'll get the door.' The pilot jumped out of his seat and pulled open the door to form the stairs. Panic arrived in that instant. What was I doing here? I was in the middle of nowhere, alone with two men I didn't know. My place was at Our Lady, next to Gail on the little settee in her apartment, watching some movie unfold in front of us. I took a deep breath. That was a silly way to think. Gail wasn't there anymore. She was off somewhere starting her real life with that man. I was here because it was time for me to do the same.

The two men were chatting easily, laughing over some shared joke I hadn't heard. I unclipped my seatbelt. Coming to Thornfield had been my own choice...the first time I had really decided my own fate. I couldn't just stay sitting in the plane watching it all from a distance.

The hot, dry air hit my face as soon as I was outside. I could almost feel the bare skin on my arms shrinking and beginning to burn under the fierce glare of the sun. The two men were watching me, and the silence was louder than any human voice could ever be.

I strode bravely up to the stranger. 'Mr Rochester? I'm Jane. Jane Eyre.'

He laughed. 'No. I'm Max Hardy. I'm the manager here.'

I held my hand out towards him to shake, in what I hoped was a professional sort of way. He glanced at it and raised a finger to the rim of his hat. 'I'll take you up to the homestead.'

My face reddened. This was not a promising start. The pilot had dumped my two small shabby bags on the ground next to the plane. So little to show for my life so far. Mr Hardy tossed them casually into the back of his ute. While he and the pilot unloaded what I assumed were supplies for Thornfield, I looked around.

There wasn't much to see. The property was mostly flat. Even here on the ground, there was no sign of fences. Low scrubby trees were scattered about, looking limp and thirsty. There wasn't much grass – and the little there was grew in ragged clumps of yellow and brown. I turned around and heard myself gasp. Standing in the distance was the biggest house I'd ever seen. It was almost as big as the main building at Our Lady that had housed dozens of us. That building had been all about function. This was something else. This was a place designed to tell you that the people who lived here were important. The very fabric of the building was imbued with a sense of power. The stone walls almost shimmered with reflected heat. It seemed strange to build a two-storey house way out here, where there was so much room to spread out, but it was very impressive. I was certainly impressed, and the schoolgirl inside me couldn't wait to explore.

Behind me, the plane engines roared back to life. The tiny aircraft bounced down the airstrip and soared away into the sky. There was no going back now.

'Come on.'

Mr Hardy slid behind the wheel of the ute. I got in next to him, my eyes fixed firmly on the house as the car began to move forward.

The sound of the mail plane leaving woke Betty from her afternoon sleep. She rushed to the window and watched it fly away.

Was Edward back? Maybe she was about to be released from these three rooms and the dreariness of the books Grace brought her to read, and the endless squares of cross stitch. That was like colouring by numbers, matching the colours with her thread. She only did that when Grace came, though. She wasn't allowed to keep her needles when Grace wasn't there.

She watched the ute moving towards her as the visitor was ferried from the landing strip to the house. It was definitely coming here. Sometimes visitors who'd come just for business went straight to the stockyards or stables, or to Max's smaller house nearby. This person was coming to the homestead.

Betty watched as the ute drew up below her window and the stranger climbed out. She was about Betty's age, but she didn't look like one of Edward's friends. Betty knew what her husband liked. He liked tall, vivacious redheads like Celine. He liked pretty little wildcats like Betty. This woman was plain. Betty didn't feel jealous at all. This woman didn't look like she'd be a wildcat in bed. But then neither did Betty. That was what Edward had liked.

The memory of the fight before he went away pushed itself into her imagination. He liked that she was wild in the bedroom. He didn't like her being wild anywhere else. The knot of fear and anger that lived in her stomach tightened, and the urge to lash out at something flooded through her body. She wanted to scream, just to remind the world that she was here. She needed to stop that. She forced herself to think of a flame, to picture it in her head dancing in front of her. To think of silent sparks flying away into an inky sky. Maybe Grace was right. Maybe she did need to learn to calm down.

Close up, the house was even more incredible, but my eyes saw something now that I had missed before. There was an unmistakable air of neglect. The place wasn't dilapidated – far from it. It was a solid stone construction that had clearly been put here to outlast its builders and their children. It was a mansion really, with its pale yellow stone walls, large windows, and veranda wrapping around both floors. But here and there, the paintwork needing a fresh coat, or a window in need of a good clean, suggested that recently the house hadn't been loved as it should have been. That was incomprehensible to me. How could somebody have all this and then just disregard it?

'Come on.'

As we walked along the side of the building, the sunlight glinted off a window on the top floor, drawing my eye in that direction. Heavy curtains made the windows seem dark and blank. Perhaps that part of the house was not in use.

At the back of the house, a door swung open and a woman appeared. 'Max, you could have brought her in the front door.'

The man shrugged and carried my bags inside. He dropped them on the floor and was gone before I'd even stepped inside.

'I'm Grace Fairfax. Come on in out of the sun.'

My new hostess was older than Max, with a crop of grey hair pulled back from her face. She was shorter than me, wearing flat sandals, and an apron over a plain cotton dress. Everything about her screamed common-sense and reliability. I felt myself relax as I took a seat at the big kitchen table.

'I hadn't realised how hot it was until I came inside.'

She nodded. 'The stone walls help keep it cool.'

I studied my new home. The table was slightly to one side of the room, and the walls were lined with cupboards. Out here, they couldn't just dash out to the shops if they ran out of sugar, and there were no neighbours to visit carrying an empty cup. The fridge and freezer at the far side of the room were big, as was the stove.

'You are probably tired after the trip. Would you like a cup of tea?'

'Yes, please…' I hesitated. Was it Mrs Fairfax? Or Miss? 'Mrs Fairfax?'

'Call me Grace. We don't stand on ceremony between ourselves.'

'Thank you. I'm Jane.' But of course she knew that. It wasn't as if they would have people just popping by for tea on a daily basis this far from anywhere.

'Well, I'm very glad to have you, Jane. I have been so busy looking after everything around here, I haven't had enough time for Adele.'

I knew from our correspondence that Adele was going to be my student, and that my role was part-nanny, part-tutor. Beyond that I didn't know very much at all. I didn't even know who her parents were. The mysterious Mr Rochester, I presumed, but there'd been no mention of a mother. My heart lurched a little at the thought of this apparently motherless child. 'Where is she?'

'I told her to wait upstairs. I thought you'd like a moment to catch your breath before meeting her.'

'And Mr Rochester?'

'On business back east. I'm not sure when he'll be coming back.' She turned her face away slightly as she spoke. 'He's a very busy man.'

'Of course.' I thought about that as I took the offered mug of tea. A part of me was relieved at the thought of not having to share this house, however big, with a strange man. 'Does Mr Hardy live in this house?'

She raised an eyebrow. 'Call him Max, and no. He has the manager's house over by the yards. Easier for him to get down to the Aboriginal camp by the creek for his R and R, if you know what I mean.'

I sipped my tea. I had no idea what she meant.

'And there's an Aboriginal girl, Peggy, used to help out with Adele, who comes up and gives me a hand when Rochester is here, especially if he brings guests.'

'Does he do that often?'

'Not anymore. But who knows who he'll have met up with back east.'

What sort of people would come all the way out here for a

party? And what would I be expected to do at times like those? Probably just look after the child. I hoped that was the case. I couldn't picture myself at the sort of party I imagined the man who owned a house like this would throw.

'So it's just us girls at the moment,' Grace continued.

'The two of us and Adele?'

She put her mug down on the table and stood up. 'If you're ready, I could show you to your room now.'

I hadn't finished my tea, but it was apparent that my time to get myself together after the journey was abruptly over. 'Yes. Of course. I'm looking forward to meeting Adele.'

'Not as much as she is looking forward to seeing you. It gets lonely for the poor girl here since...'

Her voice tailed off but I could imagine what she meant. 'She must miss her father when he is away.'

'But she's always happy with the presents he brings her back.'

I smiled at the idea of an indulgent father bringing the little girl gifts and then I caught myself. I hoped she wasn't spoiled by being the only child amongst these adults. Presents were lovely, of course, but it didn't do to over-indulge children with material things. I had learnt that from the Reeds.

We walked through a short hallway, where Grace indicated the bathroom and utility room on either side before entering a dining area. It was a large, bright room, with a beautiful table surrounded by velvet-covered chairs. Glass doors on one side led to what I now realised was a big courtyard in the middle of the U-shaped house.

'We don't eat here when the boss is away.' Grace kept walking. 'With just the three of us now, it's easier to eat in the kitchen.'

I followed her as she passed rapidly through a lovely, large sitting room.

'The same for this room. I have rooms upstairs but I'm mostly in the kitchen, and you've got your rooms next to Adele. And there's a playroom for her as well.'

We were now at the front door.

'The boss's study is down there.' Grace pointed to a closed door. 'He's a bit funny about anyone going in there – you know what men are like.'

I nodded even though I didn't know at all.

Grace continued. 'So you best stay out. At least until he comes back.'

I peered as far as I dared around the corner to the third side of the U. 'What's along here?'

She shook her head. 'That's all shut up. It was the ballroom, would you believe? Don't think it's been used since Mr Rochester turned twenty-one. His father used to throw some impressive parties, though.' She chuckled quietly at the memory.

Grace started to climb the broad, carpeted stairway to the next floor. She paused on the landing, waiting for me to join her.

'You and Adele are that way.' She pointed to our left down the corridor above the ballroom. 'The rooms on the other side are all closed up too, except for mine. So there's no need for you to worry about that.' She led the way down the hall. 'The boss is there and that's his bathroom. You and Adele have your own…'

Whatever we had, the information was obscured by a girlish squeal. A blonde head had appeared from a hallway leading to the far wing of the house. It was quickly followed by a body that hurled itself towards us.

'Adele. Child. Settle down!'

The girl slid to a halt and peered up at me from under her fringe. 'Are you her?'

'This is Miss Eyre,' Grace said. 'Say hello nicely.'

'Hello, Miss Eyre.'

'Hello, Adele.' I crouched down to bring myself to her level. She was an extraordinarily beautiful child, with exuberant blonde curls and the bluest eyes I had ever seen. Her smile was open and friendly, and without fear. I'd been picturing a sad, broken little girl, but that was not what stood in front of me. This child was joy made flesh.

'I'm glad you're here,' she said. 'I've been lonely.'

She'd already captured my heart, but the confident statement of loneliness made me hers completely. How incredible to be able to state so baldly just exactly how one feels to a stranger.

I smiled. 'Well, you won't be lonely anymore. We'll be best friends. What do you think?'

'I'd like that.' She reached for my smaller case and struggled bravely to lift it. 'I'll show you which room is yours, if you like. It's got flowers on the wall but if you don't like them we can ask Daddy to change them. But you might like flowers. They're yellow and white, and Lizzybeth said...'

'Adele!' Grace's voice interrupted the child's chatter. 'Don't yack on. Let Miss Eyre see for herself.'

I didn't argue with her, but honestly I hadn't minded the girl talking. I followed her into my bedroom. The flowers on the wall were yellow and white, like Adele had said, and also... I touched the paper lightly with my fingertips. 'Bougainvillea.'

Adele nodded. 'That's right. Boobinvillia. Do you like it?'

'It's beautiful.'

I sat down for a second and looked around my new surroundings. Grace was still in the doorway, keeping an eye on us. Adele was skipping about in excitement. The room was comfortable and clean. And I was miles away from everyone. From Our Lady. From Sister Mary Gabriel. From the Reeds. From all those memories of Helen. There was no danger here. I let myself exhale. Thornfield might just turn out to be the perfect haven.

Chapter 40

'Adele, where's your homework?'

'It's here, Miss Eyre.' Adele grabbed her books from her desk and brought them to the corner, where I was about to switch on the radio.

'Good girl.' The light on the radio glowed red and I reached for the handset. 'Thornfield Station calling Broken Hill School of the Air.'

A response came immediately from the cheerful teacher I'd had been speaking to for several weeks, but had never met.

'Hello, Thornfield. Over.'

Adele took the handset from my hand. 'You're supposed to say "over",' she reminded me.

'Sorry,' I whispered.

Adele nodded, forgiving me instantly as she had already forgiven my every lack of understanding about life in the outback. She settled herself comfortably on the chair.

'This is Adele, Mr Jennings. Over.'

'Hello, Adele. How are you today...'

I left them to it. For this forty-five minutes each weekday, Adele's schooling was someone else's duty, and I could relax. I was tempted to slip into my own rooms for a soak in the bathtub, but knew that Adele would use this as an excuse to remind me about being careful with water.

'We don't even clean our teeth under a running tap,' she'd told me on my first day. So I didn't. Nor did I take that bath. I wandered onto the veranda. I leant on the wooden railing and gazed away from the house. We really were so far away from anywhere. One day Grace had taken me into Bourke as she did the fortnightly supply run. That was two hours' journey each way, so I didn't have time to go out anywhere while Adele was busy with her lessons.

The sound of a raised voice and door slamming startled me. I turned to peer around the corner of the building. A young Aboriginal woman was scurrying away from Max Hardy's house. I now understood Grace's comment about Max's "R and R". The image of that man back at Our Lady with Gail came into my mind. It had looked so violent. There was nothing romantic to my eye. Max Hardy was apparently the same – having his way with the daughters of the workers. He looked – strong. And rough. It was a relief that he didn't live in the main house.

I tried to think of the kind of man I would like to be...with. In that way. Because that was what I wanted. To have a proper family life. The man I married would like children, of course. And he would be handsome, I supposed. I tried to imagine what that would mean. Maybe dark hair and a strong chin, maybe with a dimple like John Travolta. Or perhaps he would be blond like Robert Redford. Whatever he looked like, he would be kind.

'What are you looking at?' Max snarled, interrupting my thoughts.

'Nothing.' I stumbled over the word. Even though I knew he could no more read my mind than I could his, I felt as though I'd been caught out. I was still gazing towards Max's house when the property manager's private life was none of my business.

I hurried back inside. Perhaps I could find something to read. The long, quiet nights at Thornfield had quickly exhausted the supply of books I'd brought with me. At school there'd been a library for the students, that I'd been able to dip into freely, so buying books for myself had never been a priority. I walked through the kitchen, down the hallway and stopped at the foot of the stairs, thinking to investigate the shelves in the big living room. Then I changed my mind. Grace had said not to use those rooms. And she wasn't in the kitchen so she must be in her own rooms upstairs. I was sure she'd have books she'd be happy to share with me. Gail's apartment, I remembered, had had a little shelf of paperbacks with brightly coloured covers. Stories about romance, and murder, and intrigue. I wondered if Grace would have anything like that.

I ran up the stairs and towards the hallway that mirrored the one where Adele and I lived. But there was no hallway. Across the corridor, blocking the rest of my path, was a heavy wooden door, sealing the whole wing of the house from visitors.

I stood in front of the unexpected door. Perhaps this whole wing was Grace's flat. After all, she'd been housekeeper at Thornfield for a long time. It made sense that she'd have her own space, made private by the installation of a door. Shrugging, I knocked.

There was no answer, so I knocked again. Louder this time. When no answer came, I reached for the handle and tried to turn it. The door was locked.

Betty darted from her bed into the corridor. Nobody knocked on this door. Ever. Her heart raced. It couldn't be Grace. Grace came up the back stairs, and she had her own keys. No plane had come in today so it couldn't be Edward. Unless... Could he have driven to the property? She would have heard a car, wouldn't she? Or maybe she could have confused it with the sound of Max and the stockmen coming and going throughout the day.

She inched closer to the door.

The person knocked again.

If it was Edward, he'd let himself in, wouldn't he? Unless he thought she had keys. Her stomach leapt. Unless this whole thing was a misunderstanding. He might think she'd shut herself in here like this.

She took another step towards the door. Betty swallowed hard. Her mouth felt dry and scratchy. 'Edward?' The word came out as little more than a whisper. She coughed to clear her throat.

I was sure I heard a sound on the other side of the door. I knocked again more forcefully. 'Grace? It's Jane. Are you there?'

Silence. No voice answered my query. It was strange. I didn't think Grace had gone out. Maybe she was downstairs somewhere and I'd simply missed her earlier.

I made my way back down to the kitchen. Grace was disappearing through a doorway at the far side of the room, into what I'd assumed to be a pantry but was actually a stairway.

'Grace...'

'Jane!' She started at the sound of her name, turning quickly back into the kitchen. She had a tray in her arms with a plate of sandwiches and glass of water. She placed it on the table and quickly pulled the door behind her closed. 'Were you looking for me?'

'Yes.'

She must have seen my frown.

'These are just the back stairs to my rooms. I use them rather than the main staircase. It's quicker.' She glanced at the tray. 'I was going to have a snack.'

'I was looking for you upstairs.'

Her lips pursed for a second before her usual impassive expression returned. 'What did you want?'

I asked if there were any books I could borrow and accepted her direction to look in the main dining room. 'Mr Rochester has some in his study, but you'll be wanting to ask him before you take anything from in there.'

'Is he coming back soon?'

'I haven't heard anything.'

I nodded. 'Well, I won't keep you from your snack.'

Why hadn't Betty shouted at the woman? She wasn't sure. She could have said she was trapped. She could have asked for help. She'd had the words right there in her head, but she hadn't been able to force them out of her mouth. She stood for a long time after the woman went away, staring at the door, willing the stranger to return.

There was no point shouting now she'd gone. Her rooms were above the kitchen and the opposite side of the building to where Adele slept, so the only thing she'd get if she shouted now was a telling off from Grace. The thought of Adele sent her back into her bedroom where she curled up on the bed, pulling the pillow in close to her body as a comforter.

What must Adele think? That Betty had left her. That Betty didn't care about her anymore. That idea stabbed at her guts. It wasn't right. She would never abandon that little girl. She had to find her. She had to explain.

That evening, I let Adele take me for a walk outside. She was determined to show me the property, even though I'd had plenty of time now to find my own way around. The sun was sinking and the temperature had dropped enough to make it a pleasant evening.

'Let's go down to the creek,' Adele suggested. 'We might see a kingfisher.'

'All right.'

I stopped for a second and looked up at the darkened upper floor of the house where Grace's rooms were. I thought I saw something move at one of the windows, but the reflected sunlight was far too bright for me to see clearly. I shrugged. Whatever Grace did in her rooms was no business of mine.

'As we walk, why don't we talk about the explorers who first opened up this country? That's what the next section of your lessons is going to be. We can talk about their adventures.'

'Oh. Yes, please.'

I took Adele's hand and we set off for the line of river gums that marked the creek.

Betty could hear Adele's voice so clearly. The windows in her prison didn't open, or she would have leant out and shouted. The child was leading the mousey-haired woman away from the house. Betty could hear her chatter as they moved towards the creek, but she couldn't make out the words. If only she could see Adele, and explain. That would make things better. Another noise pulled her attention away from the window. Grace was on the back stairs. This might be a chance.

Betty ran out of her bedroom and into the corridor. Grace was holding a tray with her snack on it. 'Hello, dear. I'll pop this down.' She disappeared into the sitting room.

Betty didn't hesitate. 'I'm going to the bathroom.' She pulled the bathroom door closed from the outside, so Grace would hear the slam, and then she was away. Just as she'd hoped, the door at the bottom of the kitchen steps was still open. Betty ran through the kitchen and out into the sunshine.

Adele and the woman were disappearing towards the Aboriginal camp down by the river. Betty rushed after them. The little girl turned as she approached. 'Lizzybeth!'

Betty saw the woman frown. She didn't care. 'Sweetheart.' The little girl broke free of the woman's hand and ran into Betty's arms.

'Lizzybeth, we're going to go and see Peggy. I'm showing Jane all around the property because she's new and she doesn't know anyone or where anything is. And Grace said I was big enough to show her things, so long as we stay together and don't go further than the river.'

Betty nodded. 'That's right. You're not to go too far.' You have to stay close, she thought, where I can watch over you.

'Why don't you come and play with me anymore?'

A stab of guilt hit Betty in the stomach. She was supposed to be the one taking care of Adele, not this stranger. 'I can explain. I've just been...' She held her hand out towards that house. She'd just been... what?

'Who are you?'

Betty looked properly at this Jane person for the first time. She was plain. Really not Edward's type at all. Betty met her gaze. Something shook her. A look in the woman's eye that she'd seen before. She'd seen it in the other children on that boat years ago. She'd seen it in Edward, just for a moment on honeymoon when they'd told him his father had died. And she saw it in the mirror, every single day. This woman was lost.

The stranger shifted her gaze to Adele for a second and then held out a hand. 'I'm Jane. I'm Adele's new tutor.'

Betty looked at the hand. Nobody touched her anymore. Grace patted her head, but nobody had touched her skin to skin since Edward went away. She reached forward. The woman's hand was soft and warm. Betty held it briefly, before the woman pulled away.

'Do you live in the camp? That's where we were going.'

Betty shook her head. 'I'm not...' She didn't understand. 'I live...' She raised an arm to gesture back towards the house. Everything seemed difficult to explain all of a sudden. It was hot in the sun. Adele was skipping and hopping from foot to foot, babbling again about where they were going and about Lizzybeth coming with her. It was a lot to take in. It was too much. In all this time locked away, she had become used to the quiet.

'Elizabeth!' She knew that voice. This she understood. She looked wildly around. She wasn't supposed to be out here, was she? She didn't know exactly why not, but she was supposed to stay inside, be calm, be quiet, not make a show. She turned on her heel and started to run.

'Lizzybeth!'

Adele's cry didn't slow Betty's racing feet. She couldn't stay here. There were too many questions out here, too much noise, too much of everything.

'Where do you think you're going?'

The hand slapped onto her arm. She twisted away, but the hand was stronger. Max had grabbed her by the shoulders. A few seconds later she heard another voice.

'Elizabeth!' Grace was on the veranda. 'I thought she was in the bathroom.'

Max dragged her towards the house and shoved her at Grace. Betty let Grace shepherd her back into the kitchen, aware of Max following them a few paces behind, ready to come after her if she tried to run away.

He didn't start on Grace until they were all safely inside. 'What were you thinking? You know what Edward said.'

Grace nodded. 'I'm sorry. It won't happen again.'

'Make sure it doesn't...'

She let their voices float over her head. She looked around the room. It was exactly like it had always been, apart from the doorway to the back staircase being open. Pots, pans, plates, cutlery, groceries all exactly where they'd always been. Right down to the box of matches she'd left on the shelf. Betty forced herself not to make a sound. She just leant, very gently and very quietly, and closed her hand over the box. She lifted it as silently as she could into her pocket. She wouldn't use them, of course, but it was nice to know that she had them. Just in case everything got too much again and she needed to take herself off to that nice, calm place in the middle of the flame.

Beside me, Adele was standing with her hand covering her mouth. Whatever was going on, I could see she was upset. I crouched down in front of her to draw her attention away from the house, and whatever was happening in there.

'Adele, honey, we have another hour before bedtime. What do you want to do?'

'I want to talk to Lizzybeth.'

The sadness in her voice was heartbreaking. I glanced back towards the house.

'I think your friend is busy right now.' I thought quickly. 'Do you want to go down to the stables? Grace told me this morning that there was a new foal. Do you want to look at it?'

The little girl's face brightened and she nodded.

'All right, then. Let's go.' I kept my voice cheerful, but I was confused.

We wandered towards the stables. 'Who was that lady, Adele?'

The little girl scuffed her shoes in the dirt alongside me. 'Lizzybeth.'

She looked like a light-skinned Aborigine maybe, but I didn't know. I found my awareness drifting to the hand that she'd held just for a second. The look in those dark brown eyes, had made it seem like she knew me somehow. I tried another question. 'Why haven't I met Lizzybeth before?'

Adele shrugged. 'She went away before you came.'

But now she was apparently back and Max Hardy didn't seem to be too happy about it. The slammed doors and the numerous young women I'd seen storming away from Max's house sprang into my memory. 'Was she friends with Mr Hardy before she went away?'

'Maybe. She was friends with Daddy, I think.'

The foal distracted Adele enough to give me chance to think some more about Elizabeth. It didn't take that much thinking really. She was beautiful. Max seemed violently angry to see her. Adele thought she'd been Daddy's friend. I might be innocent about men, but I'd watched enough films with Gail to know the sort of passions that could be aroused. It wasn't hard to imagine

177

how a woman like that could cause anger between two red-blooded men. And if Max and Mr Rochester had both been involved then that was simply none of my business. I certainly didn't want to pry into some love triangle involving my employer, but the way Max had grabbed her bothered me. I understood that sort of roughness. It wasn't right.

I pushed the concern away. Grace had been there. Calm, sensible Grace. She was probably giving the woman a nice cup of tea and arranging for someone to drive her back to Bourke right now. It was a relief just to be responsible for little Adele. I wouldn't have had a clue how to deal with a jilted lover.

I glanced at my watch. It was time to get Adele back to the house for her snack before bedtime.

Getting my charge to leave the foal wasn't easy, but I soon had her ensconced at the kitchen table with a plate of her favourite biscuits in front of her. I followed the older woman out onto the veranda, clutching the cup of tea she always forced on me while Adele ate her evening snack.

'I met someone today. A coloured woman named Elizabeth.' I kept my tone light as I sat down on one of the wooden chairs Grace kept at the end of the veranda nearest to the kitchen. 'She was going down to the Aboriginal camp, I think.'

There was no answer, and I resisted the urge to ask more directly. I was new here, and it wasn't my place to do that.

'Max intercepted her and I think he brought her up here.'

Grace continued to drink her tea in silence. Maybe I was intruding. Maybe I had overstepped a mark somehow. 'I'm only asking because Adele was upset. She wanted to know when she'd see her again.'

She frowned. 'The little one asked about her?'

'Adele said they were friends.'

I watched Grace's face as closely as I dared. She was quiet again, apparently lost in thought. Eventually she shook her head briskly. 'Well, you can tell Adele she probably won't see her again.'

'Does she live in the camp?'

'She used to live here. She's not part of the place now. Mr Rochester thought…' She shifted her mug into the other hand and then back again. It wasn't like Grace to be so taciturn. 'Well, some people belong in a place like this and some people don't.'

I looked out to the horizon. 'Some people must find it quite isolated.'

Grace nodded. 'That's right. If you're used to being around people, somewhere like this could do funny things to you.' She looked at me. 'Not to you, though. You fitted in straight away.'

I was flattered that she thought so, and I tentatively agreed. Being away from the world didn't bother me at all.

'Did you take Adele down to see the foal?' Grace changed the subject.

'Yes. She adored him.'

Grace smiled, apparently happier with the new topic, which was fine. Mr Rochester's girlfriends – or Max's girlfriends, for that matter – were none of my business. Although I couldn't shake the thought that there was something wrong. There was a secret here. Perhaps one day that secret might be important for me to know. But for now, I would let it rest.

'So you're safer in here.' Grace smoothed Betty's hair.

Betty nodded. It was later in the evening now. The rest of the house would have gone to bed, but Grace was standing over Betty with her head tilted to the side in a mixture of determination and compassion.

'And it's better for Adele.'

That wasn't right. 'Adele was happy to see me. She misses me.'

Grace pulled her hand away. 'But she's got a new tutor now. It's confusing for her if you're around as well. She was a bit frightened when she saw you.'

Grace spoke with a soft, sing-song tone that she always seemed to use these days. 'There's something else I was going to tell you.'

'What?'

'Young Mr Rochester's on his way back.'

Betty sat up. 'When?'

'I don't know. Tomorrow, probably, or the day after.' Grace smiled. 'It depends on the weather. When he telephoned he said he needed to stop in Bourke for something as well.'

She didn't go to sleep after Grace had left her. She stayed by the window, looking out towards the landing strip waiting for the mail plane, even though she knew it wouldn't come until tomorrow morning at the earliest. When Edward came back though, she realised, all of this would be sorted out. They'd argued. Married couples did that. Even Mr and Mrs Mason had had arguments sometimes, she thought. But after an argument they'd made up. Edward would come back and he'd come to her, and he'd realise that she'd been in here all the time that he was away. And he'd say sorry. And she'd say sorry for being angry. And everything would go back to normal.

Betty pulled her knees up to her chest, wrapped the doona around her as the sun dropped, fixed her eyes on the landing strip and waited.

Chapter 41

Nearly two days later, the plane came. Betty watched Max set off towards the airstrip in the ute, and she watched him return with two passengers.

The first passenger jumped out in front of the house. A woman. Celine, maybe? Betty strained to see – she was blonde rather than red-haired but Celine probably changed her hair colour for every audition. The man Betty recognised immediately. It wasn't Edward. Richard Mason, sitting in the back, was unmistakeable. He was a slim little man, always looking slightly like a little kid playing with the big boys. So where was Edward?

She listened for any snatches of conversation that might give her a clue but the group disappeared quickly inside the house. Edward must be on his way. Or could he already be here? Celine wouldn't drag herself all the way out here if her little playmate wasn't around. Betty felt a stab of jealousy. Celine shouldn't be out there with Edward while Betty was shut away in here.

She forced herself to take a deep breath. Edward wasn't here yet. This was the only plane that had landed since Grace had told her he was coming back. And if he'd driven, she would've heard the car. She was sure of it. And if he was here, he'd have come to her. Whatever else had happened, even when his father had died, he'd always come to her at night. She was his wife. If he was here, she would've been the very first person to know.

I couldn't get the woman, Elizabeth, out of my mind. Something about her reminded me of Helen. It didn't make sense. Helen had been fair and blue-eyed, and petite. This woman was curvaceous despite being very slim. Nothing about the two of them physically was alike. But there had been a moment when she took my hand and looked into my eyes. Some connection that I didn't understand – as if this woman wanted to tell me something or share something with me.

Today I'd left Adele working on her art project at the kitchen table, and set out to clear my head. The track from the house leading towards the main road was rough and dusty, but at least if I stayed on the track, I wouldn't get lost. I wasn't planning to walk as far as the road – that was many kilometres away, but the track gave me the solitude I needed to think.

I thought about Helen. I didn't try to. The whole idea of coming to Thornfield was that this was a new place and a new start. This was a place where I could become normal. It wasn't working yet.

At one point I thought I heard the mail plane, but I didn't bother turning back. Grace and Max would take care of that.

The day was hot, and my cotton top and shorts were stained with sweat and dust by the time I had reached a decision. I had to ask again about Elizabeth. All I wanted was assurance that she was safe. I presumed she'd been driven over to town and would have headed off on her own from there. If that was the case, I would let it go. The way her face was playing over and over in my head was just an aberration. A sign that I was thinking about Helen. I just didn't want another terrible thing to happen to another person because I'd walked away. That was all. It wasn't because I was having those feelings again. I'd been so young when I'd been with Helen. It was normal to look fondly on youthful mistakes, and feel a tinge of regret. But those mistakes did not define the future.

Yet, sometimes, in bed at night, I could still feel the warmth of Helen's breath on my cheek. I didn't just imagine her gentle fingers on my skin as an idea in my head. I felt them. The joy that we'd found together was always there on the edge of my senses. I wanted that joy again, but properly this time, without slicing myself in two between love and faith.

I shook my head and turned back towards the homestead. I was lonely, getting used to a new environment. That was all. This was the start of my normal life, and it was like Grace had said – I fitted in here. I needed to learn to be at peace. Then maybe I'd be ready to take the next step.

I was so lost in my thoughts, I didn't hear anything until the sudden loud growl of an engine sounded close behind me. I started to turn, but lost my footing in the soft ground. I staggered and fell onto the thick red dust. A motorcycle slid past, just centimetres away from me and ploughed into the track. I saw a dark figure fall, then everything was lost in the choking dust.

'Bloody hell!'

The deep masculine voice was ragged with emotion. Anger or pain – I wasn't sure which. Maybe both.

I peered through the slowly settling dust at the man sitting on the gravel road less than a metre away. He was hugging his right leg.

'Are you all right?'

'What do you think?'

He raised one hand and clenched a fist. I stumbled backwards in fear, but he wasn't about to hit me. His hand was already covered with blood, and his fingers were biting into his own flesh as he fought against the pain in his leg.

I crawled closer to him. 'How can I help?'

'I think you've done enough already.' He spat the words at me. For a second I froze. I'd done nothing. I'd just been walking along the track. I opened my mouth to protest but stopped myself immediately. This man was injured.

I dug into my memory for the first-aid lessons I'd taken at school. Blood was seeping from the wound on the man's leg, where part of the motorcycle, or perhaps a branch of the fallen timber that lined the road, had ripped through his trousers and into the flesh.

'I need something to act as a pressure bandage. Give me your shirt.'

Moaning slightly, the man sat back and started tugging at his clothes. I put one hand on his leg. He didn't flinch. A moment later, a wad of cloth was pushed towards me.

'Hold still. This is going to hurt.'

'It's hurting like a bastard already.'

I put his choice of language down to the pain and folded the body of the cotton shirt into a pad, then pressed it firmly to the man's leg.

'Give me your hand.' I got him to hold the wad of fabric in place while I tied the makeshift bandage using the sleeves. He sucked the air in sharply as I did so.

'That'll have to do for now. We need to get you down to the homestead. If you wait here, I'll run back and get a car.'

'Don't be stupid. We'll take the bike.'

I sat back on my heels and took in the scene. The motorbike was lying across the track but didn't look to be damaged. I turned back to my patient. A pair of intense grey eyes stared back at me from a face that was handsome in a masculine, angular sort of way. There was something not quite symmetrical about it, but I couldn't see what. His eyes were perfect. His lips were full and strong-looking. His jawline was clean and his brow was clear. The only obvious imperfection in the face was a small scar, a scratch really, that ran down his right cheek. Every element was just right, but somehow the whole disconcerted me. I dragged my attention back to his leg. The blood wasn't coming through the material of the shirt yet, but the wound had looked deep. I wasn't sure he was in any state to ride a motorbike.

'Well, help me up, woman.' I found myself doing as I was told without protest, scrambling to my feet and then reaching down towards him. His large hands closed around mine and I braced myself as his weight almost pulled me over. He staggered upright, hopping on one leg. Instinctively I moved closer, slipping my arm around his body to steady him. He, in his turn, put his arm around my shoulder, resting his weight against me.

I felt a tremor. His body pressed unexpectedly against mine.

'Help me over to the bike.' I walked him towards the bike where we stopped as he surveyed the damage.

Standing still, I could feel the heat of his body, and the curve of muscle and sinew beneath that flesh, firmer and more definite than the softness I associated with an embrace. My heart was pounding in my chest. With shock. With fear for what could have happened to both of us if he'd struck me with the bike. With something else as well. I'd never been this close to a man before, and I was scared, I suppose. I could have pushed him away but he would have fallen back to the road. His arm was locked so forcefully around my shoulders anyway, that I doubted I could break free.

'We need to lift the bike. Let me get balanced here – then you go around to the other side.'

With him standing on his good leg and barking instructions at the same time, I struggled to lift the bike on my own. It wasn't as heavy as I'd feared but it was unwieldy and my muscles were tiring in the heat of the sun. At last I got the thing upright.

'Now you're going to have to start it.'

'Me?' I had barely managed to get a licence to drive a car. A bike was way beyond my experience.

He pointed to a small pedal at the same side of the bike as his injured leg. 'It's a kick-start. I certainly can't.'

Before I could say anything more, he hopped to the side of

the bike. Keeping all his weight on his good leg, he swung his bad leg over the bike and settled onto the seat.

He gestured to the small pedal again. 'That's the one. It'll probably take all your weight, there's not much to you.'

'I...' I made a half-hearted jab at the pedal with my foot.

'Come on, woman. Stamp on it. I don't know how long I can hold the bike like this.'

Reluctantly, I moved closer to him and the machine. I placed my foot on the pedal and pushed down with all my might. The pedal moved slowly downwards, but the engine didn't so much as cough.

'Harder. Put your foot on, then stand and jump on it. Come on.'

I took a deep breath, placed my foot on the pedal and half-jumped, pushing down with all my weight. The engine roared into life as I staggered away.

'Get on.'

I barely heard the command over the roar of the engine. Stepping back, I shook my head. I'd never been on a motorbike.

'I'm quite capable of walking.' I don't know what unnerved me more – the thought of an accident like the one I'd just witnessed, or the thought of wrapping my arms around that torso, and pressing myself against this stranger's body.

'Come on.' He reached out one hand towards me.

I had no choice. I moved to the bike and carefully swung myself onto the seat behind him.

'Hold tight.'

He didn't have to tell me twice. He revved the engine and as the bike leapt away like a racing horse, I wrapped my hands around him and held on for dear life.

The journey couldn't have taken more than a few minutes, but a lifetime later we pulled up in front of Thornfield homestead. The engine spluttered into silence as I sat there, my face pressed against his back, breathing in the scent of adventure, excitement and him.

'You can let go now.'

Was he laughing at me? I slowly removed my hands and swung off the bike. Then people swarmed out into the covered courtyard. Grace. Max. And two strangers. All staring at us.

'My God! Edward!'

The cry came from a beautiful blonde woman I didn't recognise. Edward? I almost staggered as realisation hit home, and I looked once more into the cool grey eyes of Edward Rochester, my new boss.

The group ferried Edward into the house and into the big living room that we didn't normally use, Max supporting Edward and frowning at his employer. 'I thought you were getting a work bike.'

Edward slapped him in the chest. 'Don't be a bore, Max. You saw how she goes. Much more fun than some lightweight little dirt bike.'

I caught the look Max and Grace exchanged, but didn't comment. The rest of the group were too engrossed with making sure Edward was comfortable to notice.

I made my way upstairs to check on Adele. With the accident I'd been away longer than I'd intended, so I was surprised that she wasn't with the group who rushed out to greet us. I'd have expected her to be desperate to be part of whatever excitement was going on. I found her sitting on her bed with her knees pulled up to her chest.

'What's the matter, sweetheart?'

Adele shrugged.

'Mr Rochester is back.'

The little girl turned towards me, her face brightening.

'I thought you'd be downstairs waiting. I think there are some friends of his visiting too.'

She frowned at that. 'I know. I saw them.'

Normally Adele was overjoyed at any visitor or new happening on the property.

I sat down next to her. 'I thought you said your daddy always brought you a present back. Don't you want to see what he's got you?'

A moment of indecision danced across her face. I waited for her to come around on her own. If I tried to chivvy her, she'd only retreat back into her inexplicable sulk.

Eventually she straightened out her legs and slid off the bed.

I followed her to the stairway. 'Now, just so you know, your daddy had a little accident on his motorbike.'

She gasped in fear.

'He's going to be all right, but he's hurt his leg, so you need to be a bit gentle. All right?'

She nodded seriously, but, as soon as we were through the living room door, any suggestion of calm was forgotten. Adele ran towards her father. 'Daddy! What did you bring me?'

'Adele. Shh. Calm down.' I put my hand gently on her shoulder. 'What did I tell you just now?'

'That Daddy had an accident.'

'That's right.' Grace was kneeling in front of Edward with a bowl of water and a cloth. The wound didn't look so bad now that she'd neatly cut a section of his moleskins away and cleaned the blood up. I kept my hand on Adele's shoulder. 'Now let's wait here until Mrs Fairfax has finished putting a new dressing on.'

The delay gave me time to properly take in the surroundings. Grace must have cleaned the room in preparation for Mr Rochester coming home. I could have cursed her for not warning me. And I could have cursed her for not telling me we were having guests as well. I took the opportunity, while everyone was distracted by Edward's injury, to look properly at our visitors.

The man was slim, shorter and slighter than Max, with a thin little moustache. His hand was tapping on the arm of the couch, out of nerves or impatience maybe.

The woman was more striking. Blonde hair, painted nails, tiny little shorts and high wedge-heeled shoes. Not the sort of thing I'd ever wear – certainly not the sort of thing anyone would wear around Thornfield. I realised that Adele was in her best dress as well – pale pink with tiny yellow flowers on it. Suddenly my sweat- and blood-stained shorts and top felt out of place. 'I should go and change,' I blurted out.

The woman raised her face towards me and nodded theatrically.

Edward shook his head. 'Don't you dare. I want lots of reminders of how brave I was and how badly hurt I am.'

My cheeks must have coloured red. This wasn't the impression I wanted to present to my employer or his friends. His blood was on my t-shirt, and when I looked down I saw that it was marking my arms as well. My knees were stained red from kneeling in the dirt, and my hair was matted with dust from the bike ride. The woman on the couch sniggered.

Grace was starting to cover Edward's wound with a dressing now. 'Look, Adele. Nearly done.' Edward smiled. 'Why don't you say hello to your mother while you wait?'

My frown mirrored Adele's but the child walked obediently across the room and stopped in front of the blonde woman, who sighed dramatically.

'Hello, Mummy.'

'How many times do I tell you?'

'Sorry. Hello, Celine.'

The stranger pulled a face. 'That's better. Anyway, Edward, we've said hello already while we were waiting for you to reappear.' She barely looked at her daughter. 'I thought you were supposed to be here yesterday.'

Edward shrugged. 'I flew out to Bourke, but then I met a guy

189

who used to do work for my dad and he wanted to buy me a beer so…'

'So you just didn't want to be rude?' The woman's voice was teasing, intimate even. Well, of course. If she was Adele's mother then she and Edward must have… My mind went back to that evening in Gail's apartment. Gail on the table, that naked man…

The woman turned her attention to me. 'So you're Adele's new nanny?'

'Tutor.' I was fighting to keep my tone civil, but I didn't know what to make of this stranger at all. A woman who showed no interest in her daughter, a daughter who was the brightest, most joyful of little girls. Children could be left without mothers for all sorts of reasons. Orphans like Helen… or children like me, taken from loving parents by the authorities for whatever reason. When I'd met Adele, I'd guessed that maybe a long time ago there was a Mrs Rochester and something awful had happened to her. Obviously I had guessed wrong.

'Good. Edward always gets the best people to take care of Adele.'

I stood my ground. 'But now you're here I'm sure you'll want to spend some time with her yourself.'

The woman smiled. 'Of course.'

'And how long are you staying?'

'Miss Eyre!' Edward's voice was sharp. He looked from me to Celine and back again. There was a hint of a laugh in his expression. 'No need to interrogate my guests.'

'Sorry, Mr Rochester.' I stuttered out an apology. He was right, of course. I was here to care for Adele. The personal lives of the rest of the household were not my business.

Grace finished her first aid and hauled herself up to her feet, then turned to Adele. 'There you are, pet. All ready for cuddles.'

Adele bounded over to her father. 'Did you bring me a present?'

'Adele!' I raised my voice in admonishment. It wasn't polite to ask for presents.

'It's all right.' Edward dismissed my shock with a wave of his hand. 'Adele understands how the world works better than you, Miss Eyre. Here she is, all pretty and smiling, and she gets a present. But you, you stand there all grubby and disapproving.' He grinned. 'So no present for you.'

I didn't know how to answer him. He had every right to raise his daughter as he wished, and I did not want to lose my job. But staying silent had never been my strongest trait. I remembered all the times in school that Helen had had to caution me to calm down and bite my tongue. Well, Helen wasn't here now.

'I don't think it's good for Adele to be quite so mercenary,' I said, nodding to the chair where Adele was even now ignoring Mr Rochester while eagerly unwrapping his latest gift. 'She hasn't even asked about your leg.'

'Neither have you, and you caused the accident in the first place.'

'I did not.' The denial was out before I had time to think. 'If you'd been riding more carefully, you wouldn't have crashed.'

I cringed inwardly. I was arguing with my employer, the man whose home I was living in, in front of his guests. This wasn't how I'd been taught at school. I'd been taught to be polite, to be demure in front of men and strangers. I risked a look at his face to gauge his reaction.

His lips twitched in a slow smile. 'Well, fortunately the leg is fine.' He gestured towards a tray on the shelf behind me. 'You could pour me a glass of liquid painkiller by way of an apology, though.'

My hands were shaking slightly as I poured whisky into one of the short, stout tumblers. Mr Rochester smiled more fully as I handed him the glass. 'Good. I like a woman who pours generous measures.'

I nodded. I had no idea how much whisky one was supposed to drink.

'And drinks for my friends?'

191

I bristled slightly at that. I was Adele's tutor, not a maid. Grace bustled past me before I could open my mouth. 'I'll get those. Whisky, Mr Mason?'

I turned my attention back to Adele, who had ripped the paper off her present and was holding it up for my attention. 'Ooh. Look, Jane… Isn't she beautiful? And she has her own car and all these pretty, pretty clothes.'

As well as the elegant blonde doll, she had a pink sports car still in the box, and a whole pile of outfits. I couldn't begin to imagine what it would have all cost. 'They are lovely, Adele. Did you say a proper thank-you to your father?'

'Thank you, Daddy.' The little girl skipped across the room to squeeze her father around the neck, before shuffling back to her mother. 'Do you want to play with me?'

The woman stiffened slightly in her seat. 'I'm sure the nanny will play with you.'

Edward laughed. 'Don't be dull, Celine. It's just dressing-up on a smaller scale. Right up your street.'

The woman moved to squat uncomfortably on the floor, holding Adele's new doll at arm's length while the child ripped the car out of the packaging. How could anyone be so uncomfortable with a little girl? I heard Helen's voice in my head telling me not to judge, but really, what sort of mother had no interest in playing with her own child?

'I'll be getting back down to the kitchen.' I was desperate to follow Grace out of the room, but she pressed a glass of whisky into my hand before she departed, indicating, I assumed, that I was supposed to stay where I was. I hadn't thought about this. Before Mr Rochester came home, everything had been so easy. We'd lived mainly in our own rooms and in the kitchen and on the veranda. Nobody had stood on ceremony because there was only Grace, Adele and myself around. Max kept himself to himself so far as we were concerned, although I wasn't sure the women down at the Aboriginal camp would have said the same.

The mood in the house had changed as soon as Mr Rochester and his friends stepped through the door. Now Max was here, apparently best of friends with his boss. Grace was clear in her role as the housekeeper, and I wasn't sure what I was or where I should be. I raised my glass to my face, sniffing cautiously at the amber liquid. Even without tasting I could feel the scent of strong alcohol burning the back of my nostrils. I held the glass down by my side, hoping for an opportunity to leave it somewhere inconspicuous.

Mr Rochester took a swig from his glass. 'Max, did I see new buildings on the Abo camp?'

Max nodded. 'They're going to pull down a couple of the older shacks. I said they could put new ones up so long as it didn't interfere with work.'

Edward grunted in apparent disapproval. 'They act like they own this place.'

Max didn't reply.

The other man, Richard, nodded enthusiastically. 'But what did they do with this land when they had it for thousands of years?'

'Exactly. My family made this place what it is. They could do with showing a bit more gratitude.'

'It's that bloody land-rights rubbish still rumbling on. Just because a few stockmen up in the Territory went on strike, graziers are supposed to just hand over land they have owned and worked for generations.' Mason was vehement.

'Not likely.' Max was equally forceful. 'And there won't be any of that here on Thornfield. If my workers stop, I'll throw them off the place and get others. They know it too. Lazy bastards that they are.'

All the Aboriginals I'd met had been polite and most seemed to work far more than Max. Peggy, in particular, had been kind to me and seemed very fond of Adele. My discomfort must have shown on my face.

'The new tutor doesn't agree,' commented Edward. There was an unmistakable hint of derision in his voice. I dropped my gaze to the floor. I hadn't meant my thoughts to show on my face.

'I don't know about these things,' I muttered.

'Clearly not. I grew up on this land. My father and his father made this property one of the richest in the country. This land would be worth nothing without the Rochesters. My family made this place.'

'I'm sorry, Mr Rochester.'

His gaze didn't leave me as he took another slug of his drink. 'I'm not sure about this Mr Rochester business. It sounds like my father.'

'Sorry, Mr...' My voice tailed off. I had no idea what to call him. The nice, relaxed, little life at Thornfield that I'd had weeks to get used to, seemed to have evaporated this afternoon.

'Because I won't call you Miss Eyre. Or do you think Jane is too informal?' The hint of laughter in his eyes, that had vanished when he was talking about the Aboriginal workers and his family's place on this land, was back.

'Well, I do work for you.' I paused, before adding, 'Mr Rochester.'

'Indeed you do.'

He leant back and took another slow drink, his eyes never leaving my face as he did. I was still marked with blood, sweat and dust from the accident. But, unlike the rest of the assembled party, I realised, so was he. It seemed then that the rest of the room and the people in it faded to nothing, leaving Mr Rochester and I together in some private place.

'And so you're determined to continue to call me Mr Rochester? Yes, yes, you are.' He answered his own question before I had time to frame a reply.

'Very well, we'll be formal, you and I, Miss Eyre. But I wonder for how long? This is the outback. Formality doesn't sit well out here. Shall we make a bet on how long it'll be before you call me Edward?'

I struggled to find an answer and he smiled, leaning forward ever so slightly in his chair.

'I think I shall enjoy having you here at Thornfield… Miss Eyre.'

I held his gaze. I had no choice. There was something in those grey eyes that seemed like he knew me inside and out already.

'You're not doing it right.' Adele's voice cut through the cloud that seemed to have descended between myself and Edward, and the rest of the room. I pulled my gaze away from her father and looked towards her as she tossed her new doll onto the floor.

A flash of anguish appeared on her mother's face just for a second, before she found a smile. 'Well, maybe it's time for the nanny to take over then.' The woman pulled herself to her feet and glanced towards the window. 'It must have cooled off a bit by now. Why don't we take our drinks out into the courtyard before dinner? Here, Edward, let me help you.'

She held out her hand. Mr Rochester slowly got to his feet and put his arm around the beautiful blonde woman.

'Yes, Celine. Let's do that. I could use some cheerful company.'

Celine put her arm around his waist, and I watched as he rested his weight against her on the way to the door. Max and Richard followed behind like puppy dogs chasing after their master. Richard muttered about him and Edward needing to deal with something private before dinner, but they were out of the room before Mr Rochester had chance to answer.

'Pick up your things now, Adele. We'll take them up to the playroom.'

I sat down in the chair, folding my arms to show Adele that I expected her to do her own tidying. It gave me a moment to gather my scattered thoughts and emotions. Before today, I realised, I'd never put my arms around a man, I'd never flirted with a man. I almost let out a laugh at the thought. Obviously Mr

Rochester hadn't been flirting with me. He was a man of the world and I was…I looked down at my own body…I was neat and tidy at best, and today I was neither of those things. And I was his employee. The idea that he saw me in the same way that he saw a stunning woman like Celine was truly laughable.

But even so it comforted me.

The door rattled on its hinges as the key was turned from the outside. He was here. As soon as she'd seen him arrive, Betty had known that he would come and see her as soon as he got the chance. In fact it was earlier than she'd expected. That was good. That might mean that Grace had told him where she was, and he was angry and had come to explain that he'd never meant for her to stay in here. He'd been angry that night, but now he'd calmed down and it was all a terrible misunderstanding. After all, they'd never had their own special time together. That time on the island when they'd been supposed to get to know each other. To learn to love each other. They'd never had that. Maybe they could have that now, and then everything would be all right. She could make him love her. She just knew she could.

She waited in the hallway as the door swung open, smoothing down her crumpled dress. She tugged at her wild hair, but she no longer had the honey and milk, or any of the fancy concoctions Mr Mason had paid for, to straighten it. Betty placed her bare feet carefully, turned her body and held herself just so to remind Edward that he loved her body.

It wasn't Edward.

At least it wasn't just Edward. She could see the tall figure of her husband beyond the door, but it was Richard who came in. He hesitated when he saw her. 'Eliza?'

She shook her head. That wasn't right. She wasn't Eliza. She was Elizabeth now. Or Lizzybeth or someone else entirely.

Richard was staring at her. 'Oh my God.'

Behind him, Edward was nodding. 'You see? It's for her own good. Grace said she got out last week. She terrified the new nanny.'

'I see.' Richard nodded uncomfortably and stepped back towards the door.

Betty panicked. They'd come to see her, hadn't they? 'Don't go!'

Richard paused. 'We've got things to do, Eliza.'

Edward's voice was low but definite. 'Grace will bring you some supper.'

It didn't make sense. They'd had a fight. They'd both been angry, but now Edward had come back and everything would get back to normal. 'But, I'm sorry.'

Edward didn't reply. He didn't even come properly onto her space.

'It was just an argument. I'm sorry.' She was begging now, feeling desperate with a fear she hadn't known was there.

'Come on.' Her husband's voice was beckoning Richard away. 'You've seen what she's like.'

What did that even mean? What was Betty like? She was like she'd always been. She was trying to be the wife she was supposed to be. She was trying to take care of Adele. She was trying to do all the right things, but they wouldn't let her.

Richard nodded. 'She was always crazy.'

'No!' Betty yelled before she had time to think. She was not crazy. If she was confused, it was because she was locked in this prison. She launched herself at Richard, catching him around the cheek with her fingers. 'Don't leave me here.'

He stumbled back. She flung herself at him again. This time he was prepared. His hands came up to defend himself and pushed her backwards. He staggered through the door and slammed it. She rushed forward again, but her way was blocked. 'Don't leave me!'

She banged on the door with her fists. It was hopeless. She

heard the key turn and then slide away. It wasn't a mistake. It wasn't a misunderstanding. It was a trap.

She leant on the wood, feeling the grain against her cheek. They hadn't gone. She hadn't heard their footsteps disappear into the house. She listened.

'The new nanny thought she was half Abo.'

'That's ridiculous.'

'Is it? She's not really your sister, is she? What do you even know about her? She could be anything. I don't even know what I married.'

Then the footsteps came and the voices disappeared. Betty was alone.

Chapter 42

The next morning Grace brought drawing paper and coloured pencils. Betty pushed them away. She wasn't a child and she didn't want to be treated like one.

'Can you stay and talk?'

Grace hesitated. 'There's a lot to be getting on with.'

'I could help?' Betty watched the other woman carefully, and the expression she was waiting for appeared. That hint of tension and fear when Betty suggested coming with her. 'You think I'm crazy?'

Grace didn't reply. She didn't need to. A night lying awake staring at the ceiling had made everything clearer. Edward thought she was mad. Grace thought she was mad. Grace thought that keeping her here really was for her own good.

'You all think I'm crazy.'

Grace gestured to the colouring things. 'Why not do one of your activities? You know how they calm you.'

Betty didn't want to be calmed anymore. She laughed out loud at the idea, and caught Grace's tiny step backwards out of the corner of her eye. The idea was laughable, though. She'd genuinely thought this was a misunderstanding. Just a row that had got out of hand. She'd really thought if she was calm when

Edward returned, this would all be over. They could make up and everything would be right again. She knew differently now. There was to be no getting out. Her husband thought she was crazy. She plucked the pad and pencils from the table and flung them on the floor. She didn't need children's things to calm her down. She didn't need to calm down. She needed to get out of here.

Grace retreated down her little stairs and Betty pulled her chair over to the window and stared out over the property. Everything was Edward's as far as the eye could see. And not just the land. The horses resting in the stockyards were Edward's. The rusted chassis of an old four-wheel drive that had clearly been left to die was Edward's too. The little girl he lavished with gifts and then handed back to the tutor was Edward's. Everything belonged to Edward whether he cared for it or not.

The plain woman, Jane, was on the veranda. Betty could hear her speaking to Adele. In response the child's happy giggle floated up to her window. There were long minutes of silence too. Betty pictured them doing schoolwork together, concentrating on reading or maths. She expected to be jealous, but the feeling she had now was something else. She didn't want to get rid of the strange woman. She wanted to join them at their studies. She wanted to make friends with someone who didn't know her, someone who wouldn't call her Mrs Rochester or Eliza, and who didn't look at her like she might explode in front of them. The woman might even call her Betty.

'Edward, I'm only saying boarding school might be the best thing. She's going to be too old for a nanny soon, and she'd have so much fun, with girls her own age rather than being stuck out here.'

Celine's voice carried clearly through the open doors leading to the big lounge room.

I put my book down and looked over to where Adele was

200

playing with her new dolls on the other side of the shady court-yard. She was singing softly to herself. I was relieved that she didn't seem to have heard the discussion inside.

'Celine, the mail plane will be here soon, then you'll be gone for who knows how long. Don't try to convince me you'll be thinking about Adele while you're off making your movie.'

'I know I gave her to you. And God knows I don't want her underfoot. But I am still her mother and I do care about...'

Rochester's laugh cut her off.

'If you're so certain she'd like boarding school, let's go and ask her.' Mr Rochester's raised voice suggested he wasn't happy.

I bent my head over my book, hoping they wouldn't realise I'd been listening. Eavesdropping wasn't nice. Celine and Mr Rochester appeared walking close together, his hand in the small of her back, her head tilted towards him.

'Adele!' Mr Rochester sat on one of the chairs beside me.

She dropped her doll on the ground and scurried over to her father. Her mother was standing to his far side, one hand, I noticed, resting on his shoulder. 'Adele, Mummy thinks you would like to have some friends your own age. Would you?'

Adele's face broke into a smile, and she nodded instantly.

'Well, you'd have lots of friends if you went to boarding school. Would you like that?'

My fingers tightened around my book as I tried to hold the tension inside my body. *Say no, little one*, I wanted to yell. Boarding school wasn't always all midnight feasts and girls together having lots of fun. It could be terribly lonely. The other girls might be her friends, but equally they might be hateful. She could be cast out, or bullied, or tempted into sin.

'Would Jane come with me?'

Mr Rochester shook his head. 'No, Adele. The school would have its own teachers.'

'Then I don't want to go.' Adele didn't stamp her foot, but her imperious tone suggested that, despite Celine's absence, there was still something of her mother in the little girl. I wanted to hug her for her love and loyalty.

'There you go, Celine – the nanny isn't as dull as you thought.' He might have been speaking to Celine, but his eyes were on me, with that expression I'd noticed that first day he came home – the one that made me feel like all his attention was mine alone. It was uncomfortable, but I wasn't sure if my own discomfort was born of dislike or unfamiliarity with any sort of attention. I risked a quick glance at Celine. The look in her eyes did nothing to ease my disquiet.

'So that's settled. Miss Eyre is going to continue on as Adele's tutor.' Rochester paused and cocked his head. 'Is that the mail plane I hear? You'd better get your things together. Max will take you and Mason down to the strip.'

Adele's face fell, but only a little. 'You're going away, Mummy?'

'Yes, my darling. Mummy is going to America. She's got a role in a new film. Can you imagine, Adele? A proper Hollywood movie. Won't that be exciting?'

'Yes,' Adele said quietly, and then she moved closer to me and put her small hand in mine. I squeezed her hand tightly.

There was a sudden flurry of movement as Max arrived with the ute, and Mason arrived with his bags. After a few minutes, the bags were loaded and the ute was pulling away towards the airstrip. To my surprise, Mr Rochester didn't go with them. He stayed with Adele and me.

We stood there until the plane was airborne, then Mr Rochester turned to his daughter. 'Adele, do you think you could find Grace and ask her to give you milk and biscuits? Miss Eyre and I have some things we need to talk about.'

'Yes, Daddy.'

As Adele trotted back inside, Rochester moved to my side.

'Miss Eyre, let's go inside.' He placed a hand upon my arm. A gentle touch but one with confidence behind it.

'Very well.' I gently moved away from his hand and then wished

I hadn't. The contact with another adult was more welcome than I could have expected.

The door at the front of the house slammed closed, and their footsteps vanished. Betty stepped away from the window where she had been watching and listening, because that's all she had. She was glad Richard had left with Adele's mother. He frightened her. But it wasn't Mason haunting her.

That touch. That little familiarity with this new woman. Edward was still her husband, and there was a small punch of jealousy in her heart. But that wasn't important. Her unrest had more to do with the woman, Jane, than with Edward. Betty was certain that she didn't want Edward for herself anymore, but she didn't want Edward to own another thing. To own another person.

Edward owned Elizabeth.. For all the bonhomie and matey back-slapping, he owned Max and Richard too. He owned Jimmy and Peggy. However much he talked about 'those kinds of people' being good workers, they meant no more to him than the cattle that ranged across the land or the chooks that Grace kept behind the kitchen. She didn't want him to think he owned this other young woman. This Jane. And she wouldn't let him think he owned Adele either.

'Please shut the door.' Rochester was pouring himself a drink. He picked up a second glass. 'The last time I offered you a whisky I don't think you drank anything.'

My cheeks flushed red. 'I didn't think you'd noticed. I don't really drink much.'

'I insist.' He handed me a heavy crystal glass. The golden liquid inside had the same familiar pungent odour that made me want to gag.

'Go on. Try it.'

I didn't want to, but he was standing so close to me I felt as if I was being subsumed within him. I could say no. I could refuse. But I wanted to face his challenge. I wanted to be worthy. I wanted to be like Celine and Richard, and the people Mr Rochester admired.

I wanted him to admire me.

Trying to avoid the sharp whisky fumes, I raised the glass and took a sip. It was horrid. I couldn't even pretend. He laughed at my pursed lips and rapidly shaking head, before he took the glass off me and placed it back on the sideboard.

I composed myself as best I could. After all, we were here to talk about Adele. Weren't we? 'Adele is doing very well with her classes.'

'Adele is one of many things I'd like to talk to you about, Miss Eyre.' He spoke my name slowly, almost rolling the words around his tongue. The words were formal, but the tone was not. I almost shivered. His low voice was practically a caress. I had never heard my name spoken quite like that before. At that moment I realised we were alone. Truly alone. Celine and Richard had left. Max was out working the property somewhere, and neither Grace nor Adele seemed to fit into this picture.

He was my employer. I suddenly remembered my silly idea about the father of the house falling in love with the nanny, like in *The Sound of Music*. I wished I hadn't. My cheeks felt as if they were flushing pink.

His lips twitched, as if he sensed my discomfort.

'So, Adele seems to like you more than she likes her mother.' He paused. 'But that's not saying much. Celine was never a natural mother.'

I didn't reply. It wasn't my place to criticise.

'Of course.' His lips twitched again, never quite settling into a smile. 'I sense that you are an easy person to like, Miss Eyre. At least I suspect you could be – would you like me to like you?'

He was challenging me again, putting me on the spot, pushing me to show that I was up to his standard somehow. In the spotlight of his attention, his approval felt like everything, but I didn't know how to say that without giving too much of myself away.

'Mr Rochester, I have always tried to maintain good relationships with my students and my colleagues and my employers.' A tiny emphasis on the last word was all I dared.

'But Adele seems to like you more than me,' he carried on. 'And I'm the one who brings her presents. How do you explain that, Miss Eyre?'

I couldn't tell if his tone was entirely serious, but this time I answered more bluntly. Caring for children was something I felt I did understand.

'Children are easily swayed by gifts, but they forget the excitement quickly. Time is what you can't buy, and she spends a lot more time with me.'

'Yes, she does.' He moved closer to me. Only a few inches separated us now. In the silence, I could hear his breathing. The voice of common sense in my head told me to take a step away. I stayed where I was.

'Maybe we should change that. If she spent time with someone else, you would have more time to yourself...to pursue other interests. I imagine you have other interests, Miss Eyre.'

My heart was beating faster. Was he flirting with me? The idea still seemed ridiculous. We weren't in a film. This was real life. I was his daughter's tutor, and he obviously had his pick of women. There was only one question I wanted to ask of him. I told myself that it wasn't for me. It was for Adele that I asked.

'There is one thing.'

'Name it. Anything I can do to please you, Miss Eyre, would be my great pleasure also.'

I was almost too flustered to speak. Only by convincing myself that I was raising this for Adele's benefit gave me the strength to continue.

'I am a little concerned about the effect of...of Celine being here. I wonder if it might be confusing for her, with her mother coming and going like that.'

His face darkened. 'Confusing?'

'I just meant that it must be odd for her. The children she sees on TV, or reads about in books, they have mothers and fathers who are a couple, or who are divorced. Adele doesn't know if her parents are, well, in either category.'

There was smirk at his lips, almost as if he knew that it was I who really needed an answer to that question.

'I was only thinking of Adele. Children need stability.'

The smirk extended into a grin. 'You're only thinking of Adele?' He stepped even closer. He towered over me. I could almost feel the heat of his body. 'You're sure you're not wondering for your own reasons?'

I tried to look away, but couldn't. The power in his face was compelling. He lifted his hand as if to touch me.

I flinched.

'What's wrong?'

I shook my head. 'Nothing.'

Helen's face appeared in my memory. The things we'd done. I'd had no problem with somebody touching me then. And I did feel something for Mr Rochester. Something unfamiliar, but weren't all feelings unfamiliar the first time? 'I'm sorry.'

'That's all right.' He was even closer to me now. 'You really have no experience at all, do you?'

'Experience?' I was proud that the tremor in my voice was almost unnoticeable.

'With a *man*.'

The way he said man startled me. I stepped backwards without thinking, searching his face for knowledge. He couldn't know, could he? Was I somehow marked by my past sin?

'Edward!' The office door was flung open. A white-faced Grace ran into the room. 'There's a fire!'

Chapter 43

Mr Rochester was almost running to the door before she finished speaking. He pushed past Grace and darted towards the main staircase.

'It's outside. The generator shed.'

I followed him at a slightly less frantic pace, worried for Adele. There was no sign of her in the courtyard, and I ran after her father. Adele was standing just beyond the house. Rochester ran past her towards the cluster of small buildings a short distance away. The generator shed was almost lost in the cloud of smoke. The dry grass around it was alight. A couple of the Aboriginal stockmen were already there, beating out the burning grass with sacks. In a flash of understanding, I saw how dangerous this fire was. There was fuel stored in the generator shed. All around the homestead, the grass was brown and tinder-dry from the summer heat. Out here, there was no fire brigade to call. The people of Thornfield would have to fight the blaze themselves, with little available water, and probably no way to direct it at the fire. This fire might seem small right now, but if it got out of control, we were all in danger.

'Stay here,' I told Adele and dashed after Mr Rochester. I took up another bag ready to join the battle. Jimmy ducked past me and thrust a similar bag into a big, open, fourty-four-gallon drum that stood by the corner of the shed. When he pulled it out, it was dripping with water. I quickly followed suit and began beating the flames. A small breeze sent a cloud of smoke towards me, and I began coughing and retching as the acrid smoke filled my lungs.

'Jane.'

Edward's hand was on my arm. He was holding a piece of cloth torn from his shirt. It was soaking wet. Quickly he tied the cloth over my face. 'That will help with the smoke.' Then he moved away, his strong arms swinging rhythmically at the greedy flames.

The mask helped, and I was able to catch my breath before tackling another part of the fire. More Aboriginal stockman came running, armed with more sacks. Gradually, the blaze was slowed, then stopped. By some miracle, the generator shed itself, and its stash of fuel, were untouched. We would have electricity still.

We stepped back from the blackened ground. I pushed the mask down from my face and took a few deep gasps of clear air. Edward was doing the same when Max Hardy appeared.

Edward glared at him. 'What on earth happened? Have you checked…?'

Hardy nodded. 'Grace says everything's under control. This was an accident.' Behind him Grace nodded.

The words puzzled me. We were the ones fighting the fire. How could Grace know if it was under control?

Max raised his voice to the surrounding stockmen. 'Did anyone toss a cigarette butt away?'

'No. We know better than that.' Jimmy answered for all the stockman, some of whom were still breathing heavily from their efforts.

Edward dropped his sack and turned back towards the house without another word.

I followed him through the kitchen door, Adele right behind

us. Grace was waiting with a jug of water. My throat was parched and I gulped down two glasses without speaking.

'Thank you ... Miss Eyre. You have once again proved your worth.'

'Thank you, Mr Rochester. I only did what anyone would do.'

'Oh, Miss Eyre, such modesty. Once again I find myself relying on you. You are becoming so important to Thornfield. How would we ever survive without you?'

His eyes sparkled as he spoke, and I blushed.

No! The flames were gone. The sound of shouting had woken Betty from her nap. She'd run to her window and seen the beautiful glow and the flickering of the flames around the outbuildings. The flames were moving across the ground, coming towards her, as if they heard her calling them. And glowing sparks flew up and away from the ground and the moving shapes of people. They were beautiful. They were free.

But the people had put the fire out. She saw Edward and the stockmen beating back the flames.

And gradually the flames had been beaten down to nothing. All that remained was a black scar on the ground.

At last, Betty turned away from the window. The flames were gone. There was nothing left. She pulled the curtains tightly shut and found the darkest place in the corner of the room. She sank to the floor and pulled her knees up towards her body, wrapping her arms around her legs until she was as small as she could be. Then she closed her eyes and let her mind fill the darkness with glowing flames.

Chapter 44

'I think you and I should eat together in the dining room, Miss Eyre.'

Mr Rochester's invitation – or was it an instruction – came a few days after the fire. I was reading lesson notes at the kitchen table, while Adele took her School of the Air class. Grace was resting in her rooms and Mr Rochester and I were alone.

'It's kind of you to ask,' I replied. 'But Adele and I eat in the kitchen with Grace.'

'Would you force me to eat by myself?'

'I doubt that I could force you to do anything, Mr Rochester.' The words were out before I could stop myself.

He laughed at that. 'Don't underestimate your power over me, Miss Eyre. Come on. Have dinner with me. I might even persuade you to try a glass of wine.'

The slightly mocking tone of his voice was another challenge. 'I think I should eat with Adele, as always.'

'Then Adele will have to join us too. As her tutor, surely you'll agree she needs to learn how to behave in social situations. We don't want her to grow up and be awkward, do we?'

Awkward like me? Was that what he meant?

He took my silence for acceptance.

'I'll leave you to break the good news to Adele. I'm sure she'll be excited.'

When he left the room, he seemed to take all the air with him.

He was right about Adele. She was excited. 'Does this mean I'm grown up now?'

'Growing up, yes.'

'What will I wear? Will you do my hair? Can I choose a pretty dress for you to wear too?'

'Let's not get too excited,' I told her. 'It's just that we are having dinner in a different room and you will have to mind your manners. It'll be a proper dinner too, not just the sandwiches you like. You'll have to eat your vegetables.'

She pulled a face at that, but the truth was that I was almost as excited as she was. I helped her pick a pretty dress to wear, although she was very disappointed at the small choice she had when doing the same for me. For once, I spent more time brushing my own hair that I did brushing her beautiful golden curls. I'm not sure who spent more time glancing at the hands of the clock as they moved slowly around the dial.

When at last those hands were approaching the correct position, Adele and I went downstairs. By habit we turned towards the kitchen, only to be met by Grace coming the other way, holding a steaming serving bowl.

'Grace, let me help.'

'No. I've got it. If you could just get the door for me.'

I opened the dining room door, and Mr Rochester was waiting for us.

Adele, of course, rushed through the door and spun around so he could admire her pretty dress.

'You do look nice,' he assured her, as he glanced up to where I was standing in the doorway.

I was in that moment more conscious of my looks than I had ever been in my life. My clothes were designed for the classroom, not the dining room of this big sandstone house. I was not the

211

beautiful Celine. Nor was I the vivacious Gail. I was…plain Jane.

'Miss Eyre, I hope you'll have a glass of wine tonight?'

'Yes. Thank you, Mr Rochester.' I might not look right, but perhaps I could at least act like a normal person. I told myself, this was part of Adele's education. I was lying, of course. It was part of mine.

We sat at the table.

'Would you do us the honour?' Mr Rochester asked.

I served a steaming casserole and passed around the dish of vegetables. As we ate, Adele kept up a constant stream of chatter, about her schoolwork and the new foal down at the stables, and the new books she was reading. Mr Rochester chatted with her, and I could see her confidence blossoming under his attention. From time to time, he would look across the table at me, and I could feel a change in myself each time he did.

It was almost as if we were a family. This was the life I had never had. And it was exactly what I had always dreamt it might be.

Things were changing at Thornfield. Even isolated in her room, Betty knew things were different.

Grace didn't have as much time for her as she did before. She still brought her food and small things to distract her. But she didn't stay and talk like she sometimes used to. She was too busy, she said. And Betty knew why.

She would watch from her window and see them together. Edward and Adele and the nanny, Jane. Edward was teaching them both to ride. Adele was younger, but she was better with horses than Jane. She was soon trotting round happily on her small pony. Edward spent most of his time with Jane. Helping her.

Betty would watch him, putting his hand on her knee. Holding her foot so she could get it into the stirrup.

Sometimes Jane would lean forward, watching as Edward gave

her instructions. Then she would try to do as he told her. He would point and wave his arms around, and she would respond by turning the horse this way and that.

'No,' Betty would sometimes call. 'Don't let him tell you what to do. Don't let him make you his.'

But they never heard her.

'Mr Rochester, I was wondering if you have any special plans for next week.'

'Next week?'

'It's Adele's birthday. Surely you haven't forgotten?'

He put the newspaper he was reading down. 'And if I had, Miss Eyre? What would you do if I had?'

'I'd be very disappointed. So would Adele. But I don't think you have forgotten.'

'What makes you say that?'

'Because the mail plane brought more than just newspapers and mail this week. There was a box for you, and my guess is that it contains a gift for Adele's birthday.'

'Nothing gets past your eagle eyes, Miss Eyre, does it?'

He smiled at me. He was not a man who smiled often, but when he did... I treasured each time I was responsible for one of those smiles.

'I was planning to make her a cake. Grace said she would, but I wanted to do it myself. To make it special for her.'

'I'm sure it will be very special.' Mr Rochester got to his feet and moved closer to me. 'You are very good at making things special, Miss Eyre. You do know that, don't you?'

As always, my heart fluttered just a little as he moved closer to me.

'Adele is a lovely girl,' I said hurriedly.

'You have become quite indispensable to her. And not just to her. To Thornfield and everyone on her. You help Grace. And as for myself, I don't know what I'd do without you, Miss Eyre.'

As it so often did, his mouth twitched into a half-grin as he said my name. I found myself wishing he would call me Jane again. Just once, as he had the day of the fire. He would say it softly, as I now sometimes whispered his name...Edward...when I was alone, in my room, late at night.

Chapter 45

Betty waited. She didn't know how long she waited. Sometimes the days would just run together. Sometimes she would just sit in her dark corner and hug herself and close her eyes to look for the flames. Sometimes, very late at night, she would catch a glimmer of flickering light down near the river. That was the stockmen's camp. They had fires there, she knew. She wanted to go down there and watch the flames.

Sometimes, when Grace wasn't there, she would test the door leading to the kitchen. But it was always locked. And then one night, it wasn't.

She turned the handle again and pushed the door open a crack. Grace had forgotten to lock it.

Betty pulled the door closed again, her breath coming in short, sharp pants.

How long was it since she had been outside her prison? Weeks? Months? A year? She really didn't know. How much she had longed to get out, but, now she could, she hesitated. She was safe in her rooms. Would she be safe out there?

But at last she opened the door and slipped through into the kitchen, where again she hesitated. She was in her nightdress and had bare feet. She couldn't run away. And besides, that would leave Adele and Jane here, on their own with him.

She padded along the hallway towards Edward's study. The door was ajar and the room was empty. Nobody came in here except Edward. If he was awake, maybe she'd be able to talk to him and explain that she wasn't the crazy woman he seemed to believe her to be. Grace wouldn't listen but that was because Grace wasn't in charge. Edward was the king in his castle. He was the one she had to make see sense.

Edward wasn't there. For a while she wandered around the room, touching things. The book covers. The curtains. The glasses on the sideboard. There was a cigarette lighter lying on the bookshelf. She picked it up. Edward didn't used to smoke and she didn't know where the lighter had come from. But when she flicked it and a small flame leapt into life, she ceased to care.

She darted back into the corridor and up the main stairs. Adele's room was to the left. Her prison was to the right. She giggled to herself, realising that she couldn't get back in there anyway. The door at this end would be locked. She was still a prisoner but now she was locked out of her cell.

Straight in front of her was the door to Edward's bedroom. Not just Edward's bedroom. Hers as well. She had every right to go in. She hesitated with her hand on the door-handle. What if he wasn't alone? What if Jane was in there with him? She didn't care. She simply had to make Edward see that she was quite herself and then everything would be all right.

The curtains were half open, and a shaft of late evening light shone across the room. Edward was alone, lying on top of the bedclothes, shirt off but still in his trousers and socks. There was an empty glass on the nightstand and the stink of whisky in the air. Betty edged into the room.

He looked so peaceful. She could almost climb into bed alongside him. How long had it been? Months at least. Months since his hands had pulled at her clothing. Months since he had looked at her in the way that meant he wanted her, that meant that she was expected to give in to him. If only she could make him look at her like that again, maybe things would be better.

She moved to what had been her side of the bed. She reached her hand towards the doona. The corner was slightly damp. She lifted her fingertips to her face. Whisky. Had Edward been drinking? Betty's hand opened, and she looked down at the lighter she was holding. To give herself courage, she flicked it open. The flame danced into life.

She clicked it shut and flicked again, watching the flame vanish and reappear at her command. She felt her breathing calm and her heartbeat slow in her chest. She knew what she was here to do.

She sat down on the edge of the bed and leant across to touch her husband lightly on the chest. 'Edward,' she whispered.

'Edward.' A little louder this time.

His eyes half-opened.

'I've come to talk to you.' It was very difficult to know what to say. Her heart was pounding again. She flicked the lighter open so she could see the flame dancing in front of her. 'You've got it all wrong.'

Edward's eyes widened. 'What the...'

His shout made her jump, dropping the open lighter onto the bed. A bright fire leapt up at her. Edward yelled again, throwing himself off the bed.

'Bitch.' He grabbed her arm. 'What are you trying to do? Burn the bloody house down?'

'It was an accident.' Her voice was low and definite, not shrill like someone who was out of their mind. It made no difference.

'How did you get out?' He was dragging her away from the room. And the bed, and the lovely flames.

'I just wanted to talk to you.'

They had reached the locked door leading to her prison. Edwards banged fiercely a couple of times.

'Grace. Damn you, Grace.'

The door opened and Grace was there. 'Take care of this.' Edward shoved Betty forward. She fell onto her hands and knees.

'No. Edward… No.'

The door slammed behind her and he was gone.

Something dragged me out of my heavy slumber. A bad dream, perhaps. Slowly I forced my eyes open and dragged my consciousness more fully into the waking world. As I lay blinking up at the ceiling, I realised I could smell smoke.

I flung myself out of bed and ran from my room. My first thought was for Adele. I opened the door to her room and she was sitting in bed, her eyes wide with fright.

'Stay there, Adele. Promise me. I'll be back when I find out what's wrong.'

She nodded.

As I ran along the corridor, the smell of smoke was getting stronger, and for an instant I thought of going back to get Adele. But there was no sign of flames. I turned the corner towards the main stairs and I saw the flickering light coming out of Edward's room. 'Oh my God!'

I was nearly at the door when I saw Edward himself. He was staggering towards me from the other corridor, the corridor that was sealed off from the rest of the house.

As he looked up, light flickered on his face. He darted past me, and without a thought I followed him. The bed was on fire. I looked about in panic. There was no way to stop the flames. Then Edward pushed me towards the door, and grabbed something from the wall behind me. He pulled the release on the fire extinguisher and fine spray spurted out. Thrusting that at me, he wrenched a curtain from the window and began beating at the flames. I directed the foam spray at the burning bed.

Then, as if in slow motion, I saw a flicker of flame grab at the fabric of Edward's trousers. With a silent scream, I turned the spray towards him. He fell to the floor, rolling in pain as the flames danced up his shin. The spray quickly put out the fire on his body, but Edward lay still on the ground. My heart pounding, I turned the spray back towards the bed. If I left that now to tend to Edward, the fire would win. Only when the last sparks were out, did I drop the fire extinguisher and fall to my knees next to the figure on the floor.

'Edward?'

He winced with pain, and then grinned. 'You called me Edward.'

I had no idea what he was talking about. 'Lie still. I'll get help.'

Just as I was getting to my feet, Grace appeared in the doorway. Her face was white with shock.

'Help me get him on his feet,' she ordered as she rushed into the room.

'But…'

'We have to get him into the shower and cool those burns.'

With one of us on each side of him, we helped Edward to his feet. His moleskins hung off him in blackened tatters. Carefully Grace started to pull them away. I helped, not quite realising what we were doing until Edward was naked. His skin was red in places, scorched white in others, but he wasn't bleeding.

'The bathroom,' Grace instructed.

Once there, I helped Edward stand upright as Grace turned on the shower, testing the water temperature.

'Now, get him in there.'

Edward cried with pain as the cool water struck him. My heart clenched with fear.

'We need to call the doctor,' I said as I too was soaked by the water.

'The flying doctor won't get here until tomorrow,' Grace said. 'We need to deal with this now.'

I don't know how long we stood there. My shorts and top were quickly soaked. Grace was wet too as we supported Edward, directing the cool water over the burns. His moans of pain gradually lessened.

'Grace? Is everything… Is she…?'

'Everything is fine,' she assured him. 'How's the pain?'

'Bearable.'

'Jane, stay with him. I need to get some things.'

I nodded. We were alone, standing under the cool flow of water. Without Grace bustling about, the atmosphere changed. We stood together without speaking, only the sound of the flowing water and Edward's harsh breathing breaking the silence.

Eventually he spoke. 'Jane, thank you. Without you…'

'Don't.' I hadn't done anything. If Grace hadn't thought to get him under the shower, the situation would have been so much worse. 'There's no need to say anything.'

'You saved me.'

I had no answer to that.

He seemed stronger now. His arm stayed around my shoulder, even though it was clear he no longer needed to lean on me for support.

'Do you know how the fire started?'

He was silent for a very long time. 'I don't know.'

Grace's return allowed me to move away. She assisted Edward back to his bedroom. Edward sat on a chair, and Grace wrapped a sheet over his shoulders, leaving the burn on his leg and stomach visible.

'Jane, pass me large sheets of that kitchen wrap.'

I picked up the roll she'd brought from the kitchen and began to do as she instructed. Carefully she wrapped the burns in the protective film. When the last of the burns was covered, there was nothing more we could do for him.

'Thank you. Both,' he said, looking slowly around at the devastation in his room. 'If you can just help me downstairs, I'll sleep in the sofa in my study.'

'You can take my room.'

He flashed me a look. 'Maybe another night.'

Slowly we made our way downstairs where we made him as comfortable as possible on the sofa.

'Get me a whisky.'

'I don't think that's a good idea.'

'I am in pain. The whisky will help.'

'So will painkillers. I'm sure there must be some in this house.'

'Whisky and painkillers. That sounds even better.'

I pursed my lips. 'That wasn't what I meant.'

He reached out and took my hand in his. 'Jane, always looking after me. Where would I be without you?'

I shivered. It wasn't exhaustion or the chill from my wet clothes. The shower. His body. His teasing. None of it had made sense. But the idea of taking care of him did. That was something, finally, that I did understand. And maybe that was all there was to being normal. You found someone to take care of and you let them take your hand.

Chapter 46

Edward healed quickly, in no small part due to Grace's first aid, which the doctor described as excellent. I supposed that in the outback, everyone learnt quickly to deal with injuries and emergencies. The plastic wrap was replaced with proper dressings, which remained in place for several days. His skin had blistered slightly, but Edward had been very lucky and I reluctantly accepted some praise for having acted so fast. He didn't leave his study for several days, sleeping there at night until he finally moved upstairs to another room. His own room was closed up, awaiting repairs. Even then he stayed indoors, avoiding the harsh sunlight on his healing skin.

Increasingly I would either set Adele to her schoolwork in the corner of the study so he had some company, or sit with him myself while my student was occupied with her lessons on the radio.

And so we talked, and I realised how starved of conversation my early months at Thornfield had been. Grace was friendly and welcoming, but she didn't read the papers or listen to the news on her radio. She wasn't a great reader or a lover of films. Edward, on the other hand, had opinions on everything. He said the Aboriginal land-rights movement was a travesty.

'They have the same land rights I have,' he said. 'They can go and buy it and work it like my family did.'

His greatest disdain was reserved for the growing campaign for New South Wales to follow other states' lead and legalise homosexuality.

'Can you imagine how that would go down out here?'

I glanced up from my own reading to see the headline he was gesturing at.

'Out here we need real men.'

I nodded, not sure what else to do. I knew that it was sinful for a man to be with another man. As I thought about that I realised that I hadn't been to confession for many, many months. Before his return I'd driven the ute into Bourke for mass. Every fortnight at first, and then once a month and now... It had been a long time since I'd last set foot inside a church.

Edward shook his head as he read to the end of the article. 'The outback isn't the place for pansies.'

'What about women?'

Distracted by my thoughts of confession, I blurted out the question without censoring myself.

He frowned. 'Well, no-one minds a bit of girl on girl. That's not the same.'

I picked up the newspaper he'd now tossed aside. The article was talking about consenting adults, behind closed doors. Something caught in my throat as I read the anonymous testimony of a man who said he loved his partner and simply wanted to be honest about it. Without fear. What could be wrong about the wish to love without fear?

'Anyway, it's just a phase for girls, isn't it? Before they settle down and get married and have children.' He pointed at the article in my hand. 'It's these blokes that are the sick ones.'

I didn't know who was right. I wanted to be a mother. I wanted to have a family. The wish for a child of my own was only made stronger by my love for Adele. I knew, with a certainty I wasn't used to, that I could care for a child. And those were the right things for any woman to want. And that meant a proper marriage, not some inappropriate and silly schoolgirl crush.

Eventually, when he was well enough to leave the dark safety of his study, Edward asked me to join him for an evening stroll down to the river. The heat of the day was long gone and the western sky glowed in shades of pale pink and yellow as we walked towards the line of river gums.

I was struck by the stark splendour of the place. 'It's beautiful here.'

He nodded. 'But isolated too.'

I couldn't disagree with him. The isolation was part of what had drawn me here after all.

'Are you lonely, Miss Eyre?'

'Sometimes.'

'I'm sorry to hear that.' He frowned. 'Do you want to leave?'

My heart fluttered. Was he about to tell me to go? The mere thought was enough to bring a tear to my eye.

'No,' I said. 'I don't want to leave. I have become very fond of Adele.'

'Just Adele, Miss Eyre?' As always he said my full name with a hint of teasing in his voice.

We had reached the river bank and he stopped walking. He didn't look at me as he asked his question, but, despite that, I felt the answer was as important to him as it was to me. If I got it right I might be able to turn this moment into something more, something that would anchor me and make the empty feeling I carried with me go away.

'Not just Adele.'

'Would you be sorry to leave me as well?'

'Yes.' I whispered the word.

He stood back from me a little, fixing me with his gaze. 'So you have feelings for me, too?'

'Yes, Mr Rochester. I have.'

He smiled. 'Do you think you might call me Edward now?'

In truth I'd thought of him as Edward for weeks now, but to admit it out loud had felt like I was giving in to something. Could it really be this simple? Could the first man I'd ever really been alone with be the one that would make all this confusion go away? Living here with him and Adele was like being part of a family. Maybe if I was brave enough I could turn that into a real family for all of us. 'Yes, Edward.'

He closed his eyes as I spoke, and bent his head towards mine. I raised my face to meet his, remembering, without wanting to, the softness of Helen's kisses. This was different. His hand on my cheek felt rough against my skin. And his kiss was as different from Helen's as a cyclone to a spring shower.

His lips were strong and demanding. His hands encircled me and pulled me close. I felt his body, now recovered from his injury, strong and hard against me. The force of his passion took the breath from my body. When his lips began to move down the side of my neck, I gasped for air. His hands too began to move. The sensation was overwhelming. I felt light-headed, over-whelmed, overcome.

In panic I pushed him away.

His breath was as uneven as mine. 'Don't push me away.'

'I'm sorry.'

He took a step back.

'Jane, are you a virgin?'

Dumbly, I nodded. I had never told anyone about Helen, and I never would.

'Really?' There was a hint of distrust in his voice.

Despite my embarrassment I was hurt. 'Really,' I stuttered. Why on earth would I lie?

When I raised my eyes back to his face, he was smiling. 'Until tomorrow then.'

'Tomorrow?'

'I thought we could take a walk tomorrow evening as well.'

I nodded. Getting outside when the harshest heat of the sun had passed would be best for his recovery.

'I have no need to rush you.'

Gratitude filled my thoughts. At least, whatever else was leaving me reeling and confused, I had no doubt that Edward Rochester was, at heart, a good man.

She didn't hear him come in. That would be one of the things Betty remembered afterwards. He'd just appeared at the end of her bed, like a spirit who'd floated in on the breeze.

He undressed quickly, briskly. Betty wasn't sure what to think. She wanted to be Elizabeth Rochester again, didn't she? That was what she was supposed to want. That would mean that she wasn't crazy. Elizabeth Rochester wasn't crazy. Elizabeth Rochester was a proper lady. She was Edward's wife. She took care of Adele. She was someone who meant something. She was someone with a perfectly normal life. Betty was supposed to rest and get better so she could get back to normal. And normal was being Mrs Rochester, wasn't it?

He lowered his weight on top of her.

This was what being Mrs Rochester meant, Betty thought. She pleased him in bed. She was his wildcat. That was what he expected.

It was what Richard had expected too, when he'd tried to bend her over the kitchen table at the Masons' house. Was it what Mr Mason had expected? He'd sold her like a brood mare. Presumably he'd expected her to breed.

Her thoughts drifted backwards, deeper into her head, further away from what was happening right now in the room. She thought of Mrs Mason. Mrs Mason had wanted her to be pretty and affectionate.

And then she thought of her father. She didn't think he'd wanted anything from her, but maybe she'd been too little to remember. His little firefly. The pet name appeared in her head unexpectedly, unremembered for years. Betty let it sit there. Daddy's little firefly.

Above her, Edward let out a moan. Betty didn't think about that.

Instead she thought about her mother. Her mother who had gone away because she was ill, because she couldn't manage, because of her nerves. It hadn't been Betty's fault – that's what her father had told her. It was just that sometimes, he'd said, people like Betty's mother couldn't cope with everything that was going on so they had to go somewhere quiet and calm until they felt better.

The bed juddered underneath them. Betty kept thinking about other things.

She wondered if she was like her mother. Was that why she had to stay here and have her tea on a tray? Was that why Grace always checked that she'd put her knife and fork back on the plate and not squirreled them away? Maybe Edward and Richard and Grace were right. Maybe there was something wrong inside her after all.

Then she wondered what the biggest fire that anyone had ever started looked like. Edward had told her about bushfires when she'd first come here. And she remembered the sight of the burning cane from the window of the plane, back when she and Edward were newly married. When she was Mrs Rochester. She imagined herself in that little plane, taking off from the landing strip and watching everything beneath her burn again.

And those were all the things Betty thought about while her husband did what he wanted. And when he finished, he pulled his trousers back on and left her without saying a word.

Betty lay on the bed and waited for the turn of the key in the lock to safely shut her back in, to tell her she was alone again.

The second time we walked along the river, we walked a lot further. As the sun sank and the stars began to appear in the sky, I stopped and looked up at those diamond lights in the deep blue velvet. It seemed to me I had never seen so many stars before. Nor had I seen stars that shone so brightly.

'It's so beautiful. It takes my breath away.'

'In this light, you are almost beautiful too, Jane.'

Edward kissed me again. This time, the kiss was softer and I was prepared. He held my hand as we walked. His skin was hard and rough, reminding me that this was something different, something new, that I just needed to get used to.

After that, we walked to the river every evening. Sometimes he kissed me. Sometimes he didn't. I didn't really mind either way, but I did like being with him. He was clever and well-read, and he didn't pressure me beyond those kisses. I liked the picture that we presented, walking hand in hand along the riverbank. I loved the idea of falling in love.

'Being with you is restful. We could have a very simple life together, you and I,' he told me. 'There'd be no drama with you, Jane.'

It wasn't the magnificent declaration of love that I'd seen in the movies Gail and I had watched together, but it was enough. In fact, it was exactly right. I didn't have the heart for a great romance. I'd thought I'd had that before and it had been taken from me, leaving me with nothing more than memories I could scarcely keep hold of anymore. The women in those films weren't like me. They were beautiful and adventurous. I wasn't looking for adventure.

One night, our walk took us in another direction, towards the camp by the river, where the stockmen lived with their families. As the camp came into view, Edward suddenly stopped. He stood in silence for a few minutes.

'Come, Jane, we should walk the other way.'

I wanted to ask why, but these evening walks had become important to me, and I didn't want anything to spoil these moments.

'You know I never expected to live here like this?' Edward said as we turned back towards the homestead.

I was confused. 'I thought Thornfield was your family home.'

He nodded. 'But I have a brother. Three years older. It should all have been his.'

'What happened?'

Edward shook his head. 'He made some bad choices. In his love life.' He laughed, a brief, bitter little laugh. 'I won't make that mistake this time.'

I didn't say anything about the 'this time.' It was clear that he was thinking about Celine, but it was even clearer to me that whatever had been between them was in the past. Now he needed a woman who could be a real mother to his child.

That night, he came to my bedroom door. He knocked. I wasn't surprised. He'd never rushed or pressured me, but this was how relationships worked, wasn't it? And being nervous was normal. It didn't mean anything.

I was lying in bed, reading. As the knock sounded a second time, I got out of bed and slipped on my dressing gown, belting it tightly around my waist. When I opened the door, he was there.

'Can I come in?' he asked.

I struggled for words, but found none. My mouth was too dry to speak, the beat of my heart too loud. Taking my silence for acceptance, he came into my room, gently closing the door behind him.

The dim light from my reading lamp softened his features and he looked very handsome. His shirt hung open, revealing the chest that I had touched when I rode on his motorcycle. Images sprang to my mind of his naked body as we stood in the shower, the cool water soothing his burns.

'Edward…'

His fingers clenched around my shoulders and he pulled me to him, his lips seeking mine with a passion that was new to me. His hands roamed my body, roughly clutching at my breast. I tried to welcome his touch. I really tried.

'Edward... Please.' I pushed against his chest. His hands tightened around me, his tongue plunged more deeply into my mouth, just for a second, before he stepped back.

'Jane? I thought we wanted the same thing.'

'I do, Edward. But this...this isn't right.'

'Why...' Then he shook his head. 'Those bloody nuns.'

Maybe that was it. A man and a woman should lie together in marriage. That was what was right. I told myself that that was what was holding me back.

'They taught you that sex was sinful, didn't they?'

Sister Mary Gabriel's lecture wasn't what he meant, but it was what I thought of as I nodded.

'It's not a sin. Never. Not between people who care for other, but I understand. I will marry you, Jane.' His tone was suddenly definite and precise. 'I can't imagine a life here without you. You agree that we should get married, don't you, Jane?'

It was as if a weight had lifted off me. My real life was finally beginning. This was how things were supposed to be.

'Yes. Yes. I will marry you.'

He pulled me back into his arms. 'It's going to be perfect, Jane. You'll be a perfect wife for me.'

I nodded as best I could while pressed against his chest. Silently I swore to myself that he was right. I would be the perfect wife. I would care for Edward, for Thornfield, and for Adele, and I would do my duty as his wife. Once we were married, everything would fall into place.

He was still talking, his voice muffled against my hair in the tightness of the embrace. 'Now I have everything I need right here,' he murmured.

Chapter 47

It didn't make sense. They were bringing deliveries to the house. An extra plane had arrived. Not the mail plane. Betty knew its schedule well. And this plane didn't deliver guests, as sometimes happened. It just bought boxes. Betty watched as they were unloaded from the ute. Grace wouldn't answer when she asked what was happening. In fact, Grace didn't talk to her very much at all recently.

'Lizzybeth!'

The girl standing in front of her couldn't be real. Nobody came into her rooms in the daytime. Only Grace. Edward came at night, but Betty didn't think about that. She closed her eyes and thought about the flames dancing over the cane fields, and her daddy promising to come back for his little firefly. Nobody came to visit. So Adele couldn't be standing in front of her, clutching a book under her arm with a determined expression on her face.

'How did you get in here?'

'I worked you out.'

'What do you mean?'

Adele padded past her and into the sitting room. 'Working

out is what I do with Jane when there's a hard problem in my maths book.'

Betty didn't understand.

'So I worked you out like that. Grace said you'd gone, but I thought about it and I watched the plane coming every time and you didn't go on the plane. And Grace keeps making up trays of food and they're not for her because she's always eating biscuits in the kitchen, so I knew she was hiding something.' The girl paused. 'I thought it might be a puppy.'

Betty's head was spinning a bit from the girl's long speech. Adele looked bigger and taller than the last time Betty had spoken to her, but she still talked like the same little girl, with ideas rushing and falling over each other in her excitement. Betty didn't know what to respond to first. 'I'm not a puppy.'

'So I waited 'til she'd just brought a tray down and then Peggy came and asked her for something so she didn't shut the door properly. Will you do my reading book with me? Jane says I have to practice every day. I'm supposed to practice on my own but it's better when there's someone to listen to me and tell me I'm doing well.'

Betty glanced towards the stairwell. The door was unlocked. She could go. She could take Adele with her right now and go.

'It's my favourite book. It's called *Seven Little Australians* and I've read it dozens of times. I'm at the part where they are sending Judy to boarding school. Mummy said I should go to boarding school, but I said no.'

Betty sat down next to Adele. 'Would you like to come away with me?'

The girl crinkled her nose. 'I've got to do my reading practice.'

'You could bring that with you.'

'Would Jane come with us?'

Betty shook her head. 'I don't think so.'

Adele looked at the floor. 'I've got maths and piano with her this afternoon.'

The little girl opened her book. 'In the next bit, Judy runs away from boarding school and finds her way home. But she gets sick.'

It wouldn't be fair anyway, would it? To take Adele away without a plan for where to go, and they'd be leaving Jane behind. The plan that had shone so brightly for a few moments faded. Betty let the child read aloud to her for a few pages. It was soothing, her voice constant, but for the odd stumble over a word, reminding Betty that she wasn't alone. At the end of the chapter, she plucked the book out of Adele's hand. 'Darling, what are all the deliveries for?'

The little girl grinned. 'For the party.'

'What party?'

'The party because Daddy's getting married to Jane.' The sound of the ute pulling up outside made Adele jump. 'That'll be her coming back. I have to go now.'

Betty barely registered Adele darting away. Jane was marrying Edward? That made no sense. Edward had a wife. Betty was his wife. Wasn't she? She remembered a white dress. And the church and the people. Something had gone wrong that day. Something to do with Edward's brother. She wasn't sure about that now, but she did remember the white dress. And the long veil.

The party must be for… Betty couldn't think of anything… for something else.

A thought nibbled at the back of her mind. Edward's hand on that woman's arm. The way he'd started coming to her again at night. Taking what he needed but nothing more. Something had changed for him, something she wasn't part of. He still needed her body but he didn't need anything else.

Grace brought her lunch tray. Betty ate slowly, thinking things through. Adele had come in to see her when Grace had left the door open. She'd sneaked out before when Grace was distracted by the fire. So Grace might forget to close the door properly if something else happened.

233

Betty waited until she heard the household coming up the stairs to bed. As usual she could see the light still on in the kitchen below her. She padded down the stairs and banged on the door. It opened a crack. 'What are you doing up?'

'I've got a headache.'

'I'll bring you an aspirin. Go back upstairs.'

Betty nodded and did as she was told. Then she hurried into the bathroom, and closed the door, running the tap to make it sound like she was washing before bed. She listened for Grace's steps on the landing. 'Can you leave it by the bed?' she called.

'All right.'

She only had a few seconds. She rushed out of the bathroom, closing the door as quietly as she could behind her, and darted down the stairs, straight through the kitchen and out into the night. As soon as she was outside she pressed herself back against the wall in case Grace realised she wasn't in the bathroom and looked outside for her, but a few minutes later she heard the woman come back down the stairs and pull the door to her prison closed.

Where would the wedding things be? They could be in one of the bedrooms, she supposed, clothes and things. But where would they hold an actual wedding? She smiled as she remembered. Thornfield had a ballroom. An actual ballroom like in a costume drama on the TV. It was all closed up, but if you were going to get married here, that would be the place. She let herself back into the house through the big front door and stood for a second in the silent hallway. The ballroom was to the right, underneath Adele's room, and the room where she guessed the soon-to-be second Mrs Rochester would be sleeping.

The ballroom door was ajar. That door was never open. She pushed it as gently as she could, praying that it wouldn't creak loudly enough to give her away.

She was right. The room was laid out for a wedding. She hunted for the final clue. It was right there on the table next to the door. A pile of neat little cards. *Order of Service for the wedding of Edward Rochester and Jane Eyre.*

Betty supressed the scream that was trying to come out of her – not of jealousy, not of hurt, but of rage. She had to stop this. He couldn't own another person. He couldn't pick another person up and then get tired of them and lock them away somewhere. She had to take this wedding apart so completely that it would be impossible to put it back together again.

She worked quickly and methodically. It would look like she'd been in a frenzy to anyone who saw the aftermath, but actually she was perfectly calm. She didn't stop, until every piece of wedding paraphernalia had been destroyed. She pulled the ribbons from the chairs and left them on the floor. She tore the neat little cards into a thousand pieces and threw them across the room. She pulled down the white tulle banner at the front of the room and trampled it.

And then she went upstairs. The best thing to do, the thing that would properly put a stop to all this, would be to wake the woman and tell her. Betty went towards Adele's room. This corridor was the mirror of her own, but without the big solid door that imprisoned her. There was just an empty corridor. She knew which was Adele's room. Just past that door was another room; exactly like the room that Grace used. That would be Jane Eyre's room, she guessed. Adele and herself both penned in by their attendants.

Betty pushed the door open. The woman was fast asleep on the bed. And then she saw it. The long white dress, with the perfect white veil, so very like the veil she'd worn that day in the church. She ran her fingers over the fabric. Without really knowing what she was doing, she lifted this veil down and draped it over her own head. Now she was the bride. But she had already done that. Hadn't she? This woman was going to take her place. Or maybe Betty could take the bride's place at this second wedding. She shook her head. It was very confusing.

Footsteps on the landing startled her. She tried to take a glimpse out of the room without being seen, but she was too slow. Grace's mouth widened in horror. 'Elizabeth!' she whispered.

Betty stood stock still. Grace extended a finger, beckoning her into the hallway. Betty inched towards the door.

'What are you doing with that?'

Betty's arms wrapped instinctively around her prize. 'Mine.'

'It's not yours. It's Jane's.'

'I'm Mrs Rochester,' she hissed. 'It's all mine.'

Grace narrowed her eyes. 'Where else have you been?'

Betty looked at the floor. 'Nowhere.'

'Well, back to bed with you, then.'

Betty followed Grace back to her room. She was tired. And she'd done what she'd set out to do, hadn't she? Jane couldn't marry him without her flowers and her ribbons and her pretty veil, so everything would be all right now.

'You need to give me the veil now.'

Betty wrapped the delicate lace around her fingers. 'Mine.'

Grace yawned heavily. 'What if you look after it until the morning? And then give it back to me.'

Betty shrugged.

'But you have to look after it very carefully.'

Betty didn't reply. Grace locked the big door and went away.

Betty went to her treasures and pulled out her matches. She carried her matches and her veil to the bathroom, and dropped the veil into the bath. She wasn't being silly. She didn't want to burn the whole place down. Just this one thing. So nobody could be a bride. So nobody had to be Mrs Rochester anymore. She dropped a match into the bath. The veil burned beautifully.

Chapter 48

Thornfield's ballroom was the perfect place for a wedding. Soft light poured in through the big glass doors that opened onto the shaded courtyard that was filled with the deep greens of the potted plants, and the bright colours of bougainvillea. The room itself had wooden floors polished to a rich golden shine, and pale lemon walls that beautifully framed the red roses that Edward had had flown in for the wedding. Grace and I had draped white tulle to create a wedding bower at one end of the room, and tied red ribbons on the chairs to match the roses. We had dotted red and white candles around the room, and made it beautiful for today's very private ceremony.

But it wasn't beautiful anymore.

During the night, someone had come into the room that I had so lovingly prepared, and they had destroyed it.

The chairs had been knocked aside, the pretty red ribbons torn off to lie like pools of blood on the floor. The roses too had been destroyed; their petals were strewn everywhere. The white tulle bower was now just a heap of torn fabric. The long tapered candles had been broken and tossed like rag dolls onto the floor.

'Who could have done this to me?'

Edward was brisk but definite. 'I'm sure it wasn't about you.

It was probably those ungrateful bastards who think this is their land.'

I shook my head. The stockmen wouldn't do this. I'd heard all the talk about land rights and I read the papers, but the protests were all peaceful and non-destructive. Besides, this wasn't about politics or land. This was something else. This was personal. Someone was trying to ruin our wedding. But who? There were no visitors at Thornfield. My only wedding attendants would be Adele and Grace, and Max Hardy would stand beside Edward, who had refused to invite his brother or any of his old friends. This was his new start, he'd said. He didn't want reminders of his old life. The Aboriginal stockmen and their families were going to watch the ceremony, and Edward was providing a lunch for them by the river bank.

Edward and I were supposed to have a meal with Adele and Max in the courtyard, which had been decorated to match the ballroom. I caught my breath and rushed to the big French doors. The courtyard was untouched. Whoever had done this had only paid attention to the decorations inside the house.

From overhead came the sound of the engine. The plane was arriving with the celebrant who was to marry us. I wiped the tears from my face. Edward turned me gently away from the worst of the devastation, and led me out of the ballroom.

'Look, what's done is done, but it's our wedding day.' There was a determination in his tone that I remembered from the night he proposed. 'We are going to be married today, so you need to go and get ready.'

His confidence calmed me a little. This was what I had chosen – what we had chosen – we shouldn't be distracted by vandalism, however heinous.

'Max and I will sort everything out down here. You go with Grace.'

I wasn't so sure, but the determined look on his face meant I was not going to argue. With Grace by my side, I headed back upstairs. I quickly combed my hair into a soft bun, and let Grace weave a handful of tiny fresh flowers though the strands. Then I applied a touch of the makeup that I so seldom wore. Then I reached for the beautiful white dress hanging on the door of my wardrobe. As Grace fastened me in, Adele ran into the room.

'You look pretty.'

She was almost right.

There had been no time to go to the city to shop. I had chosen my wedding dress from a catalogue. It had come on the mail plane just a few days ago. The puffed sleeves and gathered waist made my figure look more womanly than I had ever felt.

'You look very pretty too, Adele.' My pupil was to be my flower girl, and her pale yellow dress was another of the catalogue's best offerings.

Her smile warmed my heart.

'Adele, will you help me put my veil on?'

The little girl squealed in delight.

I turned to look for it, but it wasn't hanging from the wardrobe as I expected.

'Grace, where's my veil?'

She hesitated. 'I don't know. Perhaps you left it downstairs?'

'No. No. I brought it up here. I know I did.' At least, I thought I had. Perhaps I had left it in the ballroom. I remembered seeing the tulle discarded across the floor. I'd thought that was from the banner, but maybe... No. No. I'd hung the veil up with my dress. I remembered doing it quite clearly. 'It was in my room.'

I felt my voice rising, but there was nothing I could do to stop it. I didn't think I could stand to see anything else go wrong.

'We have to find it, Grace.'

'What's wrong?' Adele's voice shook just a little.

I looked down as her beautiful little face started to crumple. Adele had been looking forward to this wedding even more than I. I loved her dearly. It would be a joy to be her mother. I wasn't going to let anything else spoil this day for either of us.

'It's nothing, sweetheart. I think I left my veil downstairs. It doesn't matter. Are you ready? It's almost time for the wedding.'

I was relieved to see the smile return to her face.

With one final inspection of my appearance, I took Adele's hand and we made our way towards the main staircase. Grace followed us. The sound of voices rose up to meet us. The stockmen and their families must have already gathered outside the ballroom, to watch the ceremony through the big open glass doors. For the first time I dared to feel excited. This really was happening. I was going to be Mrs Edward Rochester. I'd be a mother to Adele. I was going to have a normal life after all.

For one breath of time, Helen's beloved face appeared in my mind. She looked sad. I pushed the image away. I pushed her away. This was how things were meant to be. I would marry Edward and we would be happy together.

We turned the corner towards the ballroom. Instead of being at the front of the room with the celebrant, Edward was standing in the doorway, towering over a smaller but obviously very angry man. Richard Mason.

'You know you can't do this.' Mason's finger jabbed into Edward's chest.

'It's none of your business. How dare you come here uninvited?'

Richard gasped. 'And we both know why I wasn't invited.'

Between the two of them, a short, red-faced man was frowning anxiously and peering at the papers in his hand. I moved towards them.

'Edward?' I hated that my voice was so timid.

'Jane, this is nothing. Richard was just leaving.'

'I will not leave until I see my sister.'

I had no idea who he was talking about.

'This is outrageous.' Edward grabbed my arm and turned to the chubby man. 'Come on. You came here to perform a wedding, didn't you? Get on with it.'

The man looked from Edward to Richard Mason and back

again. 'Mr Rochester. I'm sorry, but Mr Mason has made a very serious allegation.'

Edward's fingers were digging into my wrist. 'What allegations?' I finally found my voice.

My fiancé stared at me for a second, before turning back to Richard. 'Are you happy now?'

'This wasn't my…'

'You've ruined everything.' Edward spat the words at his apparent enemy.

'Edward… I don't understand…'

The celebrant cleared his throat. 'Miss Eyre?'

'Yes.'

'I'm afraid this gentleman.' He nodded towards Richard Mason. 'This gentleman is claiming that Mr Rochester is already legally married.'

Chapter 49

I looked past them all, through the open door, into the ballroom. The worst of the damage had been cleaned away. The chairs had been righted and the debris swept away. There were no roses left but the candles had been lit to cast a faint golden glow. It wasn't how I had dreamt it would be, but it was still beautiful if you tried hard enough to see it that way. Not that it mattered now.

I slowly turned my eyes to the marriage celebrant. Had he really said that Edward was already married? That couldn't be right. If he was married he wouldn't have proposed to me. This was our wedding day. I shook my head. 'That's ridiculous.'

The sympathy I saw in his eyes sent a cold shiver down my spine. I turned towards the man I was supposed to marry. 'Edward. Tell him.'

Edward said nothing.

Richard finally spoke again, quieter now. 'I demand to see my sister.'

'What?' I turned on him, my voice rising.

'My sister, Eliza Mason, is Edward Rochester's wife.'

This was crazy. 'Whoever your sister is, she's not here.' I'd lived at Thornfield for all this time. I knew it now. The only visitors we had were here to work, or buy or sell stock. Richard himself

242

had come, and Celine, but whatever her relationship with Edward might have been, she wasn't related to Richard, was she? And she wasn't here now. I talked slowly, as if explaining something to a child. 'There's only us here. Me. Edward. Adele. Grace and Max. Nobody else is here.'

Richard shook his head. 'I see why he chose you. You're an idiot.'

'Don't speak to my...' Edward's voice tailed away. What had he been going to say? My fiancée? My wife? He turned back to the celebrant. 'I demand you start this ceremony.' Although the words were fierce, for the first time I heard defeat in his voice.

The celebrant folded his papers pointedly. 'Not until this situation is resolved. I'm sorry. I'm sorry, Miss Eyre.'

Edward's shoulders slumped. The determination he'd kept up, despite the damage to the ballroom and throughout the argument with Richard, abandoned him. That shook me to my core. Surely none of this was true.

'What do you want to do?' the celebrant asked.

Richard folded his arms. 'I'm not going anywhere or doing anything until I've seen my sister.'

'What's happening?' The tiny, frightened voice at my side would have broken my heart, had it not already shattered.

'Adele, my darling.' I dropped to my knees beside her. 'I'm sorry. There's been a bit of a misunderstanding.'

'It's Lizzybeth, isn't it?'

'Out of the mouth of babes.' Mason's voice was triumphant.

I struggled to keep my voice calm. 'Adele, I need you to go to your room for a little while. Look, here's Grace. She can go up and read with you.'

'But I am going to be your flower girl.'

'Adele, my darling, I won't do anything without you.'

Her face creased with anxiety, Grace led Adele away, up the stairs and towards her room.

I rose slowly to my feet and confronted the man who was, by

243

this time, supposed to be standing beside me taking our wedding vows.

'Oh, Jane. I did not want you to know this, but, if you must know, then I'll show you. Come on. I'll show you what this bastard foisted onto me.'

I cried out with shock and pain as Edward grabbed my wrist again and began to march through the house. Mason and the celebrant hurried along behind as he dragged me up the steps and turned towards the wing where Grace lived. Towards the door that was always locked.

I froze as Edward pulled a key from his pocket. Moments from my time here at Thornfield began to flash in front of me. The noises I thought I'd heard in here. The movement I thought I'd seen at the window. And that woman…the one Adele and I had met. The one Adele knew so well. Mason was right. I was an idiot. I stumbled backwards, letting Richard move in front of me, terrified of what was about to be revealed.

'Come on then. All of you. Come and see.' Edward flung the door open and stepped back.

The hallway beyond was in shadows, bare of furniture or adornment. But at the centre of it, crouched low like an animal, was a woman. A woman I recognised. A woman I'd seen before. A woman Adele had told me from the start was 'Daddy's friend.' A woman I'd chosen not to think about.

Betty rushed out at them as soon as the door was open. She knew there'd be trouble because of what she'd done last night. Every instinct told her to hide and cower, but she didn't. This was her chance. All she needed was other people. Not Edward or Richard. Not Grace. Maybe that Jane would be with them. Or someone else. Someone who would see her and know that she was real.

Something inside had gone up in flames with the veil in the bath. She'd sat and watched until it vanished away to nothing, and she'd wished she could do the same. And then she'd realised that she was doing the same, inside these few rooms. She was disappearing into nothing. After Grace left, which she would one day, and after Adele grew up and went away, who would remember her? Who would even know that Mrs Elizabeth Rochester had ever existed? Eliza Mason was already nothing more than a name on the wind. Even inside her own head she couldn't be sure that Betty Earl had ever existed at all. She wouldn't let that happen again.

As soon as the door opened she sprang up, legs pumping, arms flailing, mouth open wide, lungs pushing her scream into the world. She was here and they would see her.

Edward and Richard were at the front. She forced her way past Richard, hearing him whimper as she pushed him into the wall. Edward was a bigger man, but he wasn't expecting her like this. He stumbled backwards. Behind him she could see Jane in her long white dress and then a stranger recoiling in horror. If she could get to Jane, she could make this right. If she could get to Jane with her sensible, open face, she could explain.

But Jane was staggering away, pulling the flowers out of her hair, tugging at the row of tiny buttons on her dress.

Edward's hands grabbed Betty, pushing her back towards that door.

'You see! You see what I've had to cope with,' Edward yelled. 'Don't go, Jane. Don't go. I need you.'

Betty shook her head. That wasn't right. That wasn't fair.

'She's mad. She tried to burn the house down.' Edward was frantic.

No. Betty opened her mouth. She had to make them see that it wasn't like that. She hadn't meant to start any fires. Well, she'd meant to burn the veil, but his bedroom had been an accident.

'Please, Jane…' His voice was wheedling now. Even as he wrestled his wife back into her prison he was trying to charm his would-be bride.

Betty's rage rose again, overcoming her confusion. 'Go, Jane!

Run away. Run as far as you can from this place. From him. He'll do this to you too.'

'Shut up!' Her husband spat the words into her face.

In the corridor Betty saw the bride slow and turn back towards them, and for a second their eyes met. One final desperate cry reached Betty's lips. 'Take me with you. Don't leave me here…'

And then the door slammed closed in her face.

I was already tearing at my wedding gown as I fled back to my room. Every touch of the satin on my skin was agony. I heard Edward shouting, but I didn't know what he was saying and I didn't care. All I cared about was getting away from him, from his lies, from the woman he'd hidden away for so long. From the pain and desperation in her eyes.

I slammed the door of the room behind me, but got no feeling of safety from the action. I dropped the gown into my bedroom floor and flung open the wardrobe, reaching for whatever clothes were to hand.

Wildly I looked around. I had no time to pack. I had to get to the plane before the pilot left. He was due to take the celebrant, and perhaps Mason, back to town before darkness fell. But after the events of the past few minutes, they were probably already on their way. That plane could not leave without me. This place that had been my sanctuary had turned into something else, something terrifying.

I slid open a drawer and reached for the small brown envelope that lay almost hidden beneath my underwear. I opened it to reveal my treasured photograph of Helen. At that moment, tears threatened to overwhelm me.

Edward's betrayal was devastating. But worse was the knowledge that I had betrayed myself, forgetting what Helen had taught me about love. Love was kind. Love was courageous. Whatever Edward had been offering here, it wasn't love. It was something much smaller, much weaker, than love.

I slid that photograph into a shoulder bag, and added my wallet, with my precious driving licence, and the few other personal things from that drawer. There was nothing else worth taking. As I opened the door, I hesitated.

Adele. I looked down the hallway to her closed door. Grace would be with her, I was sure. I took a half step in her direction. I loved that little girl. I truly did. I couldn't leave without saying goodbye.

Before I took another step, I stopped. How could I say goodbye? What could I tell her? That her father was a monster. That her friend Lizzybeth was a madwoman, locked away in this very house. That I was leaving her here, where nothing was as it seemed, because I simply couldn't stay.

I turned back towards the main staircase. I would leave without a word. Adele wouldn't understand. She'd be hurt and she'd cry. She might even hate me. It was no less than I deserved. I almost ran down the stairs.

Edward was waiting for me. His face was impossible to read. I should have been married to him by now. I knew a charming, intelligent man, not this stranger.

Who was this, the man that I had thought I loved?

'Jane, let me explain.' He reached out and grabbed my arm. 'You saw what she is like. She's mad. All of this was for her own good.'

The desperation in his voice shocked me into answering. 'You were marrying me for her good?'

'No.' His tone changed. He was charming again, definite. 'I was marrying you because you are the wife I should have had all along. You know that. You can't leave me. I need you. You make my life bearable again.'

Not a single word of love. I looked at the hand that grasped my arm. I looked at the face that I had so recently believed could make me whole.

'Let go of me.'

'Please. I'm begging you, Jane.'

I shook my head. 'Goodbye, Mr Rochester.'

I wrenched myself from his grasp and walked down the stairs and out the front door without looking back. Somewhere in the distance, I could hear Adele crying my name, but not even my affection for her could make me turn back. I had to escape while there was something of me left.

Outside, I could see the Aboriginal workers walking away from the house, whispering among themselves. I could no more face them than I could face Adele. I hurried towards the machinery shed. The car Rochester kept for his own infrequent use was there, the keys in the ignition. I jumped behind the wheel and started the engine. By the time the airstrip came into sight, I could see the ute parked beside the plane, and people moving around. I gunned the engine and sped towards them, the wheels spinning on the thick dust as I turned through the gate and slid to a stop beside the aircraft.

'What's going on?'

The pilot held up a hand as if to stop me climbing aboard the plane.

'I'm leaving with you.'

The man hesitated. His instructions obviously hadn't included this.

'It's all right,' Mason said. 'If I was her I'd run away from this place as well.'

I left Thornfield without a backwards glance. I had no idea where the plane was headed, or what I would do when I got there, but I knew that I was finished with Edward Rochester. My last thoughts as the plane lifted into the clear blue sky weren't for him. They were for the people I'd left behind – for Grace, for Adele and for the real Mrs Rochester.

PART THREE

Chapter 50

Jane

As I stepped down to the platform at Sydney's Central Station, I was jostled by the crowds hurrying to get on or off the trains. I was barely aware of the surroundings. I hadn't eaten since I had leapt out of bed, eager to be married. Now here I was, hundreds of miles away, alone, unmarried, and struggling to understand how someone could have lied to me every day since we'd met. The man who'd asked me to be his wife was already married. Edward Rochester was not the man I had thought he was. And I was not the person I had hoped to become.

A hurrying figure crashed into me, almost knocking me off my feet.

'Sorry.' The man was gone before I had even registered the word.

I followed the crowd streaming towards the exit, and stepped out through the red-brick arches and suddenly stopped. I had nowhere to go. I could not, would not, return to the Reeds. I didn't even know if they still lived in the apartment I hadn't seen for almost twenty years. But I had to go somewhere.

I sought respite in a wooden bench under the arches, and

pulled my few possessions from my bag. There was very little cash in my wallet – I'd never needed to carry cash at Thornfield. I'd never owned a bank card. I had some money in the bank, but my heart sank with the realisation that I'd left my bank book behind. My stomach churned with a combination of hunger and despair. I had no friends and not enough money for a hotel or even a hostel. Was I going to have to sleep on the street? I sat there for a very long time, watching the people marching past. Everyone had somewhere to be and, I thought, someone who was waiting for them when they got there. The exhaustion and shock of the day caught up with me. I needed to move. I needed to find help and a place to stay, but as the sun sank and darkness settled over the city, I had not one ounce of energy left.

A burst of loud laughter finally drew me from my despair. I looked up. People were still moving in and out of the station, but far fewer of them now. The raucous laughter was emanating from a nearby group of young men. They were looking my way, pointing and shouting. One of them thrust his groin forward in an exaggerated mime. I was suddenly a small child again, back in that school sports shed with John Reed and his friends.

I got to my feet, and, clutching my few possessions tightly, I walked back inside the station. There would be more people there. I would be safer with people around me. I sat down again, but this time it was a railway guard who marched over.

'You can't sleep here.'

'No. No, I wasn't…'

'Go on. Get out of here.'

I retraced my steps. The young men had gone, but the unfamiliar city was no less frightening. Sydney had changed in the years I'd been away. High-rise buildings towered over the city centre. The roads were busy, and even this late at night, the streets seemed full of people. I started to shake as the world around me spun.

'Are you all right?'

I turned towards the voice, gathering myself to run if I had to.

'Oh goodness, you are so pale. Come over here and sit down for a moment.' The woman took my arm and gently led me back to that same bench where I'd spent most of the day. 'There you go. Now don't worry. You're safe with me. Do you have anywhere to go? Anyone I can call for you?'

I shook my head slowly.

'You poor child. But it's all right. We are here to help. Do you want to come with me to the mission house?'

Mission House? In my confused state, I imagined some tropical jungle, with nuns and grass huts. 'Where?'

'The mission house. I am part of a mission.'

'You're Christians?'

She nodded. 'We just try to help people.'

It was my own little miracle. I'd turned my back on the church at Thornfield. I knew I had, but maybe the Lord hadn't turned his back on me. In my hour of need, he'd sent one of his children to reach out for me.

'It's not far. Come on. Do you think you can stand up?'

She helped me to my feet. I have only the haziest memory of walking with her through the streets of the inner city. Each time I stumbled, she caught me. She talked to me as we walked, but I let the words wash over me, too tired and caught up in my own world of despair to respond.

'Here we are.'

There was a sign on the door in front of us. I fought to bring the world into focus.

The Saint John Mission.

Inside, all was light and warmth and the sounds of many people. I hesitated, but my rescuer had her hand on my arm.

'It's all right, my dear, everything can wait until tomorrow. You can meet the sisters and Brother Jacob then. For now, you need to rest. Come on.'

She led me to a small room with a narrow bed, a bedside table and a single small wardrobe.

'You're safe here. The bathroom is at the end of the corridor. We have finished food service for the night, but if you get hungry…'

I shook my head. All I wanted now was to close my eyes and let sleep block out the nightmare that my life had become.

She left me sitting on the edge of the bed. Around me I could hear the sounds of other people – footsteps, voices, doors closing. There was no threat in the sounds, nobody coming to knock on my door in the dead of night. Slowly I lay back, letting those sounds wash over me. There was something familiar about them.

That night I dreamt of a place by the sea, with children and people who smiled all the time. There were birds, and trees to climb, and a woman, whose face I could not see, who said she loved me.

Chapter 51

Betty

Everything was so very quiet now Jane had gone. Betty didn't hear Adele chattering away on the veranda anymore. It had always been quiet up here, in her own little world, but now a lull seemed to have settled over the whole house. Grace didn't stay and talk anymore either. She put Betty's tray down and then went back to her own space in the kitchen downstairs.

But that was all right. It gave Betty time to think. Time to plan. It was all down to her. That was what she'd realised. Nobody was going to come for her. Edward wasn't going to take her back into his bed. She wasn't going to be Elizabeth Rochester anymore. She wasn't going to be any of those people they'd told her to be. Eliza Mason had died with her mother. Daddy's little firefly was just a memory. Lizzybeth was a childish mistake. None of them were real. It was time to find out what sort of woman Betty Earl had grown up to be.

Chapter 52

Jane

'We thank you, mighty Lord, for your Son, our Saviour, who came to lead us from the paths of evil into the light of your love. We ask you to look favourably upon the work we do in your name, and forgive us when we fall short of the great work you have laid out before us. We give thanks for the food you have given us this day. May it give us the strength to do your work and lead the sinners from the paths of sin into the magnificence of your light. Amen.'

'Amen.'

I dropped my eyes back to the table for the moment of reflective silence we shared before we began eating. It was strange to be praying again. The ritual of bowing my head and listening to the words being offered to God was comforting, like stepping back into a place I'd forgotten was my home. Our prayers were led by Brother Jacob. He was the leader of the mission. With his smooth dark hair cut short, piercing eyes and dark suits, he reminded me of Cary Grant in *North by Northwest*. And when he spoke, it was hypnotic. His passion for his vocation went right into my wounded soul.

Each morning, we ate breakfast in the big dining room. There were seven women at the mission. I was the eighth. After breakfast, the women would go into the streets to take Brother Jacob's message to the lost people on the streets of Kings Cross. To the women who walked the streets at night and sold their bodies. To the drunks and the addicts. And to the men who sought the company of other men.

I had yet to join these outings. I stayed at the St John Mission House, cleaning and cooking, taking some respite and comfort from the simple tasks. Living here brought back faded memories of my life before the Reeds, of a place where I had been part of a community, a place where I had been happy.

Sometimes I woke in the middle of the night, my heart pounding with fear, images of Rochester and fires burning my eyes, the sound of Adele's sweet voice and a madwoman's cries ringing in my ears. After these nights, more than anything, I wanted to hear Brother Jacob. His prayerful words formed a rock in the troubled ocean of my mind.

'Jane.'

I was standing in the kitchen, my hands deep in soapy water as I washed the breakfast dishes.

'Brother Jacob.'

'Leave those for now, Jane. Please come with me.'

I carefully wiped my hands on a tea towel, noticing as I did that they were shaking a little. I followed Brother Jacob into his office.

'Shut the door, please, Jane, and take a seat.'

I did as he asked, trying not to show my nervousness. It was the first time I had been into this inner sanctuary. It was a reflection of the man himself. Bookshelves lined the walls, their contents mostly leather-bound books with the titles embossed in gold. These were serious, thoughtful books for a serious and thoughtful man. The top of the big, dark, wooden desk was bare, except for two bibles. One was the large black leather edition Jacob used in our group meetings and prayer sessions. The other was a smaller, poorer thing; well-worn with the gold edging wearing away. This was a bible that had seen much service.

Brother Jacob stood for a moment, his eyes fixed on some distant place, his mind also caught up in his private thoughts. I was glad of those few moments. This was the first time I had ever been alone with him, and I was too afraid to ask what he wanted of me.

'Jane, have you settled here with us?' He kept his back to me.

'Yes, thank you, Brother. I am so grateful that Sister Alice brought me here. I don't know what I would have done without you. I wish I could repay you.' I knew I never could. I'd been given so much by people who'd had no reason to bring me into their world, other than the love of God and their fellow man.

He turned then, his lips twitching in a small smile. 'Well, Jane, there is a way. Are you ready to join the Mission? To devote yourself to our cause. To saving the poor sinners of this city.'

I was ready. To be part of this community, fully and completely, was precisely what I wanted. The Lord had brought me here. After Helen and Edward, it seemed clear that my faith was the only real constant in my life. It had seen me through school, and life with the Reeds. It would see me through this. God's love was the only love that was true and lasting.

'Yes, Brother Jacob. I want to join you.'

That's when he turned to look at me, his eyes searching my face. He came to me and held out his hands. I placed my hands in his as he pulled me gently to my feet.

'I knew it, Jane, right from that first day I knew that you and I were of the same heart and mind and soul.' He spoke seriously, as he always did, never joking or trying to charm. 'You are a good woman, Jane Eyre, not to be swayed by sin or by the pleasures of the flesh. You are the partner of my soul, Jane. You will stand beside me as I lead this mission against the evil growing in this city.'

'What do you mean?'

He kept my hands in his. 'I've prayed for a long time about this, and I know it is the will of the Lord.'

He placed his hand under my chin and raised my face towards him. Then he pressed his lips against my brow. 'You are an angel sent by the Lord. Together, Jane, we will be a guiding light in the darkness.'

He turned to his desk, lifted the tattered bible and pressed it into my hands.

'This is for you. A gift from my heart to yours. Keep it with you, Jane. Read it. Use the lessons of this book to help those who are lost. And remember always that just as God loves you, so do I.'

I stumbled out of the room. Everything felt so straightforward here. We were doing what the Lord wanted us to do. No other considerations mattered. It didn't matter who I'd loved before. It didn't matter that I'd spent so many years being confused. Here, there was certainty. The Lord had brought Brother Jacob and I together. If this was His will, I would give myself to it entirely.

Chapter 53

Betty

Betty waited until Grace put the tray down. She'd been working up to this for weeks now. She had been quiet and well behaved. She hadn't even lit her matches to stare into the tiny flame. She had pretended to accept her fate, as Grace began to relax again. Now, it was time.

'I don't feel very well.'

Grace frowned. 'How so?'

'Dizzy. A bit nauseous.'

'Did you throw up?'

Betty shook her head.

'I wondered if you might take me outside for a few minutes.'

Grace folded her arms across her body. 'I'm not sure.'

'Just for a minute.'

'Mr Rochester doesn't like ...'

Betty dropped her head and looked up at Grace through her lashes. She was wheedling. 'Mr Rochester wouldn't know. I haven't had any fresh air for weeks.'

Grace gave a curt nod. Betty smiled, enough to look grateful, but not enough to look triumphant.

She let Grace lead the way down the stairs and into the kitchen. 'Can I get a glass of water?'

Grace nodded. 'Be quick.'

Betty picked a glass up from the drainer and held it under the tap. It was a big old-fashioned sink. Grace was standing in the doorway, looking out towards the stables. Betty acted quickly. This was the riskiest part. Even now she wasn't sure she'd be able to pull it off. She took a rag out of her pocket and dropped it into the sink. Then she put her glass down on the counter as quietly as she could, pulled her matches from her pocket, and struck a light. She dropped it in the sink, grabbed the glass and followed Grace outside.

They sat on the small bench outside the kitchen door. Grace was jumpy. 'Just a few minutes.'

Betty leant back on the bench, raised her face to the sky, and closed her eyes. The warmth on her skin was exactly as she remembered. She waited.

Only when she was sure she could smell it, that her hopes weren't playing tricks on her, did she say anything. 'Can you smell something burning?'

Grace shook her head. 'No… Oh my goodness!' She jumped up and ran back into the house.

This was her moment. Betty was on her feet. She'd thought this part through as far as she could. She needed to get around the far side of the house so she'd be hidden from immediate view when Grace came back. Then she needed to get to somewhere that somebody would find her. But it had to be the right somebody. Jimmy or Peggy would be all right. She was sure they'd take care of her, but heading for the camp was too risky. Max could be down there or any of the other workers could see her first.

So her plan was this. She would walk away to the highway and find other people. People who would take her away from this place. She tried to remember the early days at Thornfield, when

261

she'd had a little freedom to move around. It was all hazy now, but she knew there was a road. There had to be a road, because sometimes people came and went in cars. If she could find the road she could escape. She couldn't walk down the road, of course. They'd find her too easily. But she could walk in the bush nearby, hidden from view. And then, when she got to the highway, she could flag down a car and get into town.

Then she would be free.

The first thing she had to do was get away from the house unseen. She set off at a run, knowing she needed to put some distance between herself and the homestead before Grace raised the alarm. She crossed her fingers that Grace would be so worried about getting in trouble for letting Betty out that she wouldn't call for help straight away. With luck, she'd try to find Betty on her own first.

She only managed to run for a few short minutes. Out here she should be wearing boots or sandshoes, not the flimsy thongs that were the only footwear she had. And it was hot. Not the welcome warmth on her skin that she'd been dreaming of. Truly hot. And she wasn't carrying any water. She'd had nothing to put water in. But she couldn't go back. She had a plan. She avoided the line of red gravel with the tyre marks clearly visible. Instead, she ducked into the low scrub nearby. Fixing in her mind the direction the road was running, she started to walk in the same direction. She just had to get to the highway.

Betty kept walking. The heat radiated back up at her from the red earth.

She hadn't heard any shouts behind her. There were no sounds of running feet. Maybe he wouldn't send anyone after her. She almost laughed out loud at the thought. Of course he would. Everything out here belonged to him. He wouldn't tolerate his property wandering off.

She stopped. She didn't have a watch so she didn't know how long she'd been going. It must, she thought, be an hour since she'd left the homestead. Her feet hurt. And her bare arms were covered with scratches where she had pushed her way through the scrub. She turned slowly around. There was no sign of the road. That was good. It meant anyone on the road wouldn't see her. But she should check she was still going in the right direction. The road should be over there, to the left. She veered to her left, pushing her way through the scratchy bushes and kept walking. It was strange. She should have found the track by now. She turned around. She had long since lost sight of the house, and the yards. They should be behind her. Or maybe over to the right? It didn't matter now. She would just keep walking. The highway couldn't be that far away. And then she could wave down a passing car and get a ride into town.

She scanned the horizon for some feature she might recognise, but there was nothing. Just the dry red landscape as far as she could see. But that was all right. She had a plan and she would stick to it. She turned back in the direction she'd been heading. At least, she thought it was the direction she had been heading.

Chapter 54

Jane

The women of the mission didn't have an official uniform. Not like the habits the nuns at Our Lady had worn. But we did all wear plain dark skirts that fell to our knees, and white cotton button-up blouses. We never put any adornments on ourselves or our clothes. Brother Jacob believed such adornments were the devil's work. But next morning, I did put a little extra attention into brushing my hair, which I now wore cut short like the other women. I made sure my skirt was well ironed, and my blouse tucked in straight. Today I was going out on the streets with my sisters for the first time. I wanted to do well. I wanted Jacob to be pleased with me.

'Jane, are you ready to do God's work?' Alice was waiting for me when I left my small, bare room.

'Yes. I am so excited. And proud.'

'Susan will be coming with us.'

We always travelled in threes. Jacob believed that allowing two people to be alone was an invitation to evil. A temptation to develop feelings and urges that belonged between a man and his wife in the state of marriage. Was he right, I wondered. Was that all that had happened with Helen? It still felt like a betrayal to think that, but maybe if we'd had more friends, if we hadn't been forced together, just the two of us, for so much of the time, maybe we wouldn't have fallen into sin the way that we had.

Alice, Susan and I left the mission house, heading up the hill towards Oxford Street.

'You've been spending a lot of time with Brother Jacob?' Susan's voice was excited.

'Don't gossip,' cautioned Alice.

'Sorry.' Susan suppressed her curiosity for a moment. 'You're going to marry him, though, aren't you?'

'Susan! Brother Jacob would not like you talking like this.'

I shook my head. 'Me? Marry Brother Jacob?'

Even Alice was joining in now. 'He has always taught us that a man needs a good wife by his side to help him in his work and to protect him from temptation. To be the mother of his children. I prayed it might be you.'

Pride is a sin, but I felt proud at that moment. It felt so good to hear Alice say that she thought I was worthy of him. It felt good to think that I could live the rest of my life right at the heart of this community, protected from sin. Perhaps this was it. My real chance to live the normal life that I had always longed for.

I could be the wife of Brother Jacob. I could work with him in his mission to lead the sinners back to the light. And, in doing so, I too could be redeemed for my sins.

'Look.'

Susan's voice dragged me back to reality. We were standing at the entrance to a side street. A small flatbed truck was parked in the street, and a handful of people were moving around it. On the footpath, a boom-box was blaring out a pop song, which had set everyone around it dancing.

'That song.' Alice's voice was a horrified whisper. 'They must be here for Mardi Gras.'

I didn't know the song, but the group of men around the boom-box were joyfully dancing and singing along.

'They are sinners.' Alice clutched the bible she was carrying tightly to her chest.

'We have to go and talk to them. Come on.' Susan was one of the youngest and most earnest of all Brother Jacob's followers.

'Will we be safe?'

I understood Alice's fear, but the men were dancing and laughing and singing as they draped rainbow-coloured garlands over the back of the truck. They didn't seem angry and fearful of us. And we had the Lord's protection.

'We have come to bring you the word of God.' Susan was already approaching the young men. 'We have come to pray for your souls and you will find your way out of the path of sin unto the light, for God has said that a man will not lie with another man as with a woman. It is an abomination.'

The dancing and laughing had stopped. Someone turned off the boom-box, and a loud silence descended on us all.

'Sister.' One of the men stepped forward. 'We don't want your prayers. We didn't ask for your opinion.'

'It's not my opinion. It's the word of God.'

'Not my god.' The man who'd stepped forward was holding some sort of feathered item in his hands. 'I'm not interested in any god who calls love a sin.'

'It is not too late for you to be saved,' Susan continued, holding her bible high. 'In Corinthians, God tells us that you can be cleansed through Christ. Give up your evil ways and you can inherit the Kingdom of God.'

'I'd really rather inherit my parents' home in Neutral Bay,' a voice from the back replied. 'That would really upset the neighbours.'

There was a ripple of laughter. The music was flicked back on. Susan's words were drowned out by singing and joy.

The first man who had spoken came closer to the three of us.

'Ladies, you are entitled to be who you are, just as we are entitled to be who we are. Let's live and let live. What do you say?'

'We will pray for you.' Susan turned away.

'And what about you two, will you pray for us too?' There was a challenge in his voice.

Alice nodded immediately. 'We pray for all God's children.'

He looked at me. I couldn't answer. Watching those men dancing together had brought back a memory. Helen and I had danced in our little garden, to tinny music from a tiny portable radio. It had been a different song, a different time, but we had held hands as we leapt about. Then, when the music changed to something softer and slower, our bodies had come together. With our arms around each other, we had kissed and vowed always to be together. I had repented my sins a thousand times since I'd joined the mission, but no matter how many times I pushed those memories away they bloomed again in my mind.

How could I tell someone to repent of a sin I was unable to truly repent of myself.

I turned away and followed my sisters back onto Oxford Street.

Chapter 55

Betty

Betty forced herself to keep walking as the sun began to dip below the horizon, but as darkness fell she had to admit that she didn't know which way the homestead was. Or the gravel road. Or the highway. From her room back at the homestead, she could look out the window and see Max's place and the stockmen's camp. There'd be a light or a torch or a fire going somewhere. And back in Sydney, there was always light everywhere. But here there was no light, except the brilliant sparks in the sky above her.

She turned her face to the sky and turned in a slow circle. There were so many stars. Some were brighter than others, but they were all white and cold, not at all like the red embers that warmed her. In the deepest recesses of her memory, she saw the night sky above a ship as it ploughed through the ocean, but those nights were broken by the red flares from the funnel. Out here there was nothing. She could walk five paces from this spot and have to clue to her way back. Betty sat down on the dry earth. She was defeated. She was alone, but she was free.

Something rustled off to her left. She pulled her knees in tight to her body and hugged them close. There were snakes out here, spiders too, she supposed, and wild pigs, and dingoes. She remembered all the fuss about the dingo that took the baby at Ayres Rock. A dingo wouldn't hurt a grown adult, though. Would it? She didn't know. She was still a city girl despite all the time she'd been trapped in the middle of this giant swathe of land. She knew about keeping her handbag across her body so it didn't get snatched. She knew about looking both ways before she crossed the road. She didn't know about snakes and dingoes and the way that the skin on her lips was cracking from the heat.

This wasn't her place. It was his. If it belonged to her she'd let it all burn. That wasn't true. If it belonged to her she'd go far away and leave Jimmy and Peggy and the rest of the stockmen to it. She didn't care what happened to this horrible place. It could never belong to her, and she could never belong to it.

The rustling noises were getting closer. Betty told herself to move, but she was pinned to the spot, frozen, listening to the sounds around her. The creatures making those sounds could be a hundred metres away or a within touching distance. In the darkness she had no idea. She was going to die in this horrible place. The land hated her as much as she hated it. Maybe that was it. Maybe this place had sensed an outsider the second she'd stepped off the plane and set out to destroy her.

Maybe this whole country had done that as soon as she had walked off the boat at Sydney Harbour.

The noises seemed to move away a bit. Betty screwed her eyes closed. She could tell herself that it was only dark because she had her eyes shut. She could manage alone. She'd been alone for months now. All night, every night. Sometimes sleeping. Sometimes not. She could be alone. All she had to do was wait.

She drifted away, into sleep or something else. She didn't know. It didn't matter. She'd rather die free than go back into her cage.

She woke to the sound of the voices. It was starting to get light and there were people shouting. She pulled herself up to sitting and looked around. Then she heard a distant yell.

269

'Coo-eeee!'

She scanned her immediate surroundings. She didn't have the energy to get up and run. She'd have to hide. There was a slight dip about ten metres to the left of her, partly hidden by a large brown rock. She crawled, forcing her limbs to carry her, and lay down in the dip. If she was lucky they'd give up looking before they got this far, and then, she told herself, after she'd rested, she'd be able to set off again and find the road. She lay as still and as quiet as she could. The voices kept getting closer. She listened. It wasn't a big group. Just two or three people, she thought. And someone seemed to be in charge. That would be Edward or Max. It was always one of them telling everyone else what to do.

It got to the point where she believed she could feel their footsteps through the earth. They stopped again. She listened. 'It looks like someone stopped here.'

That wasn't Edward. She listened again.

'Maybe to rest?'

She recognised the voice now. It was Jimmy. She was going to be all right. He was a friend. He'd been kind to her. She lifted her head just a touch. He was right there. A little way behind him, Max was facing in the opposite direction, swigging from a water bottle.

Betty lifted her finger to her lips.

Jimmy's face fell. He glanced back over his shoulder.

'I can't.' It was barely a whisper.

'Please,' she begged.

Jimmy turned away. 'Over here!' he yelled.

And all was lost.

The ute appeared over the horizon a few minutes later, and she was lifted onto the back. Jimmy sat beside her, not speaking until they pulled up at the house. 'You would've died if I left you.'

Betty managed to look him in the eye. 'I know,' she said.

Chapter 56

Jane

'A woman shall not wear anything that pertains to a man, nor shall a man put on a woman's garment, for all who do so *are* an abomination to the Lord your God.'

As Brother Jacob's voice rang out with clarity and passion, the women around me nodded their assent.

'Tonight, the devil will walk among us. Those who practice abomination. Those who turn their faces from God. Their actions grieve the Holy Spirit. They violate scripture. It is a pathway to other evils.'

When he was preaching like this, Brother Jacob held us all in his thrall. I tried to lose myself in his words, as I normally did when he was speaking, but this time the words failed to move me.

'God gave us a gift, when he created Eve to be with Adam. To be his helpmate and comfort. A gift to be enjoyed within a marriage between a man and a woman.'

Alice nudged me gently in the side. I knew what she was thinking – that one day, Brother Jacob would be my husband. Looking at him as he paced the room like a caged animal, I shivered. Brother Jacob paused, turning to face the assembled

271

sisters. His eyes captured mine. I saw the message there. I longed for my heart to call back to him. I longed to feel what I was supposed to feel.

I felt nothing. If anything, there was a twinge of fear as I recognised the fanatical light in his eyes.

'The rainbow is a symbol of God's promise to Noah, but they have debased it, taken it as their flag of abomination. God has spoken. Across this country they are taking steps to make these sins legal in the eyes of the courts. We say no. They say these people should be left to carry on their ungodly acts. We say no. We are not led by politicians or by the laws of this world, but by the laws of a higher power. We are led only by God.' By now he was shouting, flecks of spittle spraying from his lips. 'These acts are a threat to our Christian society. They lead to perversions, to child molestation and incest.'

My sisters were nodding fervently, but I felt a coldness grip me. The room around me seemed to blur and I was back at Our Lady, in the big assembly hall, with Helen beside me. I could hear Sister Mary Gabriel speaking.

'...depraved and counter to God's word. It is sinful and those who act this way are condemned to damnation...'

Helen's beautiful face swam into my mind. I could hear her soft voice as she told me she loved me. I could feel the warmth of her hand on my skin and the joy in my heart when we were together. Our love made us hateful in the sight of others. Made me hateful in the sight of Brother Jacob.

'But...'

Jacob stopped speaking and turned to look at me. No one ever interrupted him.

'Jane?'

'I'm sorry, Brother Jacob, but the Holy Father said such deviant feelings can be cured, with proper teaching and adherence to church law. With confession and the love of our Lord Jesus Christ, the sinners can be forgiven and taken back into the church.'

'Jane. Oh, my precious Jane.' He walked over to me, took my hands and raised me to my feet. 'Sisters, Jane is the kindest and gentlest and most forgiving among us. Her goodness shines from her like a light.'

I felt my face redden as around me, my sisters murmured their agreement.

'Jane, your goodness does you credit, but do not allow it to blind you to the truth. There is no salvation for those who practice abomination. They cannot enter the Kingdom of Heaven. They will burn in the eternal fires of damnation.'

Several of my sisters whispered an Amen.

Brother Jacob placed his hand upon my hair in benediction, and I sat back down and firmly fixed my gaze to the floor in what must have looked like penitence.

'We have a duty to the children, to protect them from such immorality. If we ignore this perversion, others will follow and our city will become like Sodom and Gomorrah, and God will visit his wrath upon us all.'

Brother Jacob swung back into his sermon.

'Tonight we will walk among them. Our faith shall be our armour. God's holy word will be our weapon. We will not suffer the sinners to live among us.'

Chapter 57

Betty

There was fuss at first. There had to be, she supposed. There was a huddle of stockmen around the kitchen door. Betty heard one of them mutter that he'd not seen Mrs Rochester for ages. Another answered that he'd thought she'd gone walk-about a long time ago. Another muttered something about Richard and all that fuss at the wedding. That sort of gossip could not be allowed. Appearances had to be maintained. Mrs Rochester was ill, Max said. It was very sad. Mrs Rochester would be cared for quietly by Grace and, of course, her loving husband.

Mrs Rochester was carried upstairs and put back into bed. She was brought water. And then some bread. She was told to rest and keep sipping from the beaker that Grace put by the bed. Mrs Rochester's loving husband was nowhere to be seen.

She sipped her water and tried to sleep. She'd failed. She'd thought that one way or another, today would be the end of it. She'd get away or the land would swallow her up. But she was back here. She'd lost.

The bedroom door clicked open. She looked up, expecting Grace. It was her husband.

He swung the door closed behind him. He hadn't come to her room for months, but she knew what he was here for. It was all he'd ever needed her for.

'You tried to run away.'

'I did run away.'

'I had to waste hours of my workers' time bringing you back.'

She'd lost the battle. She wasn't going to concede easily though. 'Why?'

'What do you mean?'

'Why did you bring me back?' She watched his face. She was expecting anger. What she saw was confusion. 'You could have let me go.'

'But you belong…'

'To you?' She swung her legs out of bed and started to stand. Now she was ready for a fight.

He closed the gap between them in one step, pushing her back onto the bed. 'You do belong to me.' He shouted the words right into her face.

'No. I. Don't.'

His hands were already on her. She knew he could overpower her, but for once she wasn't going to make it easy. Jimmy had told her she could have died out there, and he'd been right. She could die free, or live in a cage. And knowing that was a sort of freedom of its own.

She scratched, and clawed, and yelled, and kicked. She didn't stop. She didn't let her mind go to the place it normally went to protect itself. She didn't let herself think about other things. However much it hurt her she would not let herself hide from him inside her own imagination. She wouldn't let him think that this was all right, and that she was all right. She screamed as hard as she could so he would know exactly what he was doing to her.

Finally he climbed off her, and refastened his belt.

'I don't belong to you.' She extended a finger towards the window. 'None of this belongs to you.'

Chapter 58

Jane

The city was preparing for a party, and Oxford Street was its centre. All around us, people were converging on the pubs and restaurants, overflowing out onto the footpaths and the streets themselves. Shop fronts were crowded with people clutching glasses and beer cans. Rainbow flags hung from every available point.

'Disgraceful,' Susan muttered beside me.

Ahead of us, two young men were dancing, shirtless, to the music that filled the air. They undulated their hips and chests, moving closer and closer until they met in a kiss.

'Abomination!' Jacob cried. 'Fear the wrath of the Lord.'

'All right. Let's just take it easy.' A uniformed policeman stepped between Jacob and the targets of his anger.

'You!' Jacob waved his finger in the officer's face. 'You saw what they did. It was a sin, but it was also a crime. The laws of this state still support the teachings of the Bible. Take them away. Lock them in a cell before they threaten our children.'

'Sir, do you really think Mardi Gras is the right place for you to be tonight?' The officer kept his voice calm. 'We don't want anyone arrested. Perhaps you should go home.'

'We do not wrestle solely against the devil, but also against flesh and blood, the earthly powers that would foist this darkness upon us. We fight against all the forces of evil.'

'That's all very good, but you do any wrestling or fighting here and you'll find yourself locked up for the night. Understand?' The officer suppressed a grin. He didn't think Brother Jacob was a great man. He thought Brother Jacob was laughable.

'I will fight the good fight, as our Lord demands. Come, sisters.'

We followed our leader across the road. He gathered us around him. 'Let us pray.'

This time, his words didn't move me. With my head bowed, I looked around. People were laughing and dancing. Men and women, in groups, in couples, or on their own. I looked for the evil that Jacob described, and I couldn't see it. Not here.

I searched my memory. I thought of the garden at Our Lady, of the beautiful thing Helen and I had created. And I thought of Edward Rochester and the pain his nice Christian marriage had caused. I could see sin, but it wasn't in myself. It wasn't in Helen.

As the prayer ended, we linked hands.

'Now my sisters, go forth and do God's work.'

I walked away, with Susan and Alice by my side. They stayed close together, Alice taking strength from Susan's unwavering belief that we were on a mission from God. Had I shared that certainty once? If I had it was as lost to me as a dream forgotten at the point of waking.

The parade had started, and Oxford Street was awash with colour and light and sound. Two girls danced past me, their hands clasped, and disappeared into the crowd. Without thinking, I turned to follow them.

'Please. Stop for a moment.'

They did and turned to face me. The younger girl looked me up and down, and I saw her face start to close as she realised that I was not there to join the party.

'Please,' I said. 'I want to understand.'

'Understand what?' Her companion dropped an arm around her shoulders, her fingers caressing the bare skin at the top of her arm. I tried not to look, but my body responded as it had never done when Jacob, or even Edward, had touched me.

'Aren't you afraid?'

'Of what? Being a lesbian isn't illegal. Only if you're a gay man. And any day now we'll win that fight.'

'No. That's not what I meant.'

'What then?'

'I meant…' Away from the certainty of the mission, even saying it out loud was beginning to feel ridiculous. 'I meant, don't you worry that it's sinful?'

The older girl shook her head. 'Love is not a sin. Not ever.'

Her companion turned to her and kissed her.

Behind me I heard a gasp. Susan and Alice had found me.

I should turn away. I should go back to my companions. I couldn't. I wouldn't stop now. 'Aren't you afraid of what people will say once they know?'

The younger girl shrugged. 'Why? This is who we are and we are proud of it.'

She held her arms aloft. 'I am what I am,' she yelled gleefully.

No words would come. I felt tears in my eyes. The two of them saw, and without hesitation they stepped forward and hugged me, folded into their embrace, without expectation of anything in return.

'Will you be all right?' the younger one asked, as she moved away.

'I think so.'

'What's your name?'

'Jane. Jane Eyre.'

'Be proud, Jane Eyre. Be proud.'

Chapter 59

Betty

Betty let the water run over her body as she stood under the shower. She'd never really be clean but she might convince herself that she wasn't dirty.

'Lizzybeth!'

Betty switched off the water and wrapped herself in a towel.

'Lizzybeth!'

Adele was standing in the hallway at the top of the kitchen steps.

Grace appeared behind her, huffing and puffing. 'She pushed right past me.'

Betty looked the older woman in the eye. 'So what are you going to do about it?'

The woman looked at the floor. 'Actually I'm going away.'

'What?'

'To my sister's in Brisbane. Mr Rochester says my services are no longer required.' She stepped past Adele. 'I am sorry. I thought all this was for the best. For you. For your nerves.'

Betty didn't know how to reply. She wouldn't say it was all right. She couldn't say Grace was forgiven.

Grace grabbed her hand, pressing something cool and metal into her palm. Then she disappeared down the stairs.

Adele disappeared into the bedroom and sat on the edge of the bed. The little girl Betty had first met had had another growth spurt in the last few weeks. She was turning into a teenager in front of Betty's eyes. 'He's sending me away too.'

'What?' Betty's stomach clenched.

'He said I had to go to school somewhere away, because Grace is going and he's not getting another nanny to look after me, and my mum's off… I don't know where my mum is.' Adele started to sob. 'He said it would be nice. He said there were lots of other kids and it wouldn't be forever.'

In a heartbeat Betty was five years old sitting in a cold, bare office listening to her father say it wouldn't be forever, and that he'd come back for her.

Adele was gulping back tears. 'I've never lived anywhere but here. I don't want to go.'

Betty reached over and rubbed the young girl's back. 'It'll be all right.'

'I won't have to go?'

Betty shook her head. 'Not to the place he wants to send you. We'll go and find your mum. Or…' There must be somebody. 'Who else has looked after you?'

The girl wiped her eyes. 'Just you. And Jane.'

That was decided then. She would have to survive and somehow she would have to take Adele with her. 'When are you supposed to go?'

'The day after tomorrow.'

Betty closed her eyes. She needed to rest. She needed to plan. She needed more time. But Adele was relying on her. She wouldn't see another little girl sent away. 'Then we'll have to get away tomorrow.'

'Where to?'

'I'm not sure. Which way do you go when you go into town with Edward or Grace?'

'Along the road behind the house. It's over an hour in the ute, though.'

Then they'd have to take the ute. 'Can you get the keys to the ute?'

Adele nodded. 'There's a set in his office. I can get them when he goes to his room to start getting drunk.'

'Right. Wait for me in the kitchen then. Tomorrow night. Straight after dinner.'

Adele nodded. 'Thank you, Lizzybeth.'

'Aren't you a bit old to call me that?'

'Do you prefer Elizabeth?'

Betty shook her head.

Chapter 60

Jane

I walked back through the doors of the mission, knowing it was for the last time.

I looked around at the few things I had accumulated in my weeks here. There were the plain skirts and blouses that served as our daily uniform. Equally plain shoes and underwear completed my possessions. Apart from the bible with its faded gold edging.

I turned away from that and opened the window. The night air carried with it the sounds of Mardis Gras revelry. The music and the voices were muted by distance, but that only served to make them magical. I lay back on my bed and let the sounds take me. I saw again the young women I'd just left. I felt their embrace. Not with desire, but with recognition. Their faces blurred and I saw Helen, smiling at me as she had so many times all those years ago. A regretful sadness settled over me for a life cut short far too soon, and for what might have been. I'd never felt like that before. I'd been angry. I'd been guilty – for not saving her, for not being able to move on, for trying to move on, for loving her at all – but I'd never been simply sad. Helen had been clever and brave and kind and good, and I had loved her. Her not being beside me for all these years was a sadness that I'd never really let myself feel.

As I began to drift into sleep, another face appeared to me. That tanned skin, the wild red-brown hair, the dark-brown eyes – Mrs Rochester. What had become of her since I ran away? It seemed to me that I heard her voice, not screaming in madness, but crying in pain because I had abandoned her. I heard Adele too, accusing me of the same abandonment. Two faces and voices called to me over a great distance, drowning out the sounds of revelry, invading my mind.

I opened my eyes and stared up at the ceiling. How could I have done that? After I'd abandoned Helen all those years ago, I'd done the same thing again. I'd abandoned Adele, whom I professed to care for. I'd abandoned that poor woman whose life was bound to Edward Rochester. Wasn't I just as bad as the ones who vilified the people dancing on the streets outside? I hadn't seen beyond myself, and the desire I had to be considered right by the world. The world had no right to judge, not those people outside, not me, not Elizabeth Rochester.

All my life I had let other people make my decisions. From the policemen who removed me from my mother's care, to the Reeds. Even my decision to teach at Our Lady hadn't really been mine. Did I really even want to be a teacher? Or a nanny. Or a missionary?

I knew what I had to do.

I took the bible from my bedside table and set off downstairs. The door to Brother Jacob's study was closed, but I gently opened it and walked inside. I placed the bible on his desk. Should I leave a note? Jacob and the mission had taken me in when I was homeless. They had been good to me, in their own way. They deserved something.

'Jane?'

Jacob was standing in the doorway. He stepped inside and gently closed the door.

'The others told me you had returned to the mission house. They said you were sick.'

'No, Jacob. Not sick. Sickened perhaps.'

'I know. It is sickening. The depravity and…'

'Not by them. By myself.' I took a deep breath. 'And by you.'

His eyes flew open as if I had slapped his face.

'What do you mean?'

'All of this.' I spread my hands to indicate the mission and the people in it. 'I think we're wrong. I know you think you are doing God's work, Jacob, but those people on the streets out there aren't sinners, well, no more or less so than you and I. They are like us.' I hesitated, but only for a second. 'Like me.'

A cold, closed-down expression appeared on his face. 'What are you saying, Jane. Like you?'

'I loved a woman.' It was that simple.

'You have a loving heart, Jane. You give your love freely to so many people.'

'No. Listen to me. I loved a woman.' I spoke slowly, and watched the realisation spread over his face. 'She died. If she was still alive, I'd probably still love her now.' That wasn't right. 'I do still love her now.'

'But…'

The realisation was replaced by confusion, then by something approaching hope.

'But, Jane, if you repent and turn to God. By your own words, the perversion can be cured. Stay with us, Jane. You know I dreamt of making you my wife. Stay with me and be cured.'

'I am not sick. I don't need to be cured.'

'But I need you with me, Jane.'

'And I need to be who I am. Goodbye, Jacob. I do still believe in God – but my God is not your God. If I pray at all, I will pray for you.'

I left him there and returned to my room. Leaving behind almost everything, I tossed a small bag over my shoulder and left the mission. As I walked into the night I wasn't afraid. I set out towards Oxford Street, confident the people there wouldn't harm me. They might even welcome me, but I couldn't stay here. There were things I had to make right before my new life could truly begin. Tomorrow morning I'd return to Central Station. It was time to go back to Thornfield.

Chapter 61

Betty

They'd have the ute. That would make all the difference, but she still needed to be better prepared than the last time. They needed water and something to eat. Really they needed to drive further than the nearest town before they stopped for the night. Edward might still look for them there if he realised they'd taken a car.

She didn't have a map. She hoped there was one stashed in the glove box. She poured the last of her shampoo into the bottom of the shower. It was a relief to see it go. It was the same stuff Grace used, and it was useless for Betty's hair anyway. Then she held the bottle under the tap until it stopped foaming. It took forever, but she had no choice. She needed something she could carry water in and it was the only thing she had.

Her own clothes should be easier to sort out. She hardly had anything, and what she did have was old and worn. But even very little had to be carried somehow. She grabbed a pillow from the bed and pulled a pillowcase free. She remembered Christmas morning. A pillowcase full of presents. A woman's voice laughing. *You get more presents that way than with a stocking.* A woman's voice. Her mother?

286

Betty sat down on the bed. Her mother. So there really had been a time before. Before her mother got put away. Before her father couldn't manage. Before the home and the boat and the Masons and Thornfield. There had been a place where she'd belonged. There had been someone who had bought her presents and watched with a smile when Betty unwrapped them.

She was invigorated. If she'd had that before, she could have that again. And she could give that to Adele. She opened the small cupboard next to the wall and stuffed her few clothes into the pillowcase. It wasn't much for a whole lifetime, but it was all she had.

Chapter 62

Jane

'I'm sorry. We've had no luck with attempted repairs. And we've still had no word as to when another engine will arrive to take us to Dubbo. I'm afraid we're just going to have to wait it out.'

Angry responses greeted the conductor's words. He held his hands up in what was clearly supposed to be a placatory manner.

'I understand. It's hot in here and you're angry. I get it, but there's nothing more I can do. However, my colleague will be coming through soon to hand out bottles of water.'

'It's about bloody time,' a voice yelled from behind me.

'Can't you at least open a door to let some air in?' I asked.

'I'm not supposed to, but all right.'

The conductor announced his intention to the rest of the travellers, adding a warning. 'You must not leave the train. There may be trains coming on the other track. Please stay inside but it should at least cool things down a bit.'

'Thank God for that,' someone muttered.

When the carriage doors slid open, there was some movement of air, but the carriage was still stifling. We had been sitting motionless for more than an hour now. According to the conductor, the locomotive was broken down, and the railways were sending another to take the stranded train through to Dubbo. As the temperature inside the carriage rose, so too did the passengers' tempers.

Impatience flared inside me too. I was desperate to get back to Thornfield. It seemed to me that every moment I spent sitting here on this train, Adele and Elizabeth Rochester were in danger. I saw their faces twisted in fear. I saw Rochester. I smelled burning flesh as I tried to beat out the flames that engulfed him.

'I'm getting out of here.'

The loud exclamation pulled me from my haunted dozing.

'Have they brought a bus for us?' I asked as I gathered my scattered wits.

'No. They say they can't because there's no road. Well, there's a bloody road over there. You can see the cars.' The speaker was a stockman with a weathered face and worn blue jeans.

I followed his pointing hand. A moment later I saw a flash of reflected sunlight, then movement as a car raced past, followed a few moments later by another.

'The railway line runs almost parallel to the highway,' another passenger offered. 'That will be the main road into Dubbo. We can walk across the paddock.'

'Please do not leave the train.' The conductor had returned. 'It's too dangerous. You might get hit by a train on the other track.'

'There are no trains out there, mate, just an empty paddock. We won't get hit by nothing crossing that,' the stockman said.

'What about snakes?' asked a timid voice from the back.

'I ain't scared of snakes.'

I was. Snakes and spiders both had haunted me since Helen's death.

'It can't be more than a kilometre or maybe two across that paddock. So I'm off. Who's coming with me?' He jammed the hat on his head in a determined fashion.

'I am asking you once more. Please do not leave the train.' There wasn't much force in the words. The conductor seemed to have given up hope of stopping the insurrection.

I shifted lower in my seat and looked away from the other passengers, staring out the window to the distant road. Around me I heard voices weighing the pros and cons of walking. I wasn't going to do it, of course. It was against the rules. I always obeyed the rules.

The sounds ceased as the last brave person jumped from the stationary train. The remaining passengers strained to look out the windows and see them. I did too and watched as the first one climbed through the barbed-wire fence lining the railway track.

I stood up and pulled my small bag from the overhead rack.

I raced to the open carriage door.

'Wait for me.'

I jumped down and hurried over the fence. I was the last to climb between the wires. We set out across an unknown paddock towards a highway, in the hope that someone would stop and give us a lift into Dubbo.

'So,' I said to the strangers around me. 'Does anyone know if there's somewhere in Dubbo I can hire a car? I've still got a long way still to go.'

Chapter 63

Betty

Every muscle in Betty's body was tense, ready for action, as she crept down the kitchen stairs. She slid the key Grace had given her into the lock and opened the door as quietly as she could, pushing the door open a crack. The room was empty. That was all right. Adele would be waiting for Edward to retire to his room before she snuck away. Betty just had to wait. She sat in the silent kitchen, close to the wood-burning stove where she could feel the heat emanating from the firebox, as the cooking fire burned low.

There was so much that could go wrong, but she wouldn't think about it. Whatever happened, she was leaving here tonight and she was taking Adele with her. And she would find somewhere for both of them. Somewhere where they both belonged.

Eventually she heard footsteps in the downstairs hallway. She picked up her pillowcase. They needed to get going quickly, while there was still light for the drive. She hadn't been behind the wheel for such a long time. She needed to be as far away as possible before night fell.

The kitchen door swung open. It was Edward. She jumped to her feet, her arms instinctively raised in defence.

'Why aren't you in your rooms?'

She could lie. She could say she was getting some air, or pretend she was wandering around like the crazy woman she was supposed to be. No. She wasn't going to do that anymore. 'Because I'm leaving.'

'No.' The word was nothing more than a growl. 'I'm keeping you here.'

It didn't make sense. She hadn't thought of that before. 'Why? Grace has gone. Adele's going away. Why not me?'

'Because this is all your fault.' He screamed the words across the room at her.

'What is?'

'You drove Jane away. And Celine. And Freddie. All of them.'

Betty shook her head. He was ridiculous. She could see it now. 'I barely even met Jane. Or Freddie.'

'You poisoned this place.' He was drunk. As he came closer she could smell it on him. 'Before you came here, there were parties here. The house was smart. Everyone respected the Rochesters. And then you.'

She shook her head. Suddenly everything was clear. 'Not me. You. They came for your father. They came because he kept a nice house and was a good host. They came because of his name and his reputation. I didn't change anything.' She was victorious. Whatever happened next she could see that this wasn't about her. It was him. He'd inherited this vast place that his ancestors had built and tended and given value to, and he couldn't do it. 'It was you that changed everything.'

Rochester staggered away from her. 'No.'

He grabbed something off the kitchen worktop. For a second she wasn't sure what but then she saw the blade glinting in the light. She dodged to the side as he lunged at her, just stopping herself from falling onto the stove. She flailed a hand out to the side. She needed something, anything. Her fingers closed around a small metal bottle. The diesel for lighting the stove. She gripped it in her hand and swung it at his head as he lunged at her again. He caught her shoulder with the knife, but his flailing didn't have the force to push the blade into her flesh. She dodged again. Now he was in front of the stove.

'Lizzybeth!' Adele was standing in the doorway, mouth open, eyes wide.

'It's all right, darling.'

Edward roared with anger. 'Neither of you are going anywhere. You both belong to me.'

Betty knew what he did to women who belonged to him. That wouldn't be the future. Not for either of them. He made a move towards Adele, reaching his arms out as if to grab her. Betty moved first, pushing him backwards. His hand came down on the cast-iron stove top and he screamed in pain. Betty dropped the bottle she was still holding. A harsh acrid smell rose around them as liquid slowly spread across the kitchen floor. 'Come on, darling. Time to go now.'

They only had a few seconds while he was distracted by the pain in his hand. Adele tried to push past him. His good arm shot out again to hold her. Betty shoved again. He started to fall, groping for something to hold on to. He gripped the handle of the firebox, pulling it open. A red glow filled the room.

He reached out to her. 'Elizabeth.'

She shook her head. 'My name is Betty,' she screamed.

The wood inside the firebox settled, and a shower of sparks leapt from their prison onto the diesel-soaked floor.

The fire leapt up around his legs. Adele screamed. Betty grabbed her, pulling her through the flames to the door before the blaze had a chance to take them all. And then she took tight hold of the young girl's hand and together they ran.

Chapter 64

Jane

The sun had long since set, but there was still a gold and red glow against the horizon. It danced like a legendary min min light, but this was very, very real. I jammed my foot down on the accelerator. Was it a bush fire? If so it must be close to the house.

The sense of urgency that had been growing in me since leaving Sydney was now too strong to be contained. I tore down the gravel road, unafraid of the risks. A kangaroo bounded past, a flash in the headlights, but I didn't even touch my brakes. I had to get to Thornfield. I had to find them.

The car raced past the empty airstrip and slid to a stop between the house and the yards.

The homestead was ablaze. Flames licked from the kitchen up the side of the building. As I jumped from the car, a window on the top floor blew out and flames danced up towards the roof. That top story above the kitchen held Elizabeth's rooms. I ran towards the fire, the heat already starting to scorch the bare skin of my arms and face.

'Elizabeth!' I screamed. 'Adele!'

There were figures now moving at the edges of the fire.

Aboriginal workmen were yelling through the smoke. Max was there, shirtless and dripping with sweat. He swung a wet sack at the embers that were flaring to life in the dry grass, catching each tiny blaze before it took off. All they could do was try to stop the fire spreading. The homestead was beyond saving. It was going to burn.

All that mattered now was saving the rest of the property... and the people.

I ran over to Max. 'Where's Adele?' I panted.

'I don't know.'

'Elizabeth? Edward?'

He turned his face towards me for a second, and I saw the panic and desperation. 'How the fuck would I know?'

I staggered backwards, beaten by the heat. There was no way I could get into the house to save them. Tears fell down my face. I stumbled away from the smoke.

I walked away from the house, and stopped to survey the scene. Then I saw them. Two figures, huddled together, staggering across the scrub away from the burning building. I ran towards them.

'Jane!' The childish cry tore into my heart. Adele raced towards me, her face streaked with tears. She flung herself into my outstretched arms and I grasped her to me as if I would never let her go.

'Jane. You came back for me.'

'Yes, I did.' I looked over her shoulder to see Elizabeth kneeling on the ground, coughing and gasping.

I took Adele's hand and ran the few yards to the other woman. 'Are you OK?'

She looked at me in confusion. 'What are you doing here?'

Adele joined me in pulling Elizabeth to her feet. 'She came back for us, Lizzybeth. She came back.'

Reader, we let it burn.

It was over; at least for us. Max and the stockmen would

continue to fight the fire, but there was nothing left here for me, or for Adele or Betty. The three of us had virtually nothing but the clothes we were wearing. Nothing but each other. That was enough.

We drove away in my hire car without even looking back. Slowly the light of the blaze receded in my rear-view mirror and the darkness returned, broken only by the strong beam of our headlights as we turned onto the highway and headed east.

I don't know where we will go or even if we will go together.

But I am no longer alone. I am no longer afraid. And at last I know who I truly am.

Acknowledgements

This book couldn't have been written without the support of many people.

Firstly, thanks to Charlotte Brontë for her wonderful original novel, Jane Eyre.

Our thanks also go to our agent, Julia Silk, and to our editor, Clio Cornish – both of whom supported and championed the story we were telling.

Writing a novel is a curiously solitary task, even when there's two of you, so we must also thank all our friends and family for supporting us during the process. Huge thanks to all our friends in the RNA, especially the magnificent women of the naughty kitchen. And extra special thanks to John and Paul for, well, for everything really.

And finally – thank you, dear reader, for choosing this book.

Dear Reader,

We thank you for picking up and reading *The Other Wife*. We appreciate every single reader who purchases and reads one of our books, and we hope that you enjoyed it.

Jane Eyre is a novel that is loved by millions of people and we hope this story that Jane inspired might be loved by just a few of those people too.

The Brontë sisters have been a huge inspiration to writers, particularly women writers, since their books were first published. Both of us were swept up by the passion of Wuthering Heights, and inspired by the ground breaking Tenant of Wildfell Hall.

Jane Eyre, in some ways, is a book with which we have a more complex relationship. The original Mr Rochester ultimately provides Jane's happy ever after moment, and as we've got older our relationship with that ending has changed and become more uncertain. Jane is a woman who comes to know and value her own judgement, and it seemed to us that a Jane born into a different time and place might make different judgements. We also wondered, as other authors have before us, about Mr Rochester's other wife. What brought her to Thornfield and what did she make of Jane's arrival? *The Other Wife* is the result of all of those conversations. Our idea of how Jane's story might go in a more modern world might be different from yours, but we hope that you enjoyed reading it.

If you did then please tell your friends, and if you have time, it would be wonderful if you could review the novel online.

We also love to hear from readers via social media. You can contact us on twitter @JulietBellBooks or on facebook: www.facebook.com/julietbellbooks

And if you haven't already, we'd love for you to read our other Brontë inspired novel, *The Heights*. There's an extract in this ebook to whet your appetite.

Thank you once again for picking up *The Other Wife*.

Alison & Janet aka Juliet Bell

Dear Reader,

Thank you so much for taking the time to read this book – we hope you enjoyed it! If you did, we'd be so appreciative if you left a review.

Here at HQ Digital we are dedicated to publishing fiction that will keep you turning the pages into the early hours. We publish a variety of genres, from heartwarming romance, to thrilling crime and sweeping historical fiction.

To find out more about our books, enter competitions and discover exclusive content, please join our community of readers by following us at:

🐦 *@HQDigitalUK*

📘 *facebook.com/HQDigitalUK*

Are you a budding writer? We're also looking for authors to join the HQ Digital family! Please submit your manuscript to:

HQDigital@harpercollins.co.uk.

Hope to hear from you soon!

If you enjoyed *The Other Wife*, keep reading for an extract from *The Heights* – another brilliant and immersive retelling of a classic from Juliet Bell – out now!

Prologue

Gimmerton, West Yorkshire, 2007

The searchers took several hours to find the body, even though they knew roughly where to look. The whole hillside had collapsed and, although the rain had cleared, there was water running off the moors and over the slick black rubble. The searchers were concerned about their own safety on the unstable slope. The boy, they knew, was beyond their help. This was a recovery, not a rescue.

Twice during the search, the hillside started to move again, and the searchers held their breath. The blue hills were nothing but mine waste. There was no substance to them. They were as fragile as the lives of the people who lived below them on the estate that clung to the land around the abandoned pithead.

Some of the searchers had worked in that mine. Years ago. The boy they were searching for was one of their own. Almost. He had the right name, even if most of them had never laid eyes on him. They knew his family. His grandfather had worked beside them at the coalface. His uncle too had been one of them. Not the father, mind. But still, they weren't going to leave the lad buried beneath the landslip.

The family weren't out there on the slope. Maybe the police had told them to stay behind. But maybe not. Maybe they just hadn't come.

They'd been looking for a couple of hours when the photographer from the local newspaper arrived. He was told to wait safely beyond the edge of the slip. But he was carrying an array of big and expensive lenses. His camera would go to the places he couldn't.

The sun was sinking when they found him.

One of the searchers had started yet another small slip, and as the rock slid away, almost like liquid, part of the body was exposed. Carefully, they had pulled him free.

The boy hadn't died easily. Father Joseph, down at St Mary's, was an old-fashioned priest, but there was no way this lad was going to have an open casket. His body had been pummelled by the sliding rock. The rain had washed most of the blood away, but it was still enough to make one of the men turn away and heave into the scrubby grass.

Surprisingly, the boy's face was hardly damaged at all. Just a couple of small scrapes and a cut on his temple.

The team leader removed his rucksack and dug inside to find a body bag. Carefully, they lifted the boy and put him inside. There was a sense of relief when the bag was closed.

They carried him down from the hills. The photographer followed. He took a few pictures, but then seemed to lose interest. As soon as they reached the road, the photographer broke away and walked quickly to the warmth of his car.

The searchers carried the body to the ambulance and waited while he was gently placed inside. Then they too dispersed.

The ambulance and the police were the last to leave. The ambulance was destined for the morgue. The police car turned into the estate and parked outside one of the few houses that wasn't boarded up and deserted.

The young constable got out, and carefully placed his hat on his head and straightened his uniform jacket. That's what you did when you brought bad news to a family, even one that hadn't bothered to come and join the search.

He walked up to number 37 Moor Lane and knocked on the door.

Chapter 1

Gimmerton, 2008

This was the place he had almost died. Lockwood shivered. In front of him, the chain-link fence was rusted and sagging. The sign hung at an angle, the words NO TRESPASSING all but covered with dirt and grime. Beyond the fence, in the grey light of the overcast afternoon, the buildings looked dark and decayed. Odd bits of iron, stripped from the disused mining machines, lay scattered about the ground and weeds were reclaiming their place in the filthy wasteland of the deserted pit. One building was open to the elements, the remains of its roof lying in a twisted heap between the crumbling brick walls. Not a single pane of glass remained intact. The men of this town had good throwing arms. Stones hadn't been their only weapons. Nor had windows been their only targets.

Lockwood reached into his pocket and retrieved the piece of metal he'd carried with him every day for more than two decades. The nail was twisted and bent, distorted almost beyond recognition when it was fired through the side of the police van. The newspaper reports at the time had declared it a miracle no one was injured as the nail ricocheted around the interior. Lockwood knew better. A tiny white scar on the left side of his neck showed how close death had come. After everything he'd seen in this job, that was the place his brain took him whenever he let his guard drop. To this day he still woke, sweating at night, hearing the sound of the nail gun beside his ear, and the screech of metal as the nail tore through the body of the van. He could still feel the sharp stab of pain in his flesh.

Lockwood told himself he was no coward. Even then, working with the riot squad, he'd expected danger. The miners were tough, and they were angry. Desperation had seeped into the bones of their community. They were about to lose their jobs. More than that, they were about to lose a way of life that had been with them for generations, the only way of life they knew. They were looking for a fight. He'd been green and keen, and could handle himself. He'd been trained to deal with anger, and there'd been so many moments in his career when something could have gone wrong. There'd been moments when things had gone wrong, but those weren't the moments he carried with him. Instead he kept hold of this one, as clear and solid in his memory as the nail in his hand. Maybe because that was the first time things had gone wrong. Maybe because they'd never caught anyone. Maybe because of the randomness of the attack. But stay with him it had.

They might not have caught the person who did it, but Lockwood knew who it was. The squad had been out of the vehicle seconds after the incident, breaking up the crowd pounding on the sides of the van. As he struggled in the melee, his neck damp with his own blood, Lockwood had looked towards the nearby houses and seen him. A dark youth, with hatred on his face. He'd been no more than fifteen then and already familiar to the police. He was carrying something in his hands. Lockwood couldn't see it clearly, but he knew in his heart it was the nail gun, and somewhere amid the shouting he'd heard the words: 'That Earnshaw kid.'

By the time Lockwood had fought his way through the crowd the youth was gone. He'd looked at the maze of narrow streets and identical houses in the Heights estate and known he wouldn't find him. They had investigated for a few days, but found nothing they could take to court. There were more pressing matters than one split second amid weeks of violence. Nobody was charged, and the incident was forgotten by everyone except Nelson Lockwood.

Darkness was falling as he turned away from the mine and got back into his car. He pulled away from the gates and began to retrace the route he'd followed that morning. The estate was even shabbier than before. Most of the people had left when the mine closed. Rotting boards covered the windows of the deserted pub. Graffiti scarred the walls of the empty shops and houses. Here and there, curtains or a light in a window showed that a house was occupied. For some people, Lockwood guessed, there was simply nowhere else to go.

His goal was the very last row of houses. A couple of the foremen had lived up here. They were the best paid and most trusted of the mine's employees. They had also been the leaders of the strike. And they always protected their own. The hotheads who had thrown the bricks and started the fights. And a kid with the nail gun he'd stolen from the mine.

Lockwood knew what he would find at the far end of this street, where the town ended and the wild hills began. Since his last visit, someone had turned two small houses into one. It was larger than the houses around it, but not better than them. The aura of neglect and decay was almost palpable. It would take more than a coat of paint or some new guttering to erase the memories that lingered in those walls.

Lockwood didn't need to see the light in the windows to know that the house was still inhabited. He'd checked that before leaving London on this final trip to Gimmerton. He drove past without stopping. There was plenty of time.

It took only a few minutes to drive from the past back to the present. The new estate had been built on a gentle slope below the moors. The houses were all detached with well-tended gardens. They were big and new and looked away from the mine, across the valley towards the lights of the town. The people who lived in the new estate weren't part of the old world. They sent their kids to the right schools and drove their big four-wheel drives to Leeds and Sheffield to work in offices, rather than toiling beneath the ground they lived on. Their wives ate lunch, rather than dinner, and went shopping for pleasure not for provisions. The history of this place didn't touch the Grange Estate.

Except for one small corner.

The house that had given the estate its name sat slightly removed from the new buildings, surrounded by a large garden. Thrushcross Grange was Victorian – the big house built for the mine owners back in the day, then used by a succession of managers after the pit was nationalized. It remained aloof from the newer buildings that surrounded it; with them but not a part of the town's new story. Thrushcross was the old Gimmerton.

After parking his car, Lockwood removed his bag from the boot and slowly approached the house. Despite the need for a new coat of paint, it had survived the new reality far better than the Heights. But still the memories lingered. He stepped through the door and made his way to the reception desk where a young woman with an Eastern European accent waited to check him in.

'Welcome to Thrushcross, sir. Do you have a reservation?'

He nodded. 'Under Lockwood.'

She stared at the screen. 'That is for a week?'

'I'm not sure. It might be longer.'

'It is quiet time, sir. There will be no problem to extend the booking if you want to.'

It felt strange to be walking the same hallways as the people who had intrigued – no, obsessed – him for so many years. As he entered his room, with its high, embossed ceiling and big bay window, he wondered which of them had slept here. He looked around the room trying to picture them, but suddenly shivered. It must be the cold wind off the moors, and he was tired after the long drive from London. The guesthouse had a restaurant. He'd go down and get something to eat and maybe a whisky before he tried to sleep.

Emerging into daylight the next morning, Lockwood was surprised to find a bright, still day. His restless sleep had been punctuated by the deep moaning of strong winds blowing off the moors, and the tapping of heavy rain against his window. Perhaps he'd been dreaming, his mind disturbed by reconnecting with the past.

Not even dazzling sunshine could make the town centre look appealing. It had changed in twenty-four years. It had never been smart, but now the decay was overwhelming. The few remaining shops were at the bottom end of the market – charity shops, pawnbrokers, pound stores. The two small pubs didn't look at all inviting. Nor did the only food outlets; a grease-stained chippie and an Indian. A tired looking Co-op also served as post office. Lockwood had seen a nice pub and restaurant just outside the town, on a hill with a glorious view of the moors. That must be where the people from the new estate went. Their road skirted the town centre to take them away from here without even passing through the old town and risking getting the dust of poverty and hopelessness on their shiny new cars.

In a tiny town square, a group of youths sitting at the base of a statue watched through hooded eyes as Lockwood drove past. He remembered that statue. It was of the town hero, a footballer who had made it good in the first division, back when the first division really was first. It said a lot about Gimmerton that Lockwood had never heard of the town's most famous son. There were more people standing near the pub. Men leaning against the walls, smoking as they waited for the doors to open. There was nothing else for them to do.

It hadn't always been like this.

Lockwood parked his car outside the church. It had beautiful arches over ornate, stained-glass windows and a wide staircase leading to dark wooden doors. It was newly painted, perhaps to prove that God hadn't entirely forsaken Gimmerton. Across the road from the church was a magnificent gothic edifice, no doubt built when the mine was flourishing. The stone was stained with soot. Three storeys above the ground, ornate Victorian gables towered over windows that were dark and empty. Above the door, a carving announced that this was the Workingman's Institute.

Or rather it had been, when there was work.

Much of the strike had been planned and run from this building. Until the union had been kicked out. And ten years later, when the pit finally closed, so too had the Institute. It was open again, but served a very different role. The men and women who walked up those steps now were going to the job centre to sign on, hoping to avoid the interest of the social workers who occupied the floor above. But this morning, that was exactly where Lockwood was heading.

The cavernous hallway echoed slightly as he made his way to the stairwell. At the top of the steps, a young mother and two small children sat on orange plastic chairs in the waiting area. Their clothes looked as if they had come from one of the charity shops on the high street. The reception desk was at the back of the large, unloved room. Behind it stood a woman about Lockwood's own age. She had the look of a someone who'd left her better days behind some years ago and her grey hair was cut in a short, severe fashion that did nothing to flatter her lined face. She glanced up as he entered and frowned.

'Yes?'

'I'm looking for Ellen Dean.'

The shifting of her eyes told him he had found the woman he was looking for.

'And you are?'

'DCI Lockwood. I have an appointment.' He pulled his warrant card from his pocket and held it up for her to see.

'This way.'

She led him to a small office. She took a seat behind the cheap wooden desk while Lockwood helped himself to another orange plastic chair. Miss Dean sat primly, her mouth firmly shut, waiting for Lockwood to begin.

'As I mentioned in my email,' he said, 'I'm following up on a couple of incidents recently that may shed light on an unsolved case dating back some time.'

'What case?' Her eyes narrowed.

Lockwood sensed she was going on the defensive.

'It goes back to the strike,' he said, hoping to reassure her she wasn't his target. Not now, at least.

'That's long gone. People don't talk about those times much around here.'

'I'm not so much interested in the strike, as in some of the people who were here back then. The Earnshaws and the Lintons.'

He waited for her to say something, but she simply sat there, her eyes narrowing and her mouth fixed in that firm, defensive line.

'I believe you had dealings with both families in your role back then with social services.'

'In this place, most people had dealings with social services.'

Lockwood nodded. 'I'd like to start with the Earnshaws. In particular, the youngest boy. Heathcliff.'

A shadow crossed her face. He could almost feel her defences rising. Was it guilt, he wondered. He'd been in plenty of meetings with plenty of social workers over the years. He'd sat through child protection conferences, and even gone out as muscle when they took the kids away. He'd seen the good ones, the ones who cared too much, the ones who didn't care at all, and the ones who got worn down by the job. Now, here was Ellen Dean. He wasn't sure which type she was. He reminded himself that he was here to do a job. However personal this investigation was, he was a professional. He would do what the job demanded. He arranged his face into a more sympathetic expression.

'I've read the file,' he said. 'There's not much detail there. The child apparently just turned up.'

'Old Mr Earnshaw brought him back from a trip. Liverpool.'

'And you never thought too much about it? You didn't question where the boy came from or how Earnshaw got hold of him?'

The woman across the table bristled. 'It was a private fostering arrangement.'

'Really?' Lockwood's eyebrow inched upwards.

She nodded. 'Perfectly legal. There was a note from the mother.'

'That's not in the file.'

She shrugged. 'It was a long time ago. Things were different then. He were never reported missing. And besides . . . ' Her voice trailed off.

Lockwood felt a glimmer of hope. He was beginning to understand Ellen Dean now. He knew how to get what he wanted from her. 'Please, Miss Dean . . . ' He leaned forward, hoping to suggest to her that they were co-conspirators in some secret endeavour. 'Anything you could tell me about the family will help.'

The woman pursed her lips. 'I'm a professional. I don't engage in gossip.'

There it was. Lockwood forced himself to resist the smile that was dragging at his lips. She knew something. And in his experience, anyone who professed not to be a gossip usually was. He nodded seriously. 'Of course not. But if there were things you think I ought to know.' He paused for a second as she leaned slightly towards him. 'In your professional opinion, of course. And to help with the old case. It would be good to get rid of the paperwork on it.'

'Well . . . ' The woman glanced around as if checking no one could overhear. 'There was them that said the boy was his.'

313

That was interesting. 'Was he?'

'Don't know. He looked like a gypsy. All dark eyes and wild hair. Talked Irish an' all.'

'And the mother?'

'She never came looking for him. Back then, I had my hands full. It was desperate round here. The winter of discontent and all that. There were families what needed my help.' She straightened her back. 'I had important things to do. More important than wondering about one brat. He was fed and housed. He was safe. There were plenty who weren't.'

'Of course.' He smiled at her.

A sudden crash outside the room was followed by the sound of a woman yelling at her child. A few seconds later, the child started screaming. That was his cue.

'I can hear you're busy, Miss Dean,' he said, getting to his feet. 'Thank you for talking to me. I may need your help again.'

She nodded brusquely as she got to her feet. The closed, hard look on her face didn't bode well for the family who dared to create a disturbance in her office.

Lockwood spent the afternoon at the town's small library, also housed in the Workingman's Institute. The seats were empty, and a lone librarian showed him the way to their old newspaper files. The library had not yet entered the twenty-first century. Back issues of the local newspaper were on microfiche, not computer, and by the end of the day his eyes felt dry from staring at the viewer. He hadn't learnt much. He'd found a lot of stories about the miners' strike and the pit closure and the deaths that had brought him back. But nothing he hadn't already read. He had even seen his younger self in one of the photos. His face was obscured by his helmet and shield, but he knew himself. Even after all these years, he felt a twinge of pride that he had followed orders and done the job that was required of him.

The current job, however, was looking pretty hopeless.

Heathcliff had been and remained a mystery. There was nothing to tie him to any crime.

Lockwood was an old-style copper. He believed in old-fashioned investigation. People were the answer. Someone always knew the truth. The trick was to get these people to talk to him. They didn't like strangers, and most of all they didn't like a copper from the south. Old enmities died hard around here. He had a lot of legwork in front of him. And he didn't have much time. He was retiring soon. This investigation was, on paper at least, official, but Lockwood knew he'd been given the case review as a favour. No one thought he would find anything new. This case was so cold there were icicles on it. Dusk saw him back on the Heights estate, sitting in his car at the end of a street made gloomy by the lowering clouds. A small beam of light was visible from the window of the shabby house at the top of the rise.

When it was fully dark, Lockwood got out of the car and walked slowly up the hill to stop in the deep shadows beside an old and boarded-up terrace across the road from that single light. He watched for a while, but saw nothing through the grimy curtains. He crossed the road and made his way down a path between two houses into the yards at the back of the terrace row. There was a gap in the fence wide enough to let him through. From the back of the deserted neighbouring home, he could see more lights. These windows had no curtains, and for a moment he thought he could see a dark shape moving inside. He stepped onto a pile of mossy timber and grabbed the top of the fence to pull himself up for a better look.

The girl's hand came from nowhere. It grabbed his wrist, the bare fingers pale in the dim light and icy cold.

Lockwood gave a startled cry and smashed his free hand down into the girl's flesh, driven by a desperate urge to stop her touching him. His foot slipped and he fell backwards. He crashed to the ground, grimacing in pain as his shoulder hit something hard hidden in the long grass. A moment later, the door of the house next door crashed open.

'Cathy? Cathy?'

Lockwood bit back a moan of pain and sat up, to peer through a gap in the rotting fence.

The boy was now a middle-aged man, but Lockwood knew him in an instant.

'Heathcliff,' he breathed.

Time had not been good to him. His dark hair was still worn long and untidy, but now it was heavily threaded with grey. Where once he'd been muscular and lean, he was now painfully thin. His face was gaunt and lined and his eyes were sunken dark holes. He looked wildly around.

'Cathy? Are you there?' Heathcliff called in a voice shaking with emotion.

No answer came from the silent night.

Lockwood didn't dare move. Heathcliff waited, staring out into the blackness and muttering something Lockwood couldn't hear.

Something moved in the corner of Lockwood's vision. He turned his head, but there was nothing or no one there. A heartbeat later, a soft white flake drifted to the ground. Followed by another. And another. Within a minute, heavy snowflakes obscured his vision and he began to shiver and the temperature dropped even further. Still, Heathcliff didn't move. Just as the cold was about to drive Lockwood to revealing himself, a shout from inside the house caused Heathcliff to stir. Muttering loudly, he turned away and retreated inside the house, slamming the door behind him.

Lockwood waited no more than a few seconds before slowly getting to his feet. He risked another look over the fence, but there was no sign of the girl with the icy hands.

Cathy?

His mind conjured up a picture of a dark-haired girl with wild hair. She hadn't been beautiful. Not really. But something about her had been strangely compelling. She had been Heathcliff's constant companion, matching his every wildness. But then,

316

something had happened to drive them apart. He knew that much.

Hers was one of the deaths that had brought him back.

Catherine Linton. Catherine Earnshaw.

Heathcliff's beloved Cathy.

If you enjoyed *The Other Wife*, then why not try another sweeping romance from HQ Digital?